C000280440

Steep Holm

The Story of a Small Island

STAN AND JOAN RENDELL

Best wishes.
Stan Rendell
Joan Rendell

Foreword by John Fowles

SUTTON PUBLISHING

First published in 1993 by Alan Sutton Publishing Limited, an imprint of
Sutton Publishing Limited · Phoenix Mill · Thrupp · Stroud · Gloucestershire

Reprinted 1998

Copyright © Stan and Joan Rendell, 1993

All rights reserved. No part of this publication may be reproduced, stored in a
retrieval system, or transmitted, in any form, or by any means, electronic,
mechanical, photocopying, recording or otherwise, without the prior permission of
the publisher and copyright holders.

British Library Cataloguing in Publication Data

Rendell, Stan
Steep Holm: The Story of a Small Island
I. Title II. Rendell, Joan
942.393

ISBN 0 7509 0323 6

Cover illustration: *The Landing Place, Steepholme*, 1892 watercolour
by Col. R.W. Banting.

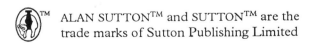 ALAN SUTTON™ and SUTTON™ are the
trade marks of Sutton Publishing Limited

Typeset in 10/13 Plantin Light.
Typesetting and origination by
Sutton Publishing Limited.
Printed in Great Britain by
WBC Limited, Bridgend, Mid-Glamorgan.

CONTENTS

Steep Holm: a watercolour by M.A. Sweeting, 1858. It formerly belonged to the Tynte family, owners of the island from 1833 until 1976

FOREWORD

Steep Holm haunts. Few who have visited it have not become, if not enchanted, at least possessed. What is this stark, silent, faintly aloof rock, so close to some dense centres – Weston and Cardiff-Penarth – of our overpopulated country? So close, and yet so far . . . it seems not quite of England, nor of Wales. There are times, approaching it, when it can seem some tropical sugar-lump from Brazil gone several thousand miles adrift. I have more than once felt echoes of Alcatraz, a bodingness, mean men in prison; at others a much more pleasant and exhilarating sense of freedom, space, light, a whiff of the Hebrides. All interesting islands have strong moods, almost human temperaments; and Steep Holm, as this book shows, has a history quite varied and colourful enough to have provoked them.

This excellent new account by Joan and Stan Rendell is rather like a first realistic painting or photograph of some figure hitherto more familiar in legend or myth. All of us who know the island and have fallen under its strange spell will feel grateful for the Rendells' labour of love. We already owe them much for what they have revealed of Steep Holm's archaeology. This thoroughly researched history leaves us – both we who already know the island and all those who have it still to discover – permanently in their debt.

John Fowles, 1993

PREFACE

The first time I set eyes on Steep Holm was on a grey day in November 1973. It was six months since Kenneth Allsop's tragic death and for much of that time a small group of his friends and well-wishers had been searching for a place to buy and care for as a memorial to his life and work. We knew it would have to be somewhere special, a place where the ideals he had striven for could somehow be kept alive. To begin with our search had been centred on Eggardon Hill, in Dorset, that great green scarp which held so much fascination for Ken himself, especially during the last years of his life, but the relatively small sum we had been able to raise was insufficient for the purchase and we were obliged to look elsewhere.

The word that there might be a chance of buying an island in the Bristol Channel was immediately enticing. I had visions of a kind of natural fortress full of seabirds, of gulls and guillemots, puffins and gannets, which says something of my ignorance of the bird life of the Severn Estuary, but never mind. The idea was exciting. I had never heard of Steep Holm, but even the name had a faint allure, suggestive of towering cliffs and ancient memories. When Rodney Legg told me about peregrine sightings, about the wild leek and the peony, I was already half convinced that this was the place we must try to buy. But first we must see it. So on a wet and windy autumn day a small party of us was escorted across to the island.

From the sea the cliffs looked wild and dangerous, the ruins of the inn romantic, but when we scrambled off the boat we could see immediately that the place had been much used and abused by human beings. On the beach itself was a great pile of rusted iron girders, scattered higgledy-piggledy among the boulders. A twisted iron ladder led up on to the remnants of a concrete quay.

At the top was another pile of girders beside a low brick building, which seemed to be full of rubble. Beyond was the tumbled masonry of the inn. There was decay and desolation on all sides.

The zig-zag path to the plateau did little to raise our spirits. The bare stems of the sycamores reminded me of the small jungles which sprang up on every bomb site in post-war London. When I saw that most of the winter vegetation seemed to be elder, brambles and privet, the initial impression was strengthened. And the rubbish! Around the steel and concrete bones of the coast defence batteries were scattered relics of the wartime Nissen huts, rusted curves of corrugated iron, broken glass, short ends of steel cable, even tin cans. That's what it's like, I thought, a bomb site covered in bomb site vegetation and bomb site rubbish.

But everywhere on the island there were also signs of the ways in which living things will always fight back against steel and concrete. The great Victorian gun platforms were covered in the remnants of gulls' nests. Mosses and lichens were beginning to colonize some of the flat roofs of the later emplacements and the foundations of many of the Nissen huts were half covered with brambles. The trees and shrubs might not be handsome, but they were undeniably vigorous. Gradually, I began to see how Steep Holm could make an ideal memorial for everything Kenneth Allsop had fought for.

Here was a once beautiful island which had been scarred by human beings in that ugliest and most wasteful of all human activities, war. The place had never been attacked, so the damage had been done by our own side. And in that process Steep Holm may stand for Britain and all the ugly wounds which we have inflicted on our own land – the industrial pollution, the vandalized townscapes, the destruction of woodland, moorland, wetland and pasture in the name of agricultural progress, all the manifestations of a greedy and uncaring society which Ken had done so much to make us see and understand. It was not the redoubt I had hoped for, free from pollution because of its isolation. It was already polluted. But it was also a refuge for some rare and interesting survivors from a time when human beings were less adept at fouling their own nests.

The outgoing tenants of the old Steep Holm Trust had cared for the peonies and the wild leeks and had helped to win recognition for the island as a Site of Special Scientific Interest. They told us of the purse web spiders and the oversized slow worms. They also showed us something which set my imagination going once more. Close to the first of the Victorian gun batteries there were low stone foundations, just visible in the scrub. It was the site, they told us, of an Augustinian priory which had stood here in the Middle Ages. To one side was an unfilled trench from an archaeological excavation. We later learned that the island's owner, Baroness Wharton, had objected to any disturbance of human remains and all archaeological work had been suspended, but at the time the abandoned dig only added to the air of mystery which shrouded many things on the island. There were rumours of Vikings, of Dark Age saints and secret burials, but very little certain knowledge.

We would have to wait a long time before we learned much more, but for the time being those of us on that first trip – Rodney, John and Elizabeth Fowles and I – had all found out enough to become Steep Holm enthusiasts. A few weeks later Betty Allsop also had a chance to see the island and she quickly came to share our feelings. The place was in a sad mess, but that in itself gave us a sense of purpose, and there were rare plants to care for, bird migrations to monitor and several scarce nesting species, ravens, cormorants, perhaps even peregrines. And there were buildings and fortifications of obvious historical importance. The combination was irresistible. Within a few months the Kenneth Allsop Memorial Trust became tenants of Steep Holm and the work of clearing and renovation began. After nearly three years of intermittent labour, of some mistakes and much negotiation, Baroness Wharton's daughter, the Hon. Ziki Robertson, generously allowed us to buy the island for a very modest sum.

Any visitor who returned to the island for the first time since then would find much changed for the better. And having done the circuit and enjoyed its pleasures according to season and weather, he or she would almost certainly join the group which gathers on the priory excavation site at 3 p.m. to hear Stan and Joan Rendell explain the work in progress. For the most part the group is attentive and well-mannered, but it often strikes me that archaeology must look a bit of a joke to anyone who sees a dig in progress for the first time. Here is a little group of grown men and women grubbing about on hands and knees, scraping at little patches of earth with a pointing trowel or even a toothbrush for hours on end, to be rewarded, if they are lucky, with a splinter of bone or a broken fragment of pottery. The walls they uncover seem no more than a few stones in a row. The finds are unimpressive. The whole site, to the uninitiated, is a muddle of tapes, planks and spoil heaps.

This fascinating book which the Rendells have now written does not go into detail about the scraping and brushing and measuring of holes in the ground, but what it does show is just how valuable those painstaking years of work have been. It also reveals the findings of many more hours spent in libraries, museums, muniment rooms and record offices of all descriptions. The sources they have traced, the old texts they have unravelled and the clues they have uncovered have now been linked together to tell the story of Steep Holm and its inter-relationship with human beings over more than two thousand years.

There are some visitors – I have heard them – who deplore the Victorian gun batteries, let alone the fortifications from the Second World War, partly on the general principle that all things military are unpleasant, partly because they resent the evident intrusion of human activity on this remote and beautiful place. We hoped the island would be really wild, they say. It will be apparent, from my own first impressions, that I understand that point of view very well. But it is to miss the point. Everything on the island – birds, animals, buildings, even the plants, as the Rendells make it abundantly clear – has been changed, modified, altered by human beings over many centuries. But the enormous difficulty of sustaining any human activity on such a remote and exposed place means that human works have soon been subjected to the forces of nature and changed in their turn. To begin to grasp how those changes have taken place and how human activity interacts with natural processes is to gain insight into what we have done and are still doing to the whole of Britain, the whole of the Earth on which we live.

It is for this reason especially that I welcome this book, but I hope and believe that it will be read by many different people for all kinds of reasons. Here are mysteries hiding deeper mysteries, clues which could lead to further clues. So much has been uncovered. So much still remains to discover. I am sure that Stan and Joan themselves will be busy on the island for many years to come with their trowels and tapes and even busier in libraries and museums, making sense of what they find. I hope very much that this book will inspire many others to follow their lead. But I also hope that the casual visitor, out for the day, with no great wish to dig too deeply into history, will find the story of this unique little island as enjoyable and enlightening as I do myself.

John Percival

ACKNOWLEDGEMENTS

We gratefully acknowledge the help and support of the many kind and generous persons who have given so willingly of their time and expertise to actively help and encourage us in our work on Steep Holm, and in the writing of this book.

It is impossible to thank everyone, but in particular we would like to mention our fellow Executive Council members of the Kenneth Allsop Memorial Trust; the Somerset Archaeological and Natural History Society, without which our involvement with Steep Holm may never have developed; Jeff Carrington, former secretary of that society for constant help, both on and off the island; Ted and Dorrien Mason, who generously gave full access to archives of the former Steep Holm Trust and to their personal research notes, and who gave us every encouragement to publish; Mrs H. Savory for the gift of photographs taken by her late husband; John and Betty Barrett, the continuing link between the two Trusts; Dr Leo Harrison Matthews for his kindness in digging out his original 1930s site records and photographs; the Maltwood Fund of the Royal Society of Arts, which made initial grants for the archaeological work; Dr C.A. Ralegh Radford for advice on medieval and earlier Christian architecture and procedures; Dr David Thackray for help with the survey work in 1977 and 1978; George Boon and Dr A.J. Parker for specialist reports on Roman finds; Dr Roger Jacobi, John Tucker, Brian Hack and Ann Everton, who examined the island flints; Dr Bob Everton for his report on human bones; Bruce Levitan for his report on animal bones; Dr Miranda Green for specialist advice and report on the Celtic stone head; Rolls Royce Technical College post-graduates for the kite photography project; Gilbert Green, who read through the geology section and prepared the geology chart (appendix); Harold Coward for Latin translations; Chris Richards and Brian Austin for local history research; Alfred Payne for recounting memories of Tom Sleeman; Mrs Mary Sandover, one of our adult education students, for telling us about her father, a coastguard on Steep Holm; Royal Artillery Institution for technical advice and information; ex-military personnel as mentioned in the text, especially Joe Walford, from whose written account we have quoted extensively; Max Flemming and Hans Messner for P.O.W. memories; present and former staffs of Woodspring Museum; Woodspring Central Library Local History Department; Bristol City Museum; Somerset Record Office; Somerset Local History Library, especially Jane Evans, Stuart Davison, Sharon Poole, John Loosley, Jane Saker, Nicholas Thomas, Mike Ponsford, David Dawson, Georgina Plowright, Derek Shorrocks, Robin Bush and David Bromwich, all of whom gave much invaluable assistance; the County Record Offices of Glamorgan, Gloucester, Northamptonshire, Warwickshire and Wiltshire; the Missions to Seamen who kindly allowed access to and gave permission to publish from the diaries of the Revd Mr Ashley; Dr David Worrall and his colleagues of the Flat Holm Project; Andrew and Lorna Gibson, former Flat Holm wardens; the following authorities for permission to quote from documents: Bristol Central Reference Library, British Library, Public Record Office, Glamorgan Record Office, Somerset Archive and Record Service, and Wiltshire Record Office; our team members over the years, who have cheerfully endured discomfort in the cause of archaeology; and the island's long-suffering boatmen – the Watts family, Pete Holder and Ashleigh Holtby – who in both good and bad sea conditions have carried us safely to and from Steep Holm hundreds of times over many years.

ILLUSTRATION ACKNOWLEDGEMENTS

Grateful acknowledgement is made to the following for use of illustrations on the following pages: Woodspring Museum (courtesy of Miss Jane Evans and Mr Stuart Davison): cover, pp. 113, 147; Steep Holm Trust archives: pp. 158, 200, 201; Steep Holm Trust archives (Harry Cox collection): pp. 96, 131, 165, 168, 170, 195; Tony Langham: p. 8; Somerset Archive and Record Service: p. 20; Local History Department, Woodspring Central Library: pp. 42, 95, 147, 161, 171; Bristol City Museum and Art Gallery: pp. 84, 136, 182; Rolls Royce Technical College: p. 231; Dept of Archaeology, University of Wales, College of Cardiff: p. 21; Dr Leo Harrison Matthews: pp. 85, 122, 129, 138, 144, 156; Joe Walford: pp. 140, 141; Captain W.G.M. Jones: p. 191; Mrs Savory: p. 174; Reg Stone: p. 187; Mr and Mrs E.J. Mason: pp. iv, 125.

Chapter One

SETTING THE SCENE

Steep Holm is a mysterious island, sometimes moodily entrenched in wild seas which refuse access to its grey and forbidding rocks – sometimes warm and welcoming in placid waters, with cliffs covered in colourful vegetation; yet still retaining a remote and austere air, as though harbouring reservations about invaders, who throughout many centuries have landed from a great variety of craft for a remarkable variety of reasons. They came to hunt or to fortify, to build or to destroy, to farm or to fish – in the hope of gaining profit or of attaining peace; to recuperate or to defy the law, in search of knowledge, or even just to sunbathe! From earliest times when the human race walked upon this part of the globe, it is likely that Steep Holm has been exploited – its natural crops plundered, its wildlife hunted and its environment altered for good or ill by man's activities. Uninhabited for centuries, yet almost always utilized for one purpose or another, this island – once a monastic retreat, twice a fortress in modern times and now a nature reserve and wildlife sanctuary owned by the Kenneth Allsop Memorial Trust – has grown in fascination despite, or perhaps because of, the changes wrought by forceful nature and inventive mankind.

For those who enjoy statistics, the island lies some five miles from Weston-super-Mare, is about half a mile long, lying east/west, and less than a quarter of a mile wide, with the broader end facing the English coastline, and the narrow point of Rudder Rock looking towards Wales. It is 256 ft from mean sea level to the highest point of the convex plateau, with sheer cliffs dipping into the sea to form the long north side. Scree, in places disguised by plant growth, forms a treacherous surface over large areas of the slightly more gentle slopes on the south side, and is a feature of picturesque but dangerous declivities in the north-west cliffs. The only wooded part of the island is above East Beach, where sycamore trees struggle to keep a firm roothold in the slanting and unstable ground. The rest of the island vegetation is at first sight principally the dominant alexanders, often varied by vivid yellow ragwort, with a mixture of native privet, elder, brambles and nettles. Other more unusual plants, such as the decorative but poisonous henbane, often have visitors guessing; but to botanists Steep Holm is especially renowned for its unique peony and the equally rare wild leek.

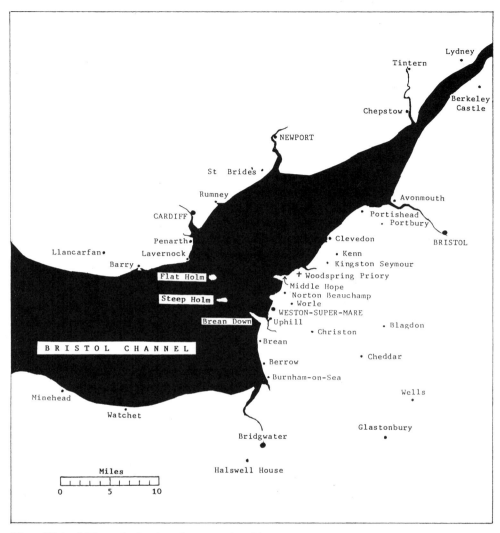

Map of Bristol Channel, showing places mentioned in text

There are two landing places; the larger pebble and rock-strewn East Beach which can be completely inundated by high tides, and South Landing – a less preferred small beach and concrete jetty exposed only at low water, but with landfall possible via the rocks at other stages of tide. From here a crumbling flight of wartime steps leads past a much earlier well-preserved lime kiln as an easy forerunner to the hard trek straight up the south slopes. To disembark at East Beach requires the use of a gangplank, with helping hands from Trust stalwarts wading in the water to aid the more nervous adventurers. Once ashore it is a simple matter to reach the steps and gate at the foot of the zig-zag path leading to the top of the

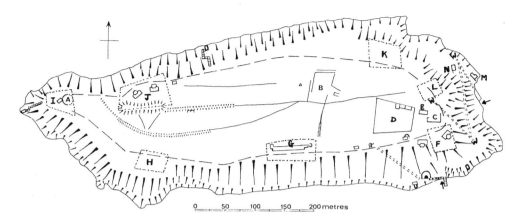

Map of Steep Holm, showing principal features. A: Roman signal station, B: possible Roman site, C: medieval priory site, D: farm enclosure, E: 1776 tenement, F: Garden Battery, G: Barracks, H: Split Rock Battery, I: Rudder Rock Battery, J: Summit Battery, K: Laboratory Battery, L: Tombstone Battery, M: inn, N: Cliff Cottage, W: winch houses

island. A steady climb, with plenty of excuses for lingering on the way, leads to the 1½-mile-long perimeter path around the elevated plateau. Here, where sea birds crowd in to breed, and migrants pause to rest, visitors may gaze in astonishment at the strange vegetation, become disorientated as they admire magnificent views across the surrounding sea to distant coastlines, and study a multitude of features which will fit into sequence as this chronicle unfolds.

From intensive research and archaeological fieldwork over many years we have discovered much of the island's past. The events, scenes and characters of history take their place as the problems arising from successive occupations are solved. Even the environment has changed, so that what we see today bears little resemblance to the landscapes of ancient times.

Chapter Two

PREHISTORY

The Ups and Downs of Steep Holm's Formation

Part of the fascination of Steep Holm lies in the fact that it is an island almost in the middle of the Bristol Channel between the mainland shores of England and Wales, where the River Severn has already widened into the funnel which is its access to the vast Atlantic Ocean. Standing on the western extremity of the island with the Welsh coast away on the right hand and the Somerset and Devon hills looming distantly to the left, one can look down-Channel to where, far over the horizon, the continent of America is the first landmass in direct line.

But from a standpoint above the north cliffs the view is quite different. The sister island of Flat Holm with its tall lighthouse built on relatively low cliffs is in the near foreground, just 2¹⁄₂ miles to the north, while to the north-east the land begins to crowd in as the Channel narrows to become the River Severn. The result of this funnelling is that the great surge of water which flows up and down this estuary has the second highest tidal range in the world. When absorbing these views it is difficult to visualize the many changes which have taken place here over aeons of time.

After the initial excitement of approaching Steep Holm and landing on East Beach, the visitor is immediately aware of the dominant cliffs of Tower Rock. Those interested in geology recognize the massive, clearly defined layers of fissured limestone – both here and below the ruined inn north of the beach – sloping at angles of 20°–30° from the horizontal. Many variations of this pattern will be noticed by those who circumnavigate either of the Holms in a small boat.

Originally formed beneath the sea, Steep Holm and Flat Holm, during much later phases of climatic extremes, became on more than one occasion prominent isolated hills which could have been reached by walking across a relatively dry valley plain. The world was already old when Steep Holm was formed. The actual rock of which the island is composed was laid down some 340 million years ago as sediments accumulating over thousands of years upon a bed of more ancient rocks which formed the surface of the earth's crust, and which had in places subsided and become submerged beneath a warm shallow sea. The compacting and cementing

Split Rock from the sea, showing complex folding of strata

together of sediment and the shell remains of billions of tiny marine creatures formed carboniferous limestone, and recognizable fossils which can be found trapped in this rock provide a fragmentary and far from complete record of the multitudinous forms of life which lived and died in the sea so long ago.

Over a protracted geological timespan varying sea bed conditions led sometimes to accumulation of shell debris limestones, and at other times to the formation of oolitic limestones – also a sedimentary rock but created under different sea conditions. Containing billions of rounded particles like minute hard roe fish eggs, this type of limestone derived from a surfeit of lime precipitated from the water and deposited as concentric layers around fine grains of sand or other tiny nuclei. The sharply contoured shapes of this gritty, more soluble rock, carved by centuries of wave action, may best be seen at low tide in the South Landing area.

With the warm climate still continuing, Steep Holm was very near a centre of volcanic activity, and along the shorelines north of Weston-super-Mare evidence is still clearly to be seen of lava and ash deposits from a fiery vent that spasmodically erupted a short distance to the west of Middle Hope.

Subsequently, about 280 million years ago, movements of the plates which form the earth's crust squeezed and buckled the neatly consolidated layers of limestone rock, raising them above sea level to form the whole Mendip range, of which Steep Holm and Flat Holm are outliers. These colossal forces lifted and folded the rocks, and in the case of Steep Holm local variations created the spectacular contortions which now fascinate geologists as they view the island's south cliffs from the sea.

Dramatic changes in the geography of the world caused tremendous climatic upheavals, and over the next 80 million years hot dry desert conditions prevailed in this area, with saline lakes forming from time to time in the depression which so much later was to become part of the Bristol Channel. At about this time arid winds and intermittent streams and torrents deposited rock waste which eventually hardened into beds of Triassic rock. On Steep Holm most of these have been eroded; although a few chunks used as building material have been unearthed during our excavations, and Gilbert Green has identified them as probably having been quarried from the plateau area, any remaining outcrop now being covered by soil.

By about 200 million years ago desert conditions had given way to severe flooding and Steep Holm was completely covered by the sea. More deposits were laid down around and above the drowned hilltop, and again the unstable crust of the earth moved and tilted.

Continued earth movements and climatic variations in subsequent epochs resulted both in repeated rising and falling of relative land and sea levels, and also in environmental extremes; the destructive action of the elements removing upper layers of sedimentary rock, soil and vegetation which once covered the island. Fissures in the limestone contain traces of lead and iron ores, which would have been emplaced from aqueous solutions in Triassic and Jurassic times, about 230 to 170 million years ago.

The 'Gooseneck' shingle spit off East Beach at very low tide

Strange reptilian creatures roamed the region for millions of years, to become extinct long before the evolution of man. Although it is unlikely that their remains will ever be discovered around the island, what are believed to be fossilized dinosaur footprints have been found recently on the South Wales coast.

Relative water and land levels continued to rise and fall until, and indeed throughout the Ice Ages – a comparatively recent era – when Steep Holm lay near the southern edge of the great ice sheets which periodically chilled northern Europe over some two million years. Slight indication of this phase is given by 'foreign' flint pebbles found with greensand cherts among the much more numerous local rock pebbles which form the 'Gooseneck', a shingle spit visible off East Beach at low tide. These almost certainly derive from a glacial deposit somewhere nearby in the bed of the Channel, but the suggestion that scarring of the island's north cliffs was caused by a glacial movement along an east/west axis is open to doubt.

During these glaciations relatively slight lowering of average temperatures caused so much of the water drawn up from the sea to fall upon the land as snow, which was crushed into ice, that at times the sea levels fell by as much as 300 ft. These were also times when Steep Holm ceased to be an island and was no more than a hill on a desolate plain.

At the opposite extreme, in inter-glacial periods of warmer weather, when the ice sheets retreated farther and farther north, sea levels were exceptionally high, creating beaches at correspondingly higher levels than those of the present day. These can readily be traced at intervals along the Bristol Channel shorelines, and there is possible evidence of similar raised beaches around the cliffs of the two limestone islands. On nearby Flat Holm, in the nineteenth century, military work to adapt a cave system into a huge water reservoir revealed one such raised beach at a height of 53 ft above existing sea level. It was reported that the beach sand was quite hard, with pebbles and shells. Other remains, including antlers of red deer, were also found. On Steep Holm, a survey of caves in the 1930s uncovered similar bone evidence. Within one 'old swallet' on the north cliffs, approached with great difficulty, was an inner chamber. Here, in red cave earth beneath a sheet of stalagmite, were found 'fragments of sub-fossil bones, one of which was identified as that of red or rein-deer'.

No one knows exactly why, during each succeeding inter-glacial period, the rising sea levels appear never to have attained the maximum heights reached previously.

The Channel Flooded

After the last great glaciation which affected this country, and while sea levels remained low, the average temperature gradually rose until the summers were warmer than at present, and initially tundra vegetation, then woodland began to colonize the hospitable soils of the valley which was destined to become the Bristol Channel. The winters, however, remained long and cold, and it was not until the

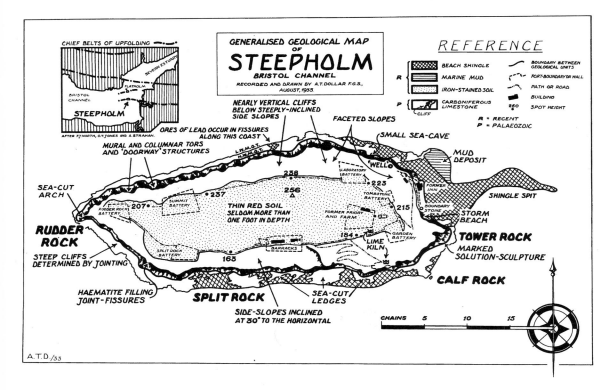

Geological map by A.T. Dollar, 1933

rise in sea levels which followed the release of water as the ice cap retreated northwards, that a more moderate climate prevailed. The post-glacial valley woodland was slowly submerged by higher tides until eventually the coastline settled to more or less its present appearance, with Steep Holm and Flat Holm again becoming islands. Petrified remains of fallen trees, relics of the drowned forests, can still be seen at low tide in places along the Channel shores, and some of those locations have produced tools in the form of worked flints from prehistoric times. Often, when the sea scours away some of the layers of mud in the inter-tidal area, peat deposits from decomposed vegetation are also exposed – a legacy of patches of reed swamp which once grew where the Channel now flows.

Although rapid by geological standards, the increase in sea levels would not have brought dramatic and devastating overnight flooding, but a scarcely noticeable rise of perhaps a centimetre per year. When the Bristol Channel was dry some ten thousand years ago, it would have been possible to walk across to Lundy (now 11 miles from the nearest mainland point). Even about eight thousand years ago, long after Lundy had become an island, it would still have been possible to reach Steep Holm and Flat Holm by walking from what is now the coastline. Here it is interesting to note the comparison in age between the 340 million-years-old limestone of the two Holms, and Lundy's slate beds which were laid down about 370 million years ago; the dominant granite of that island being a mere 52 million years old.

The First Prehistoric Evidence

That man had begun to explore and exploit Steep Holm some time between ten thousand and six thousand years ago is suggested by the tentative identification of one or two mesolithic flints discovered during archaeological work on the island. Whether these were deposited before or after Steep Holm became an island is at present uncertain, and indeed, in the absence of an assemblage, specialists find it difficult to agree on the exact dating of these flints – one of which shows evidence of having been retouched for use at a later date. What attraction would Steep Holm have had for mesolithic (Middle Stone Age) man?

Before it was flooded, the wooded valley plain around Steep Holm afforded hunting grounds; and the recent dramatic discovery of preserved footprints sunk into the alluvial clay below ancient peat beds in the inter-tidal region on the Welsh side of the Channel provides evidence of such activities. Impressed more than six thousand years ago, these are the earliest traces of human footprints known in Britain.

Steep Holm, before it became an island, was a natural extension of the valley territory, its higher location offering an environment for different plants and animals. Migrating birds and those nesting on the hillside crags could have been caught for food, and their eggs gathered in season. The isolated hilltop would have provided a base which was comparatively easy to defend from marauders.

As the sea gradually encroached, encircling and converting the hill into a 'new' island, mesolithic man could utilize the rich resources by gathering limpets which colonized sea-washed rocks, or trapping fish in the widening and deepening estuary. In its transitory stage the area abounded in wildlife, and mesolithic man is known to have established regular seasonal camps for the exploitation of environments such as this. Whether such a camp existed on Steep Holm is still open to speculation, although it is intriguing to read nineteenth-century guesses at the date of ancient shell middens which were observed 'above the landing place', where workmen had dug through a bed of shells. Did the 'very dark [earth] abounding in limpet shells and bones of animals' date only from early historic times, as suggested by the Revd John Skinner and Thomas Clark, both of whom visited the island in the 1830s?

The Earliest Channel Sailors

The territories of roaming bands of hunters became greatly restricted by the steadily rising sea levels. Broad tracts of low-lying coastal regions were lost; the 'link roads' to Europe were cut by the English Channel (previously also dry land); the former woodlands of the Bristol Channel valley plain were flooded; and Steep Holm, with its sister island, was surrounded by fast-flowing seas.

Given these circumstances, the skill and imagination to fashion a raft, a dug-out canoe, or a shallow basket of withies covered with watertight skins was not beyond the ingenuity of late mesolithic man. Difficult as such craft might have been to control in shallow estuarine waters, it is more than likely that the islands' resources would have been sufficiently tempting to encourage him to make the effort. His successor, neolithic (New Stone Age) man almost certainly did so, although the evidence is tenuous. Pottery-making skills were known to the neolithic communities. Their pots were fired at low temperatures, and typically were round-based vessels, sometimes decorated, and with lugs for hanging them over fires. When a team from the Bristol Naturalists' Society was excavating on Steep Holm in the 1930s it was aided by H.W. Maxwell, Director of Bristol City Museum, who identified the finds. The published report includes his comment: 'The pottery is very mixed, the oldest fragment being part of the foot of a Neolithic bowl.' Dr Leo Harrison Matthews was a leading member of the excavation team, and years later commented on the artefacts: 'Maxwell had them all at the Bristol Museum. They may well have been destroyed in the Blitz. . . .' The museum was indeed badly damaged by bombing during the Second World War, and many items deposited there were lost.

Neolithic man used different techniques in fashioning his flint implements. He also established a more settled lifestyle, learning to grow crops and domesticate animals. This era which was to set the basic pattern of living for thousands of years to come, lasted from about six thousand to about four thousand years ago. No Bronze Age evidence has been identified on Steep Holm, although Bronze Age settlements have been excavated both on Brean Down and between Barry and Sully, while Flat Holm has produced a fine bronze axe.

That the Severn Estuary and Bristol Channel in prehistoric times were narrower and more shallow than at present is confirmed by Welsh archaeologists, who found Bronze Age hurdle trackways preserved beneath many centuries of accumulated mud deposits in what is now the inter-tidal area along the estuary's western edge. There is little doubt that similar evidence awaits discovery in the inter-tidal region of the estuary's English shore line.

Iron smelting was a natural sequence to the working of copper and bronze, and it employed new techniques which were made possible by achieving higher working temperatures; but even at this time traditional tools of stone were not completely superseded by the new implements. Some of the flints from Steep Holm appear to be of Iron Age date. Flint scrapers were used for such tasks as cleaning animal skins, while flint blades (also identified) were used as knives. The presence of these flints on Steep Holm is proof of at least seasonal use of the island in the later prehistoric period, by which time boats had become far more robust and seaworthy and were quite capable of transporting whole families with animals and stores; while trading vessels and immigrants had long been crossing the English Channel.

In the last 500 years before the Roman conquest the general picture of Celtic society in Britain is principally that of a loose-knit community of restless and sometimes warlike tribes who expended much energy and organization in building increasingly complex and sometimes immense hillforts to protect their possessions from neighbouring raiders. There are several examples of these forts on the mainland a few miles from Steep Holm. Viewed from the more ordered civilizations of Greece and Rome this way of life may have seemed almost barbaric, but the British were not uncultured. They had certainly become skilled in such crafts as intricate metal-working and leather-tooling; and many examples of exquisite ornaments from this and even earlier periods in this country's history adorn our museums.

During the comparatively cool, damp climate of the Iron Age, Steep Holm itself would not have been sufficiently hospitable or indeed large enough to support many people or animals over a long period unless there was some form of mainland link to alleviate seasonal hardship; and it therefore seems doubtful whether the island was occupied permanently in this prehistoric period. Visitors to the island in the past, however, have pondered the possibility of some features on the plateau having ancient origins. In 1832 the Revd John Skinner repeated hearsay information of a possible prehistoric burial – although it could equally relate to the Dark Ages:

An old man – who inhabits the hut at the summit of the rock . . . informed me that while digging within the small inclosure which he calls his garden, he came to a vault or cist, seven feet long by four wide; the walls formed of stone without cement, and covered with flat paving stones as he called them; within was a human skull, and skeleton with the skulls of sheep, and other bones, some of which appeared to have been burnt, but there was no appearance of any weapon or vessel.

A year earlier the Revd David Williams had written: 'Two or three bands run across the island from N to S . . . they were probably outliers to the encampment, as at Worlebury [hillfort] on Weston Hill.' Tentative inference that a possibly even more ancient feature existed was made by John Strachey in the 1730s: 'on ye Sumit or Ridge runs a Single foundation to a Circular Enclosure of Like Loose Stones at ye Western poynt, whither a Watch tower or Tumulus [prehistoric burial mound] is Very Uncertain.'

Remnants of the line of stones, of the circular enclosure and of the bands running North to South still exist; and undoubtedly the residue of the 'circular enclosure' is one of the most ancient relics on the island. At present, though, it cannot be said positively that an Iron Age outpost or small settlement was here, although there are hillforts large and small on virtually every hill and promontory on the neighbouring channel seaboard. In the detective work which gradually builds up the archaeological record there is always a chance that the vital clue will materialize to decide the point. Meanwhile there are alternative theories to explain the enigmatic features on the island plateau – but they will be discussed in another chapter.

Chapter Three

A ROMAN OUTPOST

New Discoveries

The final stages of the Iron Age culture in Britain were cut into abruptly by the rapidly widening powers of the Roman Empire. South-western territories were under Roman control well before AD 49, by which time the Mendip mines of Charterhouse were exporting to Italy Imperial stamped lead and silver. The Roman conquest and long occupation of this country is familiar territory for history scholars; but how does Steep Holm fit into the story of Romanized Britain?

Until the current archaeological work, the island was not credited with having any connection with the Roman occupation, although in the last century some visitors found clues which were not followed up. Recent discoveries and identification of numerous Roman artefacts, including fragments of flue and roofing tiles, show that the Romans can claim the honour of being the first authenticated permanent residents of the island. That their presence on Steep Holm was maintained for several centuries is indicated by the wide-ranging dates of Roman ware recovered over the last fifteen years.

What is particularly intriguing is that one of these Roman finds – a small sherd of Italian produced red gloss Arretine pottery – pre-dates the Roman conquest of Britain by more than thirty years. In its imitation of earlier metal prototypes from classical Greece, Arretine ware, the predecessor of the later and more generally found Samian pottery, was renowned as the very best quality tableware; and the sherd found on Steep Holm lives up to that reputation. Bearing a delicate vine leaf scroll beneath the rim, the sherd is part of a 'crater', or wine bowl, shaped like an inverted bell on a pedestal foot, and standing some 6 in high. The bowl of the pot would have been decorated with moulded figures standing out in relief. The style of the pottery was perfected by highly skilled Greek slaves or freedmen who were working in Italy; the workshop concerned in the manufacture of the wine bowl ceasing production in AD 10. Steep Holm would seem to be the last place where one might have expected to find elegant pottery of so early a date; and how such a costly import from Arretium (now Arezzo) came to be on the island remains an unsolved mystery.

George Boon, to whom we are indebted for a specialist report on the Arretine sherd, points out that Steep Holm is by far the most westerly location at which decorated Italian Arretine ware has yet been found. We like to think that the crater was brought to Steep Holm after the conquest by a Roman officer who treasured it either as a family heirloom or as loot from previous campaigns. Discoveries by archaeologists of examples of the later Roman Samian pottery carefully repaired by riveting or by inserts of lead, are clear indications of how such items were valued.

The presence of fibulae on Steep Holm is readily explained, for these early brooches were used to fasten clothing in both Iron Age and Roman times. Two brooches are of La Tene III type – a simple but ingenious bronze safety pin – which continued in use into the first century AD. These were obviously lost or thrown away when, as commonly happened, the securing pins snapped.

Moving on from the overlap period between Iron Age and Roman cultures represented by these finds, it is easy to re-create some of the atmosphere of Roman Steep Holm. One can visualize the difficulties of unloading from a supply vessel the latest consignment of heavy two-handled amphorae filled with olive oil or fish oil – these commodities having various uses; in cooking, for dressing salads, medicinally, or as lamp fuel.

The top of one such globular amphora was discovered in 1980 on the site of the previously mentioned circular feature at the western extremity of the island. Its surviving handle fortuitously still bore a clear potter's stamp which neatly dated its manufacture to between AD 90 and AD 140. This storage jar, of a form known as Dressel 20, had originated in the Baetis river valley region of Southern Spain. Another handle from a similar type of amphora was rescued when many tons of rock and other debris were being cleared from within the ruined nineteenth-century inn building which stands just above East Beach.

Even today, to live permanently on Steep Holm would be possible only if there were an efficient and regular supply service to the island. That the Roman occupation of Steep Holm was not one of a peasant smallholding family scratching a living from the soil and surrounding sea is proved by the type and variety of artefacts which have now been found. Broken pieces of the high-quality decorated tableware which superseded Arretine pottery, and which was imported from Gaul, again make it clear that luxury goods could be afforded by the Roman inhabitants of Steep Holm. Samian sherds of the Form 37 type, in the shape of deep 'fruit' bowls, with moulded figures similar to the Arretine decoration can be quite accurately dated, being contemporary with the amphorae, and in use during the second century AD. Other Samian fragments, unearthed during path-widening above East Beach, represent rather more than half of an attractive shallow dish of Form 36 type, with a sinuous vine leaf decoration around the rim. A colour-coated pottery base which was found on the plateau could have been part of a vase or an oil lamp; while a delicately decorated sherd of Castor ware, and a fragment of an indented beaker add to the picture of affluence.

Neck and handle of amphora found at Rudder Rock in 1979, with handle (left) from a second amphora from above East Beach

In considering other luxury items which helped to ease the rigours of island life, it is tempting to speculate upon the excavation of a small bronze bracelet and a thimble, which at present cannot positively be assigned to the Roman era. A broken spindle whorl is another object which cannot be closely dated in its unstratified context. But a disc brooch certainly points to stylish Roman elegance; and an ornamental bronze tip resembling a tiny clenched hand was perhaps snapped from a large hair pin – or even from a stylus, once used for letters or lists of stores, written on long-since lost tablets of wax.

For cooking and storage purposes coarse pottery was in daily domestic use; and sherds of the ever popular black-burnished and grey wares have been excavated, some with distinctive lattice patterns on the shoulders of the unglazed pots. Culinary discoveries also included a piece of a pottery strainer. These had many uses, some of the less obvious being for cheesemaking or for the mixing of medicines.

Cream cheese may have been made using *mortaria*. Several different types of these wide shallow dishes with thick rims and a pouring lip are represented. They are readily identified by their heavily gritted inner surfaces, their normal use being for the crushing of seeds and herbs, or for compounding herbal remedies, using a pestle of wood, stone or pottery.

New Plants Introduced?

Steep Holm's flora includes several species which were used by Roman herbalists to treat various ills. Henbane, although poisonous, was recognized to be a powerful narcotic to ease toothache, alleviate seasickness or even to soothe madness! Hemlock was used as an ointment for rheumatic pains – although it was deadly poison if taken internally in the minutest quantity. Valerian was renowned for its essential oil, used as a sedative for headaches or nervous disorders. Could the present plants be descendants of Roman introductions, or were they brought to the island much later?

Roman cooks liked to use a remarkable mixture of herbs and flavourings when preparing meat, birds or fish for the table. Native plants were available, like the prolific nettle and the now rare wild leek (*allium ampeloprasum*) which still survives on both Steep Holm and Flat Holm, but the new style of cookery demanded a number of plants of Mediterranean origin. These included *smyrnium olusatrum* (since medieval times usually known as alexanders because of its link with the Egyptian city of Alexandria), and this has become the dominant vegetation on Steep Holm. Although understandably there is no botanical record of it on the island until 1562, it is known to have been introduced into England by the Roman conquerors, along with many other plants for seasoning. Such was the pungent quality of cooking in the utensils of the day that some Roman recipes advocated 'Take a new pot.' If the old pot, even though undamaged, was contaminated by absorption of strongly spiced flavours which would spoil another recipe, it was customary to destroy it – the earliest documented use of throwaway ware!

Quite apart from plants having medicinal or culinary uses, some were also valued for magical or superstitious ritual. The Mediterranean peony (*paeonia mascula*), so named after the Greek god, physician and herbalist Paeon, could be used medicinally (although poisonous), and was prized as a charm against evil spirits – the seeds being strung together as a necklace, or the tubers being carved decoratively and similarly worn. Gaius Plinius Secundus (Pliny the Elder), first-century Roman soldier, who was killed in the AD 79 eruption of Vesuvius, mentions this plant in his prolific writings. We shall never know who introduced the wild peony to Steep Holm, but we can indulge in a little intriguing speculation! Even the harmless and useful elder which is a feature of the island plateau has been from ancient times surrounded by an aura of superstition.

Evidence of Living Quarters

Although flue tile fragments have been unearthed from infill debris on the medieval priory site, the Romans' living quarters were probably near the summit of the island, where fragments of *tegulae* (pottery roofing tiles) have been found – some still with traces of mortar on their edges. Also on the plateau we have identified more pieces of box flue tiles bearing their characteristic combing pattern to aid the adhesion of mortar. The latter tiles clearly indicate the former presence of a heating system, or perhaps a bath house – and a tiny isolated fragment of finely finished lime wall plaster, painted yellow, which was found in surface soil, is almost certainly Roman.

Examination of surviving archives shows that some further evidence was found in the nineteenth century, but disregarded and subsequently lost. The Revd John Skinner visited Steep Holm on 26 July 1832. He was a noted antiquarian who spent a large proportion of his time travelling to ancient sites, often paying labourers to dig 'one or two' in a day, to see what could be found. Fortunately he employed no team of diggers for his day on Steep Holm, but he did make some tantalizing notes and sketches. In his diary he wrote:

> As we ascended by a zig zag footpath to the summit, I picked up fragments of the grey Roman pottery, and noticed also specimens of coarser ware, some lacquered over; the earth here looked very dark abounding in limpet shells and the bones of animals, showing that it had been a permanent, not a precarious abode as far back perhaps as the time of the Romans.

Later, almost certainly on the plateau, he noticed 'tiles and bricks some of the former hollowed out after the Roman manner; but they might also be attributable to a later period'.

Whether or not Skinner's identification of the 'grey' pottery was correct cannot now be proved, or disproved; but our experience of pottery finds from current archaeological work on the island would suggest that his 'specimens of coarser ware, some lacquered over' were from a later period. There seems no doubt, however, about the accuracy of his observation of tiles 'hollowed out after the Roman manner'.

Being obsessed with theories of Danish connections with the island, Skinner did not pursue the implications of what he thought were Roman finds, and if he made a collection of Steep Holm sherds this has not survived.

Coins

Detailed study of local newspapers of the last century produced another vital scrap of evidence. A gentleman, writing under a *nom de plume* to the *Weston Mercury* in 1887 (Queen Victoria's Golden Jubilee Year), tells of a week's recuperative stay in the island's Holm Hotel. His account includes the following intriguing comment:

> Some years ago some Roman coins, now in the possession of a Weston gentleman, were discovered; and the intelligent and courteous Master Gunner of the island, Mr Ware, a short time ago exhumed a small Roman coin which was submitted to a good authority on numismatics at Weston. The opinion of this gentleman in a letter dated July 23rd 1887 greatly excited my curiosity and attention. It is to the following effect, 'The coin which I enclose herein is of bronze make, and represents a conquerer leading a soldier or a slave captive in

a kneeling position. The lettering is much effaced and indistinguishable but the work is fine, and shows that Roman artists 1,600 or 1,800 years ago were much in advance of the present day, to wit, this year's Jubilee coinage. It is undoubted evidence that the Romans had a station on the island . . .

The same incidents appear to be elaborated in an account written fifteen years later, in 1902, by author and local historian F.A. Knight, who refers to a tradition that 'a former tenant of the island once dug up a pot of coins, but all trace of them now appears to have been lost'. He also recorded that during the fortification work of 1867 'a coin bearing the figure of an archer was found'. Knight made no attempt to date these coins and it is apparent that already the earlier rumours of alleged Roman finds on Steep Holm had faded from memory.

Recently, more evidence of Roman coins on Steep Holm has been passed to us by Mr E.J. Mason. This is a letter written from Switzerland on 7 February 1960, by the late 9th Baron Wharton, then fifty-two years old, whose family had held the island for well over one hundred years. He was answering a general enquiry about what he knew of the family's period of ownership:

> . . . I remember as a child seeing a handful of silver Roman coins in very good state, which had been dug up by my great uncle on the island. The date of the coins was not long after the date of the Roman conquest . . . I should add that my great uncle found also, or rather dug up, a certain quantity of Roman pottery, some of which was badly broken, but some of which was almost perfect. I cannot tell you what became of the coins, but I am perfectly sure that the Roman pottery was consumed in the fire which destroyed the large front of Halswell Park [Halswell House, the family home in Somerset].

During current archaeological excavations, five small bronze Roman coins have been discovered ranging in date from AD 269 to AD 335. Of these coins, one (Tetricus I, AD 271–3) had been clipped, and another (Claudius II, AD 269) is a counterfeit. This practice was widespread in Roman times, and there are several caves in the Mendip hills which were used as Roman counterfeiters' dens.

Rare Glass

With the latest of these coins we move into the fourth century; and with additional pottery finds the evidence of occupation in that period is reinforced. But it was a tiny piece of glass which was to become the most important discovery from this later era. Greenish, streaky, slightly bubbly and with small marks on the surface, superficially it appeared insignificant; but from previous experience of fragmented glass of this type, we knew that it had to be from an engraved glass bowl of the extremely rare Winthill type – an identification soon confirmed by the Director of the City of Bristol Museum. Only three examples of these bowls had been identified previously in England, and none are complete, although one from the Winthill site is almost so. Made at Cologne, Germany, in the period AD 300 – 350 these bowls were shallow, with mythical, hunting, or Biblical scenes engraved with a flint burin on the underside, so that the design could be seen through the glass.

At the beginning of the Roman chapter in Steep Holm's history expensive Arretine ware is present, and dating from 300 years later another remnant of a rare import occurs. What is the significance of these finds? To us it seems unlikely that any wealthy civilian would have chosen to live permanently on the island. Like the Arretine wine crater, the engraved glass bowl probably belonged to an officer of the Roman Army, or at least to someone who held an important and lucrative island post under the Roman administration.

An Island Signal Station

Why were the Romans so interested in this remote and rocky island that they established a permanent base there over several centuries? We are sure that there can be only one answer.

Use of Steep Holm for a signal station, watchtower or lighthouse has to be the most convincing explanation, and a site at its western extremity is ideally situated for this purpose. The position of this site is significant, providing magnificent panoramic views of the Channel between England and Wales. The fact that the Victorians built a gun emplacement to one side, and that the army engineers of the Second World War chose this same spot for the only battery observation post on the island emphasizes this point. A Roman signal station or lighthouse here would have been perfectly positioned to have contact with shipping, as well as with both the English and Welsh coasts and the sister island of Flat Holm. Study into the technicalities of Roman signal stations generally is still at an exploratory and slightly controversial stage, but use of the island for this purpose seems to be the only logical reason for such a long and important occupation.

In good visibility, at approximately 30 miles range, the first-century Roman signal station at Old Burrow on the North Devon coast might possibly have been in contact; perhaps through a chain of temporary shore stations. The Welsh tribes were never entirely subdued by the Romans, and at that time there was a constant danger of raids across the Channel by the Silures. Later, when a Roman presence had been established on the South Wales coast and fortresses had been built, there was still the risk of Irish raiders coming up the Channel.

The estuary then, as now, was an important thoroughfare for shipping, with cargo boats carrying supplies to towns and military bases; while fast rowing galleys with camouflaged sails maintained frequent patrols, ever watchful for marauders.

In the first century Sea Mills, near the confluence with the River Avon, was established as a temporary port for supplies for the Roman Army in the West Country; but there were also numerous harbours and landing places at the mouths of many of the smaller rivers. Uphill, where the River Axe meets the Channel in the shelter of Brean Down (site of a late Roman temple) was probably the nearest of these minor ports to Steep Holm; and remnants of a possible fort at nearby Bleadon can still be seen, while a rather elusive but partly traceable Roman road leads to it from the direction of the Mendip lead and silver mines.

At what appears to have been the site of the probable signal station, almost immediately above and to the north of Rudder Rock, partly sheltered by being below the island plateau, are the substantial remnants of a curving stone wall, slightly tapered, and with a base several feet thick. Within the curvature of this walling are the 'underground' ammunition stores of the Rudder Rock Victorian gun emplacement.

Close examination of this area during field survey work in 1977 revealed that the Victorian builders had ingeniously incorporated their military works into peripheral remains of a much more ancient feature. Confusing the picture further, the Second World War battery observation post also encroached on to its edge.

With the recognition that part of the pathway from Rudder Rock to the next Victorian gun battery above the north cliffs was in fact the top of a second section of ancient curved walling came the realization that there are two segments of a circular construction. After this discovery, comparison with aerial photographs and research into documentary material provided valuable additional information.

John Skinner, in a diary account of his visit to Steep Holm in 1832 wrote: 'At the very extreme point northwards nearly opposite to the Flat Holmes and Pennarth Point on the Welch Coast, I noticed an oval outpost or signal station. . .' His reference to a northern extremity of Steep Holm was at first puzzling, in view of the island's long north coast. Reconciliation of his account with others, and with known facts was not possible until we realized that he had mistakenly supposed the island to lie along a north-south axis, instead of east-west. When corrected, his 'extreme point northwards' became the Rudder Rock area at the *western* extremity, and his account then tallied with our discovery.

Skinner described the feature: 'It measures within the oval about 20 paces by 18; the walls formed of loose stones might have been about 4 feet wide; the uprights being fixed in the soil, or rather the rock, and the inner space filled up very similar to the workmanship of the vitrified forts in Scotland.'

On what seems to have been an even earlier visit, probably in 1818, he noted 'a Beacon the circular mark of the area where the fire was still remaining'. Preoccupied by Danish connections with the island he ignored the significance of what he described as 'fragments of Roman pottery at the N [i.e. west] extremity', and assumed the feature to be a Danish work.

More early evidence comes from Thomas Clark, in 1831, who after a visit to Steep Holm wrote: 'At the Western end I observed an oval space, also surrounded with a ridge of stone but still ruder and less conspicuous [than another ridge of stones which he had noticed elsewhere on the island].'

The earliest known description, however, was found in manuscript notes prepared in the 1730s by John Strachey, who was gathering material for an intended topographical history of Somerset. He records 'a Circular Enclosure of Like Loose Stones at ye Western poynt, whither a Watch tower or Tumulus is Very Uncertain.' His 'watchtower' observation might well have been very close to the mark!

These early writers were fortunate to see the feature before it was so well disguised by the later fortification work that it was 'lost' to view, and its existence forgotten. Its eastern half now lies buried beneath the rubble which was piled upon the Victorian shell and cartridge stores built within the oval, and it was from among this rubble that the large chunk of Spanish amphora was retrieved in 1980.

The oval ridge of stones is curious in that it is not typically Roman, yet it does bear resemblance to plans of some small signal stations which have been identified in other parts of this country. It is possible that this was an adaptation of an Iron Age construction, perhaps originally a cattle or sheep pen. To assign a firm date to the feature, it will be necessary to carry out detailed and skilled investigation of this much disturbed area.

Usually Roman signal stations consisted of a square tower within a boundary wall. The problem here is that the Victorian ammunition stores were built exactly where a tower might have been. The importing of fuel to the island to feed the fire or light must have caused a few headaches, especially as there is no convenient landing place at the west end.

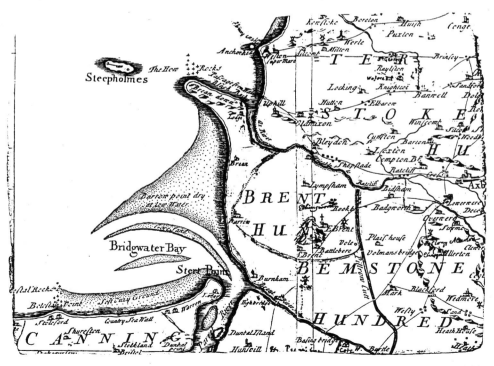

Map of the area by John Strachey, showing features marked on Steep Holm, dating from the 1730s

Connecting the signal station/watchtower/lighthouse with their living quarters and landing places, the Romans undoubtedly had a trackway and this almost certainly would have followed the course of the line of stones which was traced along the dorsum of the island plateau during field survey work.

On a map of old Somerset drawn by John Strachey as part of his unpublished notes, Steep Holm is a mere ¼ in long. Looking closely at tiny marks within this outline, it can be seen that he had drawn the oval feature and trackway which was traced in the 1977 fieldwork. But this drawing also implies a second possible signal station at the east end of the island, where gun emplacements now stand, adjacent to the summit of Tower Rock. This position would cover an expanse of Channel and coastline not visible from the Rudder Rock area, and a station here could account for the quantity of Roman artefacts which have been found in this part of the island. Unfortunately, however, Strachey does not clearly identify his second circle in his text – and on such a small scale map the mark could indicate another quite different feature.

A Romano-Celtic God

An exciting discovery on 28 June 1991 by a member of the archaeological team suggests a new dimension to the Roman presence on Steep Holm. In the sycamore wood above East Beach, Mr Terry Gore noticed a human face carved on a small algae-covered stone, lying among loose scree which from time to time slides down the steep slope. The impure Jurassic limestone on which the face is carved is local to

Close-up of Celtic carved stone head found on Steep Holm, 1991

the region, but not to the island; and pink discoloration indicates that at some stage it has been subjected to fire. It measures 3.6 in high; 3 in wide; and 5 in deep; the sculpting of the features being typically Celtic, with pear-shaped head, hollow, uneven eyes, elongated nose and wide-open mouth.

Dr Miranda Green (who has prepared a specialist report on the head) and several other experts in Celtic imagery agree that the 'shouting' aspect of the mouth was intended as a symbol of life. The cowled head could have been inset into a building as a talisman; or fixed into the gable end of a shrine erected to venerate springs of 'life-giving' fresh water which emerged from the cliffside. Had the face been associated with a tomb monument, it is more likely to have been fashioned with a closed mouth.

Although these rare 'god-heads' cannot usually be dated accurately to within 500 years, unless stratified, Dr Green suggests a connection with the signal station. A small garrison could have included Celtic soldiery, and Roman tolerance of native religions allowed the Celts to erect and venerate their own pagan gods. The Steep Holm god-head was in no way stratified, but the area in which it was found regularly produces Roman pottery and building material, as animals or the elements disturb the surface.

Whether this intriguing find pre-dates, or is part of the Roman scene; or even how it reached the position in which it was found, is at present yet another mystery!

Another Celtic Head?

Shortly after Terry Gore's discovery reports were circulated of another Celtic carved head, given to the present warden, and said to have been found on the island in the 1930s by Dr L. Harrison Matthews. Two totally different Celtic stone heads from Steep Holm would indeed have been exciting; but the claimed provenance for this thumb-sized artefact has been contradicted by Dr Matthews's own evidence. No such find was recorded in his archaeological report or in his personal notes, and a letter from him affirms that 'the finds . . . did not amount to much, and Maxwell [director] had them all at the Bristol Museum'.

Chapter Four

DELVING INTO THE DARK AGES

The First British Historian

We now reach the point where the history of Steep Holm always used to start – with the legends of the so-called Dark Ages which followed the withdrawal from this country of Roman protection, in around AD 410. Generally the Romanized way of life continued for some time after the official Roman presence was removed; but it slowly disintegrated under increasingly bold petty raids, incursions and invasions by the Picts, Scots and Saxons. One survival from this confused era is the first positive name for the island, then known by the native races as Ronech.

Firm evidence is missing for any occupation of Ronech during the period immediately following the abandonment of the Roman base. Legend creeps in with the story of St Gildas and his 'stormy' sojourn on the island. Many of the tales recounted of him are heavily embroidered with miraculous events, some of them not always in keeping with the saintly image which would be projected nowadays. But this fifth/sixth-century northern chieftain's son who later became a much travelled monk, has a claim to fame as the author of what is regarded as the first 'history' of Britain – written as twenty-six introductory chapters to a religious tirade on the ills of this country.

Liber Querulus De Excidio Britanniae (or 'Lament over the Destruction of Britain') is not an entirely accurate narrative, and Gildas has been criticized for this; but he had to rely mainly on 'word of mouth' traditions and memories as there were few written references to past events in Britain. More to the point, the main purpose of his work was not to write a history but to highlight the evils of his day – in particular the continual quarrels and wars between certain petty chieftains – in comparison with bygone days, when Roman rule, although sometimes cruel, had guaranteed stability and relative peace to Britain.

Some oft-repeated legends say that Gildas lived on Ronech for seven years, having built there an oratory (a small chapel for private worship). Others add that he wrote his history while on the island, flinging into the sea those pages mentioning Arthur in a fit of pique following a quarrel with that king – which neatly explains the lack of even a mention of this famous contemporary character in the history, but does nothing to resolve the controversy over the true identity of Arthur. Could the absence of his name in *De Excidio* be explained by Gildas being more concerned with scolding the bad chieftains than praising the good?

The literal accuracy of his biographies is suspect, but it can be conjectured that Gildas was born in about AD 476. In turbulent times he had to flee to Wales with his family in about AD 506. On the death of his wife a year later he turned to a religious life, tonsuring his head and leading an ascetic existence.

On his way home from a journey to Rome, Gildas landed on the islet of Rhuis in southern Brittany where he was able to obtain a grant of land to found a monastery in around AD 520. Shortly afterwards he is said to have returned to Britain in search of recruits for his new community; and the legends of Steep Holm are connected with this part of his life. Seven years spent either abroad or touring Britain appear to have been transposed by later writers to seven years of solitude on Ronech. For perhaps two or three years he was at Llancarfan Monastery in South Wales (in around AD 527–9), where his friend Cadoc was abbot. During that comparatively short stay he probably followed the custom of withdrawing to a place of retreat each year during the season of Lent, returning to the monastery by Palm Sunday in preparation for Holy Week and Easter.

Some early accounts say that both St Gildas and St Cadoc spent Lent on Echni (Flat Holm), which is credible as, unlike Steep Holm, it came (with the similar 'hermit' island of Barry) within the ancient boundary of Llancarfan Monastery. Others say that Cadoc favoured the more hospitable island, while Gildas stayed alone on the rugged cliff tops of Ronech. No early oratory foundations have yet been unearthed either on Flat Holm or Steep Holm, which is perhaps not so surprising. Following the Roman discoveries we now know that the recluse could have adapted one of the abandoned Roman buildings. Other holy men are known to have followed a similar practice.

Contrary to what is said in popular versions of Gildas's sojourn on Steep Holm, if he was there he would not have been entirely alone. He would have been accompanied by at least one or two novice monks to minister to his practical needs, and basic furniture is likely to have been placed in his cell – even if he did sometimes feel inspired to sleep out on the rocks! Remembering the likelihood of earlier pagan Celtic veneration of the fresh water which emerged from the cliffs, it is of interest that Gildas is credited with having elicited a spring on the island. Did he also perhaps destroy what might have remained of an existing shrine – one bearing a god-head antefix carved from stone?

Gildas's diet is said by some modern writers to have consisted of fish and the eggs of sea birds. Of necessity fish may have formed part of his daily fare, although this was not always favoured by the early Christian Church because of its associations with the Roman goddess Venus. Indeed, Gildas himself is said to have tried to destroy a statue of Venus by burying it beneath the foundations of his Rhuis monastery. Fish on Friday was not to become the normal custom until a later period; and unless domestic fowls were transported to the island Gildas would have had few breakfast eggs. During the early spring months seagulls gather in their thousands on the islands to select their nesting places – but they seldom lay their eggs during Lent. It is too early in the season. More probably the birds themselves were trapped (following the earlier Roman practice of using bird lime or nets), as their flesh, and even that of seals and other sea mammals, was not then considered to be 'meat', and so was acceptable during periods of fasting.

Ronech's vegetation contained more than one vital plant in prime growth and plentiful supply during the season of Lent. Alexanders, with nettles (still equally prolific on the island) would have made a nourishing supplement to a diet of cereals and pottages (stewed mixtures of whatever was available); while flavours were further enhanced by the fresh spring growth of the wild leek. Mead, ale or, more normally, water completed the meagre meals taken in the weeks of abstinence.

During comparatively short stays for prayer and fasting on Ronech or Echni it would not have been possible for Gildas to write such a long epistle as *De Excidio*. He himself said that it took ten years to compile. Quite apart from the effort of composing and writing such a long treatise between frequent obligatory prayer sessions, the preparation of expensive vellum and freshly mixed 'inks' from a variety of ingredients was a laborious and lengthy task.

Wild leeks on the Holms

Alexanders growing on Victorian Garden Battery

Modern stories that Gildas regularly rowed across the five miles of sea between Steep Holm and the mainland at Uphill to preach at a church there are fabrications loosely based on John Leland's sixteenth-century statement that the saint preached in a church by the sea shore. His preaching venues would have been along the Welsh coastline. Confusion derives from the island's much later (documented) religious connection with Uphill's Norman church in the twelfth and thirteenth centuries.

Legend says that eventually Gildas was driven from Ronech by the unwelcome attentions of raiding pirates, and that he removed to Glastonbury. John Leland, Antiquary to King Henry VIII, quoted William of Malmesbury's 1125 history of Glastonbury, which stated that Gildas had died there. Leland himself visited Glastonbury before the Dissolution and had access to the monks' impressive collection of manuscripts; but he was writing a thousand years after the death of Gildas, and with reference to a library which had been re-created following the disastrous fire of 1184 which had destroyed most of the abbey buildings. After the fire, and in an attempt to attract desperately needed funds from pilgrims, the monks displayed relics said to have been found by them during preparations for the rebuilding work. These relics included bones purporting to be of Gildas and of King Arthur and his queen, among others, but there are doubts about the authenticity of these remains. Moreover, in replacing the abbey library by copying ancient manuscripts borrowed from other religious foundations, it is generally suspected that original versions of histories may have been elaborated to include rather more than was first written.

After leaving Wales, Gildas could have spent a short time at Glastonbury, and it is true that pirates were troublesome in the Severn Estuary, perhaps to the extent of interrupting his devotions; but his early biographer says that he had returned to his own monastery at Rhuis by about AD 534 – no doubt with a band of recruits to add to the numbers of that community.

Rhuis has a better claim than Steep Holm to being where Gildas wrote his treatise, for it is calculated from events mentioned in the text that it must have been written by about AD 544, ten years after his return to Rhuis, and during a period of forty years' comparative peace. Even though foreign invasions were temporarily halted, petty West Country chieftains were still engaged in bitter power struggles and vendettas.

A year after *De Excidio* was written Gildas's brother and sons are said to have been forced to flee from Wales because of his virulent comments about the chieftains there. Would Gildas have written his vigorous attack on the evils of the ruling princes of the West if he was within easy reach of their wrath?

The later years of Gildas's life, apart from occasional short visits to Britain and Ireland, were spent at his monastery at Rhuis, and he is recorded as having died there in about AD 570, having attained the remarkable age of ninety-four years – if the calculations of his biographer are correct.

That Gildas had local knowledge of the River Severn area emerges from his pioneering history, when he bewails the lack of order and peace in Britain during constant strife, and the ending of a former trade in luxury goods which once had plied up and down the estuary. Whether he is recalling hearsay from far-off days when the strong Roman presence made the waterway safe, or whether his complaint stems from the stoppage of later trade is not clear. But we would like to think that it refers to Roman commercial traffic, as indicated by the artefacts found on Steep Holm.

From the historian's viewpoint, if Gildas did indeed stay on Steep Holm, even for just a few short weeks during Lent, what a pity that such a prolific writer left no description of the Isle of Ronech at that time!

Brave King Tewdrig

Saxon invaders of Britain gradually consolidated their positions and pushed farther westwards until eventually, instead of just raiding the countryside, they infiltrated and settled around the Severn Valley. By the ninth century their influence was strong enough for the Bristol Channel islands to be commonly known by their rather ungainly Saxon names – Bradanreolice (Flat Holm) and Steopanreolice (Steep Holm): Bradan meaning 'broad' and Steopan, logically enough, 'steep'. 'Reolice' derives from the Irish *reilig* (cemetery) and the Latin *reliquiae* (relics), so these names clearly indicate veneration of the two islands as burial places. The inference is that there was a cemetery on each island, perhaps with a small oratory or hermitage – possibly dating from the time of the saints Gildas and Cadoc.

The *Book of Llandaff* records an incident from the seventh century which has some bearing on the former tradition of burial on the islands. It recounts how, in his old age, King Tewdrig had ceded power to his son and had retired to live as a hermit near Tintern. To help his son against Saxon infiltration he came out of retirement in about AD 620, and led his army to victory at the Battle of Tintern. Although mortally wounded in the fighting he refused to go back to court with his son, but insisted on returning to his hermitage. His dying request was to be taken 'hence to that desirable place where I wish to lie after death . . . to the island of Echni' [Flat Holm]. With all due honour his body was taken to the shore on a wagon drawn by stags, then conveyed across the water, and interred on the island.

If Echni was considered a suitable place for such a royal burial, other prominent people would also have arranged for similar burial rites; and the indefatigable Strachey provides an example in his Steep Holm notes: 'Cambden Says the Holms were famous for The Burial of Gualch a Britton of Great piety whose Disciple Barruk gave name to Barry Isle on ye Opposite Welch Shore.' The connection with Barry Island may give Flat Holm the distinction of being the venue for this renowned Dark Age burial, rather than Steep Holm; but the Saxon perpetuation of tradition in renaming both places 'reolice' indicates that the same veneration must have applied equally. The cist burial on Steep Holm as described to Skinner in 1832 could as readily be associated with this era as with prehistoric times.

Many isolated offshore islands were regarded as holy places where those who had the resources wished to be buried, because of earlier associations with former saints who were remembered in folklore for regularly setting out across the turbulent waters to withdraw into solitude for uninterrupted contemplation and prayer.

Lundy's large cemetery, which is still in use, has strong evidence of traditional island burial rites. Around an ancient cist, presumed to have been the place where a holy man whose name is lost was buried, other interments were made over several centuries, some marked with early Christian memorial stones. One of these seems to indicate the burial place of a fifth- or sixth-century local chieftain's son.

A fragment of stone slab bearing an incised cross, dated to between the seventh and ninth centuries and found on Flat Holm, may be connected with an early religious foundation there – or could it simply have been part of a memorial to King Tewdrig?

The Vikings

For two hundred years from the time of St Gildas, until the late eighth century, there were no significant attacks on this country, but by 870 the dreaded Viking ships had penetrated the 'Severn Sea', raiding up the rivers which flowed into it. The Parrett, the Axe and other waterways became thoroughfares up which the sleek boats moved on their way to ravage inland as well as coastal regions, the raids becoming more extensive as the morale and resistance of the Saxons faded.

That 'Steopanreolice' played a part in later vicious attacks is apparent from what must be the *Anglo-Saxon Chronicle* extract most quoted by West Country historians – the gist of which shows that by this time the advantage was with the defenders.

The *Chronicle* records that in 914 a great force of ships commanded by two Danish earls came from bases in Brittany and ravaged North Wales and across the country, seizing hostages and demanding ransoms. The king paid the enormous sum of £40 for the return of one bishop who was captured. But this time the men of Hereford and Gloucester successfully fought against the marauders and in turn demanded hostages to ensure that promises to withdraw were kept. All along the south coastline of the Severn Sea men were organized to watch for the retreating forces and to prevent another landing. Twice more the Vikings attempted night raids, at Watchet and Porlock, and each time many of them were killed, only a few escaping to their ships and fleeing to Steopanreolice. The survivors were soon starving, and many of them died of hunger, until some were able to make their way to safety in Ireland.

Nothing is straightforward when trying to unravel the history of Steep Holm. One copy of the *Chronicle* – regarded as the earliest – actually names the island of retreat as Bradanreolice (Flat Holm) while all the rest refer to Steopanreolice (Steep Holm). Whether an error was corrected, or whether copies were carelessly rewritten cannot now be verified; but with the Viking tendency to utilize suitable islands as bases and jumping off points for their raids, it is virtually certain that both islands were used in this way. Steep Holm was more easily defended, although each would have posed problems for the safe mooring of ships.

John Strachey elaborates on this point when he noted (in the 1730s) that Steep Holm was used 'for harboring ye Danish Pyrates in their ravages on these Coasts wch Shews they were put to great Extremitys for here is both ye foulest Ground for Anchoring and ye most Dangerous Rocks Roughest Tydes & Generally most Tempestuous Biding in all this Channell . . .'. The unfortunate Strachey must have suffered a rough voyage!

For food supplies the Vikings generally gained more than enough from their plundering – when all went well. On this occasion, being unable to replenish stores after successive defeats in battles would have accounted for shortages on what should have been a well-stocked base.

The *Anglo-Saxon Chronicle*'s reference to the Vikings stealing away by night to raid coastal settlements may point to partial verification of John Skinner's theories that what we believe to be an older feature – the oval enclosure at the west extremity of Steep Holm – was put to use by them as a beacon to guide their ships up and down the river to selected targets, and back to the safety of the islands. If this were so, the old watchtower or signal station area could easily have been adapted to this purpose.

No archaeological evidence of Viking presence on Steopanreolice or Bradanreolice has yet materialized; but following the raids which continued with varying success throughout the tenth century, permanent and peaceful Viking settlement became established on the mainland. From 1016 England was ruled wisely by the Danish King Cnut for nearly twenty years; and the Saxon names of the two sister islands became changed by long usage to the Danish 'Holm', meaning 'river island'.

The last successful invasion of British soil, in 1066, forever ended the question of Danish or Saxon dominance and enforced another great cultural change in this country; but the once hated former raiders' name for the islands was never again replaced. With only minor variations of spelling over the centuries, Steep Holm, a local legacy of the violent era of the Vikings, became fixed on the map of history.

Chapter Five

FOUNDING A MEDIEVAL PRIORY

A Flat Holm Comparison

To Steep Holm's sister island the aftermath of the Norman invasion brought a moment of prestige. *The Anglo-Saxon Chronicle* records that in 1067, following her son's defeat and death at the Battle of Hastings, Queen Githa, mother of King Harold, found refuge on Bradanreolice (Flat Holm) with many of her ladies. There they remained for some time – not on Steep Holm, as some writers have assumed.

While on the island, however, where did the queen and her entourage stay? It is unlikely that a peasant's farm would have been able to feed and accommodate them for long. Did Flat Holm have a religious establishment capable of providing for the queen and her court for 'some time'? We are sure that it did.

A sixth-century connection with St Cadoc, and a seventh-century king's desire to be buried there have already been commented upon, and of Cadoc we find a revival of tradition recorded in a mid-twelfth century deed by William, the powerful Earl of Gloucester and Lord of Glamorgan. By this deed William gave three acres on the Welsh mainland to the brethren [at the religious House] dedicated to 'Sancto Michaeli et Sancto Cadoco et Dolfino [on the] island in the sea off Penarth'. The particular use of these words seems to exclude any high water islets close to the Welsh shore and pinpoints Flat Holm as the location. No St Dolfin has been traced, and this was probably the scribe's Latinized error for the Celtic St Dyfan, pronounced 'Duffun'.

Another twelfth-century charter by Earl William names Flat Holm when granting to the newly formed Bristol Abbey of St Augustine (now Bristol Cathedral) the ownership of 'Platam Holmam . . . with the chapels . . . in that island'. By yet another deed he gave, for the 'use and sustenance of the Augustinian Canons living on Flat Holm', the advowson of the church of Rumney, Cardiff.

Charters of St Michael of Stepholm

Steep Holm's own tradition of having early religious associations was also continued in the twelfth century, when a small Augustinian priory was established there by 'Robert, Son of Richard'.

The period after the Norman Conquest had seen the establishment of many small, independent and often poorly endowed religious houses founded by feudal landowners, following the more ambitious pattern set by William I, who had sought to atone for the slaughter at the battle of Hastings. In return for patronage the Brethren were obliged to offer regular prayers for the founder, his ancestors, family and successors.

By the end of the twelfth century many such establishments had sprung up. The priory of 'St Michael of Stepholm' was one of them, having apparently been founded in the latter half of that period, some years earlier than the nearby mainland Augustinian priory of Worspring (later Woodspring), and completely separate from that or any other foundation. Documentary proof of its existence came with five surviving twelfth- and thirteenth-century charters which were discovered between 1886 and 1892, when the contents of Berkeley Castle muniments room were being sorted and catalogued by I.H. Jeayes of the British Museum Manuscripts Department. The earliest of these charters was dated by Mr Jeayes from its style and handwriting to the time of Richard I (1189–99). Translated from the Latin, the charter reads:

> Know all [men] both present and future that I Robert son of Richard, for the sake of God and for the health of my soul and of my predecessors [ancestors] Have given and granted, in so far as it belongs to [the] lay parson, the Church of Saint Nicholas of Uppilla [Uphill] in pure [unconditional] and perpetual alms to Saint Michael of Stepholm and the brothers serving God there, with all liberties and with all things pertaining to the same church [Uphill]. And so that this my gift [act of giving] may remain valid and unchangeable I have confirmed it with the present writing and the protection of my seal.
>
> A list of witnesses completes the charter.

This is the earliest known reference both to the priory and to the old Norman church of St Nicholas, Uphill, which is slightly earlier than the-first of the Steep Holm charters. But until Mr Jeayes's discoveries its connection with the island's priory had long been forgotten, any vague memory of a link with Steep Holm having been transposed to the Gildas legend.

A subsequent charter by Robert has not survived, but fortunately its text has been preserved in a confirmatory deed by his son-in-law, John of Ken (Kenn, near Clevedon). Members of the family which took the name of the village as its own were lords of the manor from about 1150 until the end of the sixteenth century. The little church at Kenn still has a Norman window survival amid mid-nineteenth century rebuilding, and a carved memorial tablet to the last member of the family to bear that name. John of Ken's charter was evidently drawn up to preserve the rights of the Brothers of St Michael of Stepholm after Robert's death. Dated to the time of King John (1199–1216) the confirmatory deed reads: 'Know [men] both present and future that I John of Ken have authenticated in this word the charter of Robert, son of Richard, my ancestor.'

Uphill old church of St Nicholas, with Brean Down (left)

John then sets out Robert's charter:

Know all [men] both present and future that I, Robert, son of Richard have given and granted, for the sake of divine piety and for the health of my soul, and of my father and my mother and my ancestors and my successors, to Saint Michael of the island of Stepholm and the brothers living together there, half a virgate of land in Uphulla [Uphill] which Ailric of Rewa held with all its appurtenances in pure and perpetual alms, free and quit from all secular service. Similarly free multure [grinding] in the mill of the aforenamed township [Uphill]. Similarly in my pasture in the same township four cows and twenty sheep.

Finally, John adds: 'I, undoubtedly the aforementioned John of Ken, holding [it to be] valid and firm [binding], have confirmed this gift with the present writing and by the affixing of my seal.' So, as well as Uphill church, the canons of St Michael had been given by Robert half a virgate of land (approximately 15 acres) in that parish, free use of the mill, and apparently four cows and twenty sheep with pasture.

This is the earliest known reference to a mill at Uphill. As windmills were then only just beginning to be used in this country it may have been water-driven, and was probably tidal. There is a ruined (partially restored) windmill tower near Uphill church but this dates from a later period. A tidal mill on the tortuous creeks of the River Axe was marked on Greenwood's map as recently as 1822.

Who was Robert, son of Richard? As he was able to give both the church and the right of free milling we can assume that he held the lordship of the manor of Uphill. Most probably he was a descendant of one of the four knights who at the time of the Domesday Survey held Uphill and Christon in quarter shares under the overlordship of the Norman Baron Serlo de Burci, in return for service in time of war. From one of the charters we know also that Robert's daughter and heiress was Agacia, the wife of John of Ken.

Writing in 1916, and repeating most of Jeayes's 1892 account of the Steep Holm charters at Berkeley, E.H. Bates Harbin attempts to identify the founder of the priory by working backwards along the family line of a known mid-thirteenth century patron. On that basis he surmises that the priory was probably founded by a member of the wealthy de Ewias family.

That conclusion is by no means certain. The known patron was Lord Robert Tregoz, owner of the island in 1260. Although Bates Harbin was able to show that it was through his de Ewias grandmother, Sybil (one of a family with Benedictine sympathies) that Lord Robert had inherited the nearby manors of Brean and Burnham, it must at least be open to doubt whether the ownership of the island, and the patronage of its Augustinian priory, also came to him through that connection. In view of the known Uphill and Christon grants enjoyed by the Brethren of St Michael, it would seem more likely that the priory founder was connected with those manors – at that time quite separate in ownership from the de Ewias family's holdings of Brean and Burnham, which were not part of the original Serlo de Burci overlordship.

Julia, wife of Lord Tregoz, was a de Cantilupe, and this family, which owned vast estates, including lands in Somerset, was of Augustinian persuasion. It was also Julia's family connections which influenced the eventual pattern of closure for St Michael's. We believe that Steep Holm came to Lord Tregoz through his wife.

Long before Lord Tregoz came into the story, many of Serlo de Burci's original landholdings had been acquired by the Fitzmartins of Blagdon who, at the time of King John, granted a further charter to the Brethren of St Michael of Stepholm. Drawn up by William, son of Robert, son of Martin, this in turn confirms another now lost document by Robert, son of Richard, which had given to the 'Church of St Michael of Stepholm' a virgate of land in Uphill, formerly held by Ailric of Rewa. Although most of the early charters can be dated only by the style of handwriting, this Steep Holm deed can be quite accurately pinpointed as not later than 1209, when William Fitzmartin died.

Was there a first charter which is also missing? The endowments which can be traced through the surviving archives are relatively slender – not unusual for such small monastic houses. But the island itself is not included. For the canons to have actually owned Steep Holm might not have been necessary, but one would expect some form of document conferring upon them the rights of use and occupation.

One of the charters of St Augustine's Abbey is very similar to the first known Steep Holm charter in phraseology but it is not entirely certain that this was indeed the abbey's foundation document. For example, in the case of nearby Woodspring Priory there was an initial letter written about 1210 to the Bishop of Bath from the founding patron, William de Courteney, grandson of William de Traci, one of the assassins of Archbishop Thomas à Becket. This letter, in which de Courteney proposed to give all his land in Worspring for the establishment of a religious house there, was Woodspring's original foundation document, and is a useful guide to the similar (but earlier) aims of Robert son of Richard:

> I turn for help, more diligently beseeching your fatherhood that you may deem [it] worthy. . . . I had and have [in mind] to found at Worspring, in my demesne, where a chapel has been built to the Blessed Thomas the Martyr, a certain conventual house of the order of St Augustine's Canons of Bristol, or of any other order which you will have preferred to arrange, namely for the soul's health of Robert de Curtenai, my father, whose body rests there, and my mother, of my own self, and of my wife, of my ancestors and of my descendants; for the accomplishment of the founding of which [religious] house I have given and handed over all my land of Worspring both for the religious men there at the time serving God and the Blessed Mary, and the Blessed Thomas the Martyr, and I have also given a certain revenue for the foundation of the said house . . . also I beseech you to transfer as far as you may wish, the church of Worle, of which my advowson is vacant, to the religious men who will have been established at Worspring by you, so that the revenue of the said church of Worle may be converted to the sole use of those who have been established in the aforesaid place of Worspring by your authority.

The Church

Those visitors to Steep Holm who know little of its history are surprised to learn that a substantial religious establishment could have existed on this small rocky place, several miles out to sea. Life within those medieval walls was not easy, nor was it intended to be so.

The Augustinian priory of St Michael of Stepholm was not large. It probably never had more than twelve canons, the prior, and a number of lay brothers. For the most part there would have been far fewer brethren in residence. It was the lay brothers who, although under vows and wearing the habit of the Order, chiefly carried out the manual work. Unlike monks in other Orders, Augustinian canons did not normally take part in the physical labour involved in looking after their priory buildings and attached lands. On Steep Holm, however, the problems of such a small community living on the island must have resulted in some departure from this general procedure.

When the priory was founded it would, of course, have been necessary to build a church and accommodation for the brethren. This work was almost certainly begun by the lay brothers with skilled assistance, before the prior and the canons arrived on the site. Technically everything – from buildings to books – had to be ready for the canons before they moved in, so that they could at once begin 'to dwell there and immediately to keep the [Augustinian] Rule'; but it is probable that in this case, as with so many others, temporary structures were used while the lay brothers toiled to complete the permanent buildings. With such a low status establishment a full conventual plan for the priory would seem unlikely, and some intended buildings may never have been entirely finished. The later foundation of Woodspring Priory, near Weston-super-Mare, was fortunate in having from its commencement the use of an existing small chapel; but records show that it was over seventy years before the Augustinians there managed to complete their new church, which was to be modified and embellished several times – the last building programme being unfinished at the Dissolution of 1536.

The remains of Steep Holm priory comprise foundations of a long, narrow building of carboniferous limestone quarried from the island rock, with many facing

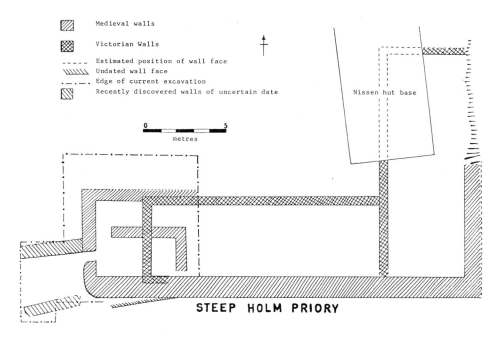

Plan of Priory of St Michael of Stepholm, also showing later occupations of the site

stones of the robust walls roughly dressed with a claw hammer. In places it had been necessary to cut away bedrock on which the priory was to stand, to achieve a suitable surface on which to build. The bedrock floor had been partially levelled by making up hollows with closely packed small stones. Excavation of the whole of the area enclosed by the walls has not taken place, but there was no sign of tiling, or mortar at floor level, only compacted soil and small stones above bedrock. The occasional positioning of slabs of sandstone beneath the stonework of the north and south walls may indicate re-use of materials from an earlier building. It could not have been an easy or speedy task to finish the erection of even this modest structure, and probably some years elapsed before it was completed – if indeed it ever was.

Over the centuries there have been various occupations of the island for diverse purposes, and a great deal of disturbance has taken place on and around the priory site. Stones from the walls have been extensively robbed to construct later buildings, so very little survives of the original complex. The contours of the surrounding ground have been greatly altered, removing evidence of any outbuildings or of the cloister area. All that is positively identifiable at this stage of excavation as being contemporary with the priory building are foundation walls of random stonework forming a long narrow rectangle, with interior measurements of 73½ ft by 15 ft, and a gap in the north-east corner. Until excavation of the site has been completed and more evidence discovered, much of the detail must remain conjecture. Nevertheless we can build up a basic picture.

The walls were substantially built to support the weight of a steeply gabled roof tiled with roughly shaped pennant sandstone slabs from the Clevedon/Nailsea area, fixed with either wooden pegs or nails. Wood does not survive on the well-drained limestone soils of the island, but many corroded nails have been found. Crenellated ridge tiles of coarse pottery with a thick green lead glaze completed the waterproofing. Fragments of these ridge tiles which were probably manufactured in Bristol, may have been the 'coarser ware, some lacquered over' which Skinner saw and pondered over on his visit in 1832.

The scant remains, with no surviving architectural embellishments, do not indicate where partitions or the original doors or windows were positioned, but the interior of the building would certainly have been rather gloomy because of the small deeply recessed round-headed windows of the period. Shattered fragments of imported stone found among the remaining debris hint at simple decorative or supporting features. One large, shaped piece was probably from a column base, although it was not found *in situ*. Broken slabs of blue lias may have been grave markers; others could have been from an altar, and well-tooled triangular pieces were apparently archstones; but sadly few architectural furnishings have survived the centuries in recognizable form.

This simple rectangle must have contained the chancel with its altar at the east end of the church. But to accommodate no more than a nave (for the lay brothers), and chancel (for the canons), its length is disproportionate to its width. Although no evidence has come to light yet, with the long north and south walls having lost much of their stonework, one wonders whether there could have been a squat tower in the centre of the building, as was the case with similar small early churches which are close parallels to that on Steep Holm. Adjacent to the chancel (possibly to its north) there should have been a sacristy, where vestments, holy vessels and books needed for services were kept. Another essential was the chapter room, where a chapter of the Scriptures and of the Rule of the Order was read aloud each day by the prior or a senior canon.

Lost Structures

The most practical position for a cloister area was to the south of the priory church, where there was just sufficient space for small adjoining secular buildings, with a roofed pathway around a kitchen garden – the normal use for the cloister square in those days. Domestic quarters had to comprise at least a dormitory, reredorter and refectory, with the attendant kitchen and bakehouse if possible separated from other buildings for fear of an outbreak of fire. To avoid spreading infection the infirmary was similarly isolated. There should also have been a dovecot, barn and other necessary minor structures connected with husbandry. Normally the prior would be entitled to at least a room, if not a modest house, apart from the rest of the community; and ideally the lay brethren would not share accommodation with the canons – but it is dubious whether this separation was ever achieved on Steep Holm.

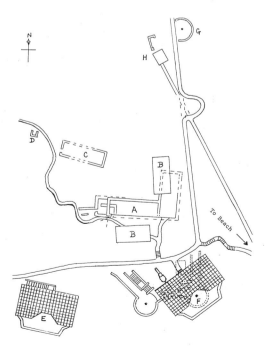

Plan of the south-east 'corner' of the island, showing how the priory remains and surrounding area have been intensively reused by successive occupations for widely varying purposes. A: Priory ruins, B: Nissen hut bases, C: ruins of 1776 tenement, D: privy, E: Second World War gun emplacement, F: Second World War gun emplacement partially over Victorian double gun battery, G: Tombstone Victorian gun battery, H: Second World War winch house and remains of Victorian side arms store

With the exception of the church, all evidence for such a complex of buildings on Steep Holm has disappeared beneath later military structures. But there are intriguing glimpses of what might have survived until the eighteenth and early nineteenth centuries. John Strachey, who visited the island in the 1730s, noted: 'On the Top of ye Hill are ye foundations of Walls divided into Rooms the whole being of Large Extent ye Stones seem to have been Laid without Mortar.' In fact the walls of the priory building were bound together with a friable brown sandy mortar, which might not have been evident without close scrutiny. Separately, on a very tiny drawing of the island – part of a map of the whole county of Somerset – he shows a minute plan of a rectangle divided into three such rooms. This may have been intended to show only part of the feature which he described as being of 'Large Extent'. If Strachey drew what we now know as the priory church, our excavations have shown that at least one of the dividing walls on his plan, although medieval, may not have been part of the original structure. There were several post-priory alterations to the building, and these will be discussed in sequence.

To further establish what has been lost to the south of the priory church, an analysis of what Thomas Clark wrote, a hundred years after Strachey, told us that the 'piony' (peony) grew on the flat top of the island, with caper spurge, henbane, abundant alexanders, privet and wood sage. 'Great round-headed garlic' (wild leek) was prolific on the high east cliff ledges. These plants, he and his brother decided, must have escaped from a space at the south-east corner of the island. He described the feature: '. . . near the house [built to the north-west of the priory church ruins in 1776] there is a space perhaps 50 yards square which we supposed was once a garden. . . . This place is surrounded by a ridge of stones which I took for a dilapidated wall. . . .' A year later, in 1832, a garden was being cleared and cultivated with modern vegetables by an occupier of the 1776 house, when Skinner was roaming the island gathering notes for his diary.

Thirty-five years after these invaluable observations were recorded, the ancient contours and features of this entire area were destroyed, and few traces of what were probably less permanent structures than that of the church can have survived to be still awaiting discovery. For during Victorian fortification work of the 1860s, the 'foundations of the priory were in great part laid bare' in constructing what came to be known as Garden Battery, which was placed on the traditional site of the priory garden – or cloister and ancillary buildings precinct.

Remnants of Gatehouses?

It was, of course, important to preserve the priory's seclusion from unexpected or unwelcome visitors who might intrude, even on a remote island. Clearly there were gatehouses; and writing in the 1730s John Strachey – an historian who took care to note what he observed even if he did not always know what it meant - records:

'Steepholmes . . . Is Inaccessible Except at 2 places & those bad enough so yt [that] not above one man Can Clamber Abreast. At the Entrance of both places were the freestone Jambs for Linterns with hooks for hanging of dores in a thick Wall. One of these was Washed away in ye great storm 1702 [1703].'

Which one remained? A chance remark by the Revd Mr Lightfoot, who in 1773 visited Steep Holm on a botanical excursion, described the wild leek as growing by the 'stone gateway above the Landing Place', but the wild leek grows in rock crevices above both beaches; so this observation could have referred to either landing place. Although nineteenth-century and later construction work has destroyed all traces of the old stone structures, Lightfoot's cryptic note confirms that as late as 1773 one of the gateways was still identifiable.

Some years ago, after rough seas had scoured the pebbles, what appeared to be a curved stone lintel from an old archway was found among the rocks of East Beach. The return boat being close in to shore, the stone was dragged with some difficulty to what seemed to be a safe temporary resting place above high tide, and lashed down to a mooring ring. Before it could be rescued or properly studied and recorded, a storm severed the heavy ropes and smashed the stone to fragments. Was this the last recognizable survivor of the remaining gateway above East Beach?

From research, excavation and exploration we now know something of the foundation of the priory itself – and of its layout. But what of the Brethren who lived and worshipped within this isolated island retreat?

Chapter Six

LIFE AT ST MICHAEL'S

Daily Routine

Mariners passing the island would have been cheered on their perilous journeys by the clear ringing tone of the priory bell, and the haunting melody of chants which drifted across the sea from the candle-lit church. The community may even have kept a light in the form of a fire basket (a cresset) slung from a vantage point to act as a beacon, which in clear visibility could be seen for miles around to guide ships safely on their way – a common practice at coastal churches.

Although the Augustinian Rule was less rigid than that of other Orders, obligatory attendance at frequent services throughout the day interrupted other routine tasks to such an extent that there was often anxiety to return to unfinished work. No wonder the canons of St Augustine's Abbey, Bristol, had to be reproved for unseemly haste, and told not to 'as bees fly out of the choir as soon as service is ended, but devoutly wait, as becomes holy and settled persons'.

There is no positive evidence that the island's 50-acre plateau was being farmed by the brethren, but not to have done so would have been illogical. In such an isolated location there had to be maximum use of the land to raise crops and rear animals to provide a modicum of self-sufficiency. Drinking water for farm stock would have been collected by digging shallow depressions lined with clay or mud to form dewponds. Over the centuries these have disappeared, but fieldwork has revealed lynchets (banked field boundaries) which were also recorded on a sketch prepared in 1832, although evidently there had been no arable farming on the island since the days of the priory.

Duties and Responsibilities of the Prior

The Steep Holm priory, with its island setting and few canons in residence, had to dispense with some of the normal posts such as novice master, almoner and guest master, or combine them with other duties, but certain appointments were essential. The overall responsibility for running the establishment, caring for the welfare of the inmates, and keeping strict discipline, fell upon one of the senior canons, who was appointed prior for life by the vote of the brethren. This was a solemn and complicated ceremony: after all, they were choosing the person who was to hold their entire lives in his hands. As absolute master of the canons, the prior presided at business meetings held in the chapter room. By his dedication, teaching and leading of daily worship, it was his duty to set an example to all those within the priory walls.

For a while all seemed to go well for the little island priory, and early in the reign of Henry III, Thomas de Muncketon, a witness to John of Ken's earlier charter, added his own gift to the brothers living on 'Stepholm'. Unfortunately this charter is mutilated, so words are missing, but what he gave was: '. . . all my land in Curcheston [Christon] namely that half virgate which Ailman Boving at one time held with . . . land belonging. . .' He explains: 'I [have] held . . . land better, and more freely, and more quietly [free from interference] for one pound of cumin to be paid annually to John of Ken or his heirs to . . . service and suit [of court] belonging

Augustinian Canon, from Sir William Dugdale's Monastici Anglicani de Canonicis Regularibus Augustinianis, *1661*

to them.' The pound of cumin – a spice known in this country since the first century AD – appears to have been an annual charge, probably in lieu of service, although Thomas was the actual landowner. Completing his charter Thomas adds:

> But this aforenamed land Robert son of Richard gave to me and my heirs – his charter testifies. Which for greater preservation I have handed over to the aforesaid Brothers together with the confirmation of William, son of Martin and the confirmation of John of Ken and Agacia his wife, daughter and heir of the aforesaid Robert son of Richard.

So he actually handed over the earlier charters to prove the community's rights to the gift; but this does not seem to have protected the canons from later losing their claims. The cost of litigation and the fear of losing land or privileges, especially on the death of a patron, was a constant worry for many religious houses. Despite the paucity of records it is clear that St Michael's was no exception.

We know the name of only one prior of Steep Holm, and that simply because he was involved in an apparent dispute over property in 1236, and by a lucky accident the court's ruling survives. The Somerset Fines for the twentieth year of Henry III include an Assize of Mort Ancestor in which Henry, son of Richard, quit claimed to 'The Prior and his successors and his church of Stepholm' half a virgate of land in Kercheston (Christon) – probably the land referred to in the above charter by Thomas de Muncketon. In return Prior William 'received Henry and his heirs into all benefits and orisons [prayers] in his church of Stepholm for ever'.

In simpler terms, it would perhaps seem that the court had to settle a dispute following the death of a patron; the prior winning his petition and Henry, the heir, having to relinquish his claim to the land in return for the traditional intercession of prayer by the brethren. What is more likely is that both parties were in agreement, and took the matter to court so that their wishes should have greater legal significance. By the thirteenth century the vague wording of many early charters was causing confusion, and it had become a necessary expense to draw up new firmly worded charters to settle titles to lands.

Another case which is relevant, although the Steep Holm brethren were not a party to it, took place twenty years later, in 1256, when Robert de Sparkford – a name that twice appears among the witnesses to the earlier charters – with others, quit claimed the right to the advowson of Uphill church to Reginald le Long and others. In return, Reginald and the others acknowledged Uphill Mill to be the right of Robert and his fellow petitioners. From this division of privileges formerly granted to the priory, it appears that by this date the brethren of St Michael's had already lost at least two vital grants which they had earlier enjoyed.

Robert and his allies and Reginald and his allies were on opposing sides in this matter; but in a further court case heard the same day Robert de Sparkford and all the other parties to the case concerning Uphill church and the mill joined forces to acknowledge the right of William de Cricheston (Christon) to hold of them an acre and a half of meadow there for a nominal yearly rent. Payable at Easter, this was to be one clove of gillyflower (a dried flower bud of the Eastern clove tree, used as a spice). In return, William gave up 'all his right in all the pasture under the wood of Cricheston towards the south' (except for enough for him to keep two oxen).

It is obvious that after a lapse of time, grants previously awarded to the priory were being claimed by the various heirs of deceased former patrons. Despite the apparently firm wording of the earlier charters, the intentions to donate 'for ever' had become very tenuous as far as the island community was concerned; the loss of income from Uphill church and withdrawal of free milling concessions must have created financial difficulties.

Backtracking a little, to 1243, a court case of a different kind would have caused more headaches for Prior William or his successor. In the list of Somerset Pleas for the hundred of Wynterstoke for that year is recorded:

> 780. Brother Gregory of la Houme [Steep Holm] and Robert his brother, accused of larceny, withdrew themselves, and they are suspected of larceny (*de latrocinia*) therefore let them be exacted and outlawed. Brother Gregory was not in tithing, nor was his brother, because they were lay brothers of priory of la Houme, and because the Prior has them not to right, to judgement on the Prior.'

It was one of the rules of the Order that no one was to leave the priory precincts unless accompanied by at least one other brother, and it should be emphasized that the two mentioned in the court case were not full canons but lay brothers. They would probably have been sent on a domestic errand, perhaps to collect tithes, or rent for property owned by the priory – or even to fetch supplies. They would certainly not have been sent to preach at Uphill church.

As head of a religious house, the prior was responsible for all the household, and could have been fined for not bringing the delinquents before the court. Whether the two lay brothers were innocent or guilty will never be known, for this is another unfinished case, and the fate of the brothers with alleged criminal tendencies – perhaps unjustly accused – is a matter for conjecture.

The Canons of St Michael

If the prior had to be away from the priory his normal duties were carried out by the senior canon, along with such responsibilities as overseeing the continual round of prayers for the patron and his family. Others kept the church clean and cared for, with herbs or hay spread on the earthen floor – for no trace of tiles has been found inside the building, and it is probable that limited funds never allowed such luxury, even for the chancel. The establishment had to be kept stocked with a multitude of necessities; by no means easy when relying on erratic transport arrangements from the mainland. Elaborate ritual had to be maintained, despite the difficulties of obtaining regular supplies; and a loss or breakage could be a disaster. Some ridge tiles excavated from the priory appear to be later replacements – evidence perhaps of emergency repairs to the roof.

The most popular or the most tolerated of the officials was the kitchener, depending on his skill in preparing the simple fare. Meat was seldom allowed. Sheep were kept mainly for their wool and milk, but to eat chickens, geese and ducks was permitted. Sea birds were plentiful and palatable – as well as augmenting the supply of fresh eggs in season.

Fish, especially on an island, was a mainstay to meals. Indeed it is probable that 'leisure activities' on Steep Holm would have included the mending of long nets and traps which were strung out in traditional fashion from stakes along the shingle spit of pebbles off the island's East Beach. Eels were regularly caught, and salmon were among the fish trapped. In the priory excavations, thornback ray and cod bones are among the fish remains which have been identified, and it is obvious from our finds that shellfish such as limpets and oysters were also an important element of diet. The various seaweeds were invaluable, either as a nutritious addition to the stewpot or to provide a mulch to enrich the kitchen garden soil.

A typical meal, served in a bowl, might have consisted of roughly ground cereals, which were basic fare, compounded with vegetables in the inevitable 'pottage' (or stew) which included fish, or even a little meat on festival days. Thick slices of coarse bread were normally used as side 'plates', the repast being washed down with ale, mead, or elder wine, with water being served on fast days.

In preparing these fundamental dishes the island's natural vegetation was skilfully used to supplement plants cultivated in the priory garden. Much of Steep Holm's flora is reputed to have been introduced by the inmates of the priory; some herbs could be descendants of escapes from the traditional site of their garden, just south of the main building. Others are obviously more ancient in origin, and such plants as ground ivy, wild leek, nettle, mallow, the white deadnettle, and elder, which are still to be found growing on the island, all had their uses to improve (or disguise) the flavour of food, or for brewing. The occasional appearance of a puff ball fungus must have been greeted with delight for this could be sliced and cooked; and again we may speculate on who really did introduce the wild peony, for in medieval times the seeds were a very discreetly used 'hot' spice.

Alexanders, at their best in early spring, came into their own during the long weeks of Lent. A quote from a later century is equally relevant to the priory days. The plants were 'much used to make broth with the upper part of the roote which is the tenderest part, and the leaves being boiled together, and some eate them either raw with some vinigar or stew them, and so eate them, and this chiefly in the time of Lent to help digest the crudities and viscious humours [which] are gathered in the stomache by the much use of fish at that time.'

Relics of meals around the priory's refectory table include sherds of English and French mediocre coarse pottery found during excavations, and tiny fragments of a rather special vessel which is particularly distinctive – a beautifully decorated polychrome wine jug also imported from France. A pottery rim fragment, thick, coarsely made and of large diameter also found during excavations could have been from a curfew – a large inverted 'bell' which by Norman law had to be placed each night over the ashes of every fire as a safeguard against conflagration. On Flat Holm, too, there is another parallel, with the similar identification of a pottery sherd from a curfew.

Both for drinking and to maintain cleanliness a plentiful supply of fresh water was needed, and the absence of this must have added to the problems of living on Steep Holm. The Brethren were surrounded by unlimited sea water, with the salt in the air slightly tainting the rain water collected in catchments from the roofs of buildings. In dry seasons this was by no means a plentiful supply, and to sink a well from the plateau to the fresh water table would have necessitated an impossibly deep shaft. But at various places low on the cliffs fresh water percolated from fissures in the rocks, and this was collected. Even in dry summers springs continue to emerge from various places above East Beach. At one point there is what is known traditionally as the 'Monks' Well' – a simple catchment in the rocks, which may have its origins in the days of the priory. Although much altered in more recent years and now covered, the catchment is situated close to the route of the original (now impassable) path straight up the steep slopes from the rocks north of East Beach to a point near the priory site. John Strachey, writing in the 1730s, recorded that 'There is also a spring of fresh water on the N.E. side of ye hill which is brim full but doth not run over.' On the other hand, a manuscript written in 1625 says the

Henbane in flower

following: 'And there is in the West side of the said Ilande one little Springe of fresshe water never drie, but not to be gone unto without some danger, because it is in the side of the Ilande between the Sea & the highest of the Ilande.' If the writer of this earlier account had his compass bearings correct, this would suggest another spring in the cliff side at the opposite end of the island from Monks' Well – in a very dangerous position.

Many of the plants used still grow on Steep Holm. Henbane (once known by the more descriptive name 'henbell') was used by the infirmarian for the treatment of nervous disorders, as a 'hypnotic' painkiller and even for seasickness, but it had to be administered with great care – for there was a high risk of killing the patient. Other potentially lethal plants such as hemlock, members of the nightshade family, the single peony and caper spurge survive in greater or lesser abundance. All had their place in former medicine, as did the more innocuous herbs.

Mortars were indispensable to both the kitchener and the infirmarian when pounding ingredients for 'pottages', or mixing herbal concoctions; and a fragment of heavy stone bowl found among rock debris at the nineteenth-century inn site above East Beach could have been from a mortar used by the brethren of St Michael. The flat topped rim and external supporting lug are typical, but no part of the base remains, and the added refinement of pecked decoration on the exterior may suggest a better class of vessel.

Caper Spurge

Like the kitchen, the infirmary was usually a separate building. Monastic custom was that the 'canons in the Infirmary should be relieved while sick, and be provided with victuals more nice than for the healthy, and with medicines their sickness may require'. Should anyone 'feign himself sick when he is not so', he would be punished.

Quite apart from the treatment of sick canons by a self-taught infirmarian, there was no skilled veterinary surgeon to look after the animals. Burdock, peony, mullein, nettle, wild leek and ivy were only a few of the plants used to treat various disorders, and the animals were encouraged to graze brambles, hounds-tongue, ground ivy, plantain and scurvy-grass (a rich source of vitamin C) to keep them in good condition. One typical traditional dose for a sheep suffering from rheumatism was one root of peony, finely sliced and brewed in water and wine. Mullein was useful for respiratory troubles in animals, and burdock for treatment of skin parasites. 'Strong brews' of these and other herbs were nearly always readily available; preparation was simple, the doses not too critical and the cost minimal.

With the far greater general appreciation of simple remedies, and the plants which produced them, it is possible that surplus herbs were 'exported' to the mainland to augment priory funds. Steep Holm's vegetation still includes not only medicinal and culinary survivals from that long distant age, but another plant the value of which has been forgotten. Weld, still plentiful on the island, was once the source of a yellow dye, used by the medieval cloth makers of Bristol. Nothing was wasted, for as Kipling wrote:

> Anything green that grew out of the mould
> Was an excellent herb to our fathers of old

For everyone, life at St Michael's was simple and hard. The whole point of being there was to be cut off from the temptations of the secular world, and to live a communal life of poverty, prayer and intercession. Virtually every habitable offshore island had its community, and vestiges still survive on many – a few even now retaining their religious houses. Locations such as Steep Holm and Flat Holm were chosen particularly for their associations with former saints. During the short days and chill long nights of winter (despite the slightly warmer climate of the island when compared with the mainland), life could not have been pleasant as the canons worked and tried to concentrate on their prayers in and about an almost unheated priory. Apart from the kitchen bakehouse only one small open brazier was allowed, around which the brethren were permitted to gather in their spare moments. They knew that the bitter east winds howling around the buildings, and rough seas crashing tons of pebbles high up the beach to batter the cliff face, meant indefinite delays in the landing of stores perhaps desperately needed; while the eerie feeling of total isolation and silence when thick fog swirls across the island has to be experienced to be understood.

Yet, for all the privations, there must have been many days when simply to feel part of the mysticism of the island and the elements – or to meditate on the glory of God as made evident by the fantastic views around the Channel seaboard – was compensation enough.

Chapter Seven

DEATH – AND CLOSURE OF THE PRIORY

Those who Never Left the Island

In the years of the priory's existence, comparatively few though they might have been, it was inevitable that some sick canons were unable to respond to the nursing care and medicine dispensed by the infirmarian. Mention of numerous burials on Steep Holm may surprise those who normally associate graves with clearly defined cemetery areas, as on the mainland. Yet, long ago, there was indeed a graveyard on the island. We have already made reference to the ancient custom of 'holy island' burials for prominent citizens, and the derivation of the former Saxon name which perpetuates the tradition. The siting of a religious house on Steep Holm had some connection with the former reverence for such places, and the custom of burial on the island naturally continued in the days of the priory.

Over at least the last 160 years of Steep Holm's history, skeletal remains have been disturbed from within and to the north of what is now known to be the priory site. Nor were the bones originally all from unmarked graves. Broken and re-shaped pieces of imported blue lias stones have been recorded during our excavations, reused as building material incorporated into later medieval alterations at the west end of the priory building. Some of these appear to be fragments of grave markers. More specifically identifiable is the large piece of blue lias stone still remaining from a thirteenth-century tombstone carved with an incised floreated cross and having moulded edges.

The story of this stone's discovery will be told in a later chapter. It is a significant find, for like all the other blue lias on the island, someone had to go to the trouble and expense of importing it, the nearest source being in the Watchet area of the Somerset coast. It is the only piece so far discovered which has been carved in this way, and it was obviously intended to mark the grave of someone of note; either one of the priors (perhaps Prior William himself) or a member of the patron's family who had special rights of burial in or near the priory. Could it even have marked the resting place of Robert, son of Richard?

Land to the east and south of the priory precincts fell away sharply. To the west were fields for crops and grazing animals. With only a small amount of space available for all the needs of the community it was logical to use the less hospitable land lying north of the church as the burial ground; and it was in this area that the tombstone was discovered.

Stories of skeletons being found on Steep Holm originate in the last century. The first to be recorded was when an early burial was accidentally disturbed by an elderly tenant on the island who, in 1832, told Skinner of his discovery. Rather more than thirty years later, in the 1860s, a great deal of fortification work was being carried out, which resulted in the contours of the island being reshaped for ever; and tales of 'giants' buried in the shallow soil began to circulate. An 1885 newspaper reported: 'Many human bones have been found on this island and the horns of a deer, with animal bones some few years ago.'

Frederick Henry Harris, who had lived on Steep Holm 'all his life' was interviewed by a visiting reporter in 1913. He said that 'when he was a boy he dug up seven skeletons of gigantic men, skeletons 7 ft long, lying with every bone and every tooth perfect in shallow graves, side by side, divided from each other by dwarf walls'. As he was then seventy years old, his adventure could have pre-dated the fortification work of the 1860s. But the Harrises were seldom very accurate with dates and ages, so it is more probable that as a young man he had been thrilled to have the opportunity of helping the navvies at that time digging foundations all over the island. No hint was given of the location of these burials.

F.A. Knight, in his classic *Seaboard of Mendip* of 1902 perhaps recorded a version of the same or a similar incident, when he writes that 'one chamber [of the priory] was so well preserved that it was repaired and used as a living room by the foreman in charge of the works. In clearing out the earth, in order to lay down a wooden floor, it was found that the whole space inside the walls of this building was packed with skeletons, lying close together side by side only a few inches below the surface'.

Moving on to the 1930s, when Bristol Naturalists excavated trenches alongside walls at the east end of the priory building, the uncovering of a 'recent hearth' tempted them to surmise that this might have been the chamber which the foreman chose for his living quarters, and where the skeletons were found. More recent fieldwork and investigations have disproved that tentative theory and it is now believed that the 'loosely laid bricks surrounded by much ash' are from organized Victorian picnic feasts.

When preliminary survey work was being carried out on the priory site during weekends in June 1977, an illicit 'dig' by a holidaymaker staying on the island between two of our visits uncovered numerous broken and reburied human bones from just within the south wall of the priory. These were left by the digger in a cardboard box, with a rough sketch to show where they had been found. Subsequent limited investigation revealed that not all the bones had been located or removed by him in this regrettable incident – but the rest were allowed to remain *in situ*. Those which had been disturbed told us something about the former inhabitants, but nothing about the location of the cemetery.

The late Dr Bob Everton examined these fragmented human remains from the medieval period, and immediately pointed out evidence of spondylitis, osteo-arthritis, and similar afflictions which had affected the bones. One old man had suffered from severe arthritis of the elbow. Apart from disease, an injury – possibly a badly-treated fracture – had led to deterioration of an arm bone. Another forearm bone had a fracture which had reset itself with overlap and some angulation; and a finger had been broken and allowed to mend without medical attention. Not only the accidents, but the aftermath of irregular healing must have been extremely painful for the unfortunate persons. There were also very sturdy bones from at least one man who had been accustomed to heavy work. Post mortem damage indicated that at some time in the past these pathetic remnants had been dug up roughly, and as clumsily reburied. Victorian bottle glass was found with the bones. Did the workmen reinforce shaken nerves by indulging in 'Dutch courage'? At least thirteen individuals were represented, including a minimum of one adult female (probably three), one child of about ten years of age, and one younger child. At once this pointed to the custom of members of the founder's (or patron's) family exercising their right to burial in the priory cemetery.

More information about those associated with the priory was gained by these finds, but the probable location of the cemetery still depended upon a vague surmise based on stories of the last century. These seemed to point to the foreman's 'hut', and therefore the burials, being within the present foundations, yet the crucial tombstone was found outside and over to the north. True, it could have been moved from its original position, but perhaps something was wrong with the earlier assumption.

Excavations from 1979 onwards extended to the west end of the priory building, and new evidence began to emerge. The whole interpretation of where the cemetery was situated was changed when an attempt was made to identify positively the line of the north wall, from which most of the stones had been robbed. First a heap of reinterred human bones was uncovered from a shallow depression just outside the wall. Again all but the very small bones were broken, but this time they were the sad remnants of a single burial, compared with the relics of thirteen or so individuals which had been unceremoniously 'dumped' inside the south wall. It was possible to establish that this person was male, and had been 5 ft 4 in tall – far from being one of the race of 'giants' of Fred Harris's story. Similarly, tales of 'giant' skeletons being discovered on Lundy and elsewhere appear to be exaggerations, but this may be partially explained by a natural elongation of the framework of bones as it is compressed in the ground over many years, so extending the apparent height.

Shortly after the finding of these skeletal remains came the real breakthrough, with the first ever archaeological discovery of an *in situ* burial on Steep Holm, just a little to the north-east of the reinterment. It now became obvious that the priory cemetery must lie to the north of the building, with inhumations in such very shallow depressions that virtually any digging below top soil must disturb them. Initially only the skull and collar bone with the upper vertebrae were exposed, the

'Brother Cuthbert' – C burial. The first complete in situ *burial to be excavated, 1984*

teeth of 'Brother Cuthbert', as we dubbed him, being perfectly free from decay, but very worn – mute evidence of the fare dished up by the kitchener of long ago: a sugar-free diet, but one which included coarse stone-ground grain and tough fibrous food which quickly wore away the biting surfaces of the teeth, so exposing the core. As shown by eloquent wood or stone carvings in many churches, the misery of toothache was by no means unknown in medieval days! Further excavation showed that this was someone who had been 5 ft 7 in tall.

A second skeleton, somewhat crushed by the weight of stones above but otherwise undisturbed, was discovered just to the north of Cuthbert. This male was quite robustly built, and 5 ft 8 in tall; again with undecayed but worn teeth. He had suffered from osteo-arthritis to such an extent that some of the vertebrae had become 'frilled' and one or two spinal bones had fused together.

This burial had actually cut into an earlier interment, the lower bones of which had been carefully lifted and deposited alongside the later inhumation. Yet again, this rather small-boned male showed symptoms of severe osteo-arthritis. As it is Allsop Trust policy not to lift or unnecessarily disturb skeletal remains, it was not possible to measure accurately the height of this, the earliest priory burial yet found. The condition of the bones and teeth confirmed Fred Harris's detailed memories of his nineteenth-century adventures, when he had helped to remove other skeletons in

Excavated burials C, D, and E, in rock-cut graves, with bedrock 'walls' between and to right, 1990

the way of the Victorian building operations. For the burials which were found in the 1980s must have been very similar in appearance and arrangement to those so vividly remembered by the old man.

Fred Harris's 'side by side' recollections of his finds were proved accurate, and indeed his curious description of 'dwarf stone walls' was verified. Not walls, but bedrock laboriously chipped sharply away to leave ridges between very shallow graves — the dividing rock to a casual glance resembling low walls. Despite the painstaking efforts to achieve greater depth, the burials were still only a few inches below the old ground surface, although over the centuries deposits of soil, stones and midden material (rubbish) had accumulated. This was hardly a hygienic situation, especially as these burials, apart from being very shallow, were close to the north wall of the church, and in slightly rising ground. There was absolutely no indication of coffins with these particular burials, and it is virtually certain that they were shroud interments.

A Mystery Solved

These *in situ* medieval burials, with their Christian east/west alignment, and, of course, no grave goods, justified our suspicions that it was not the priory ruins themselves which had been the site for the Victorian foreman's living quarters, with the skeletons below the floor. The crowded cemetery area was outside and to the north of the priory walls. Apart from broken fragments scattered from the crudely reburied bones by the south wall, no human remains have so far been found interred inside the building. Indeed, it was not normal practice to bury within the church until after the thirteenth century.

But just a few yards north-west of where Brother Cuthbert and his companions lie are the dilapidated ruins of an old tenement. This late eighteenth-century cottage, built with stones robbed from the priory walls, was partially renovated in 1830, when it was the only noticeable structure on the island plateau according to contemporary nineteenth-century accounts. On studying these descriptions, it was found that the priory building, recorded by John Strachey in the 1730s as triple-chambered foundation walls, was, according to William Withering in 1826, 'a little enclosure with ruinous walls and few remaining vestiges'. John Rutter described the priory as 'no longer visible' in 1829, while Thomas Clark noted only a ridge of stones forming an enclosure in 1831. Skinner, in 1832, saw nothing which he recognized as a priory building – commenting only that pottery sherds and rubble 'perhaps . . . belonged to the small religious House said to have been established here . . .'.

The evidence of these observers shows that no part of the priory building was in such good condition that it could readily have been renovated for the foreman's home in the 1860s. At that time there was only one structure on the plateau which was sufficiently intact for adaption to the foreman's use – the old tenement or cottage. Once again ruinous, it could easily have been mistaken for the remains of a priory room. Situated in what is now proved to be the cemetery area, it has to be the 'chamber' from which so many skeletons were dug by Fred Harris and his navvy friends. It is also obvious that they reburied the bones in a hastily dug hole beside the priory south wall – to be uncovered again by the unauthorized 'dig' of 1977. The recent archaeological work has at last corrected false assumptions originating from Victorian stories which had become legend.

Even within the small community of a priory which was in existence for a comparatively short time, the normal incidence of death through age, accident or illness may well have meant that some thirty or more canons and lay helpers never left the island – in addition to members of the founder's, or subsequent patrons' families who were brought to Steep Holm for solemn last rites. In later years the canons who died were not always replaced, and the diminishing number of brethren remaining had to continue as best they could with prayers of intercession, and with the sometimes grim struggle to survive on a rapidly reducing income. Inevitably the round of worship was neglected.

The Priory Transferred

As already shown, in the mid-thirteenth century the brethren of St Michael's had lost at least some of the rights which early patrons had granted to them 'for ever';

and it is clear that as the years went by enthusiasm for maintaining this remote priory had waned. We have seen that in 1256 members of the former patron's family were exchanging the right to the advowson of Uphill church – perhaps the most important source of income formerly held by the canons.

The final blow was struck only four years later. By 1260 inheritance and marital rights with other subsequent disposals of property had taken the priory out of the hands of the family which had first founded it; and Lord Robert Tregoz held the patronage. Apparently he had acquired it through the dowry of Julia, his wife. Confusion has arisen for researchers in the past because Julia's father, grandfather, and great-grandfather were all called William. Of the three generations, the first William de Cantilupe (Julia's great-grandfather) died in 1238. It was he who had re-endowed a small priory which previously had been transferred from an unsuitable site at Wicton to Studley, in Warwickshire – but in the diocese of Worcester. Here he had been buried as patron. Julia's grandfather gave the Studley canons lands for the support of a hospital at the priory gates for the poor and infirm. Her father endowed Studley Priory with lands in Locking, Worle, Kewstoke and Norton – all on the seaboard of the Severn Estuary; and in 1250 her father and mother together donated land at Trent, near Yeovil.

With the priory of St Michael clearly failing, it was not unreasonable that Lord Tregoz should wish to transfer it into the care of this other priory, so much favoured by his wife's family. He had to seek ecclesiastical consent, and the final Steep Holm charter from the muniment room of Berkeley Castle, dated 1260, is by the Bishop of Bath and Wells (at that time William Bitton I – only the second bishop of the newly formed combined see). After the preamble, it reads:

> . . . the noble Lord R[obert] de Tregoz patron [of] the religious place which is called Stepholm [has] conferred the house itself with the whole island and all other appurtenances to the religious [men], canons of the order of St Augustine of Stodlegh [Studley, Warwickshire] . . . in pure and perpetual alms as patron of the house, for the sake of charity having the necessary power and seeking the increase of religious worship because at the aforesaid house [Studley] divine services are usually celebrated more frequently.

This either tactfully referred to the lack of rigid routine on the island, or provided a suitable excuse for the move.

The deed confirms that the bishop gave his consent to the transfer 'in so far as it is up to us', but he decreed that at least two canons from Studley 'shall remain constantly on the aforementioned island, and that the canon who ought to be in charge there should be presented to us and our successors the diocesan [bishops] of the house by the Prior of Stodlegh . . . and shall be called Prior of Stepholm, by no means to be removed by the said Prior [of Studley] without our consent. . . . If . . . on [account of] his unworthiness he himself should happen to be removed, we will and grant that the same Prior of Stodlegh shall have the power freely to present to us and our successors another of his canons to the said house and its rule. And that at the time of a vacancy the above mentioned Prior shall obtain the supervision [charge] of all goods at the said house and also the care [protection] of the house itself. . . .'

So, in 1260, Studley appears to have acquired both the priory and the free tenancy of Steep Holm, provision being made for two 'caretaker' canons to reside on the island, and with Lord Tregoz retaining the overlordship. Those, however, were troubled times. King Henry III was at loggerheads with his barons; and although the barons were Royalists, disagreements with the King caused a state of semi Civil War to exist. In such circumstances it is not surprising that no other record of the arranged transfer has been traceable. But in any case Studley could not have held the property for long. In 1265, only five years after the transfer was approved by the Bishop of Bath and Wells, the decisive Battle of Evesham took place, and in the fighting the barons' leader Simon de Montfort (Earl of Leicester) and Lord Robert de Tregoz were among those slain by the King's supporters.

On 17 September a general peace was declared, but the lands of every accomplice of Earl Simon were attainted. They were taken back into the King's hands, and many of them were given to his followers. That may explain why, not long afterwards, we find the island in completely different ownership; that of Thomas de Bec, Bishop of St David's in Wales – but significantly formerly King Henry's personal chaplain.

By 1268 some of the Tregoz lands had been re-acquired by the family. John Tregoz, son of the unfortunate Robert, obtained King Henry's favour to the extent that he was excused payment of a substantial portion of the heavy fine still outstanding for restoration of his inheritance, and was later created 1st Baron Tregoz. The Manor of Brean (but not the advowson rights) was included in the regained lands; Steep Holm was excluded.

While the Bishop of Bath and Wells, by the deed of 1260, had clearly indicated that a religious presence on Steep Holm should still continue, with at least two canons from Studley on the island, national politics had by 1265 defeated this intention.

Studley after 1260

The priory of Studley, apart from losing the dubious asset of distant Steep Holm, had other troubles. In 1269 it was desperately in need, as shown by a letter of that date preserved in a collection of manuscripts at Oxford. Sent from the Bishop of Worcester, the letter (in Latin) sends greetings in customary style to an unidentified community and reports that the brethren at Studley were '. . . as much through their own simplicity as [on account of] the tumult of the most recent upheaval, burdened with more than double of the true annual value of their whole substance . . . with the insupportable burden of the continually increasing expenditure'. What the immediate cause of the trouble was we are not told, but evidently the Studley canons had been caught up in an aftermath of the Baronial Wars, and the priory was unable to support all those living there. Explaining that '. . . dispersion of the Brothers [is] having to be borne for the time being . . .' the bishop's letter asks the other community to 'look after two Brothers of the said place, certainly prudent and discreet men and of respectable conversation, for the space of one year and a half'. It has been conjectured that these were two brethren who perhaps ought to have been on Steep Holm, but that interpretation is not tenable. The Studley community had lost Steep Holm approximately four years before the 1269 letter was written. Indeed, from the text of the letter it appears that a general dispersion was necessary temporarily, with brethren going in pairs to several religious houses. Presumably the bishop expected that by the end of the specified eighteen months Studley would again be able to care for the canons. The problems were eventually overcome, and there was an expensive rebuilding of that priory, followed by re-consecration in June 1309; and Studley Priory continued in reasonable prosperity until its dissolution by King Henry VIII in 1536. Long before that time the Steep Holm priory buildings had been adapted to other uses.

Chapter Eight

MY LORD'S CONEY WARREN

Having indulged in a brief excursion into the history of Studley Priory, we must now return to Steep Holm to discover what had happened to the island following the removal of the remaining brethren and their chattels. Despite the directive of the Bishop of Bath and Wells that at least two canons from Studley 'shall remain constantly on the aforesaid island', the troubled times made it extremely unlikely that this ever happened. When the forfeited lands of Lord Robert Tregoz were partially restored to his son John by the king in 1268, Steep Holm had already been included in the lands granted to Thomas de Bec (or Beke), and had entered a new era, for Bishop Bec had no ambitions towards re-establishing a religious house on the island.

During excavations of the priory building in 1979, walls were found that should not have been there, containing materials not used in the main construction. It was obvious that someone had lived and worked in this part of the building in conditions quite different from those kept by the canons. Artefacts associated with these walls, although still medieval, post-dated the closure of the Priory. This was more like a 'squatter' occupation.

As the excavation work continued, the events on Steep Holm after the closure of St Michael's began to be clarified. Let us first, however, look at what the archives can tell us. Among the royal grants to Thomas de Bec were the 'villes' of Uppehull (Uphill) and Crucheston (Christon), manors traditionally linked with Steep Holm through early gifts of land to the former priory. All these holdings were still kept together by being leased to Robert de Berkeley, and this is the first time the Berkeley name appears in connection with the history of the island. Thomas de Bec died on 14 April 1293, and his property was inherited by his eldest brother, John de Bec, Lord of Eresby (Lincolnshire). The new overlord quickly disposed of the island, associated manors, and the advowson rights of Brean, so that by 1305, when he in turn died, all the holdings had been granted to Henry de Lacy, Earl of Lincoln. The ageing earl did not keep his acquisitions for long. Official archives here do not entirely agree, but it is recorded that years before the earl's death in 1311 at his London mansion (Lincoln's Inn), his young son had drowned in a well at Denbigh Castle, and his daughter, although three times married, had failed to produce any children. The earldom was in abeyance: Robert de Berkeley had died, and Sir Maurice de Berkeley held the properties.

After a hiatus of a few years comes the much discussed and quoted flurry of activity highlighted by an entry in a now missing 1315 (8 Edward II) bailiff's account roll of the Manor of Portbury. Referring to this in his *Baronage* of 1675, Sir William Dugdale claimed that Maurice 7th Lord Berkeley '. . . built a Friary in a place called the Holmes . . .'. This was not correct, but until I.H. Jeayes published the twelfth-century charter of Robert, son of Richard, Dugdale's statement was taken as evidence to date the foundation of a religious House on Steep Holm to 1315, or soon after. The *Baronage*, however, misquoted John Smythe's *Lives of the Berkeleys*, written earlier in the seventeenth century. Smythe's account actually reads: 'This Lord Maurice new built the friery for the fryers and brethren in the Holmes, an Iland in Seavern and not far from his Manor of Portbury.' There is a significant difference in the wording of this earlier history – 'new built' in this context meaning a rebuilding.

John Smythe was steward of the vast Berkeley estates – a position of great importance, his authority being second only to that of the nobleman himself. In this trusted position he served successive Lords Berkeley for fifty years, and during that time he had free access to the collection of documents preserved in the muniments room of the castle. His devotion to the Berkeley family extended to an avid interest in their distinguished genealogy, which he detailed in hundreds of pages written over a number of years before 1628. Although writing three hundred years after the rebuilding took place, Smythe must have been familiar with the earlier charters kept in the muniments room, and others since lost, referring to the twelfth-century priory of St Michael. That there was no mention of these documents in his long history was surely because he was concerned only with events directly connected with the Berkeley family, which did not enter into the Steep Holm story until after the priory closed. Nevertheless, his knowledge of the priory's earlier existence flavoured his interpretation of entries which he found in the Portbury bailiff's accounts – thus he assumed that Lord Maurice, whom he called 'the Magnanimous', had rebuilt the priory for the benefit of the religious community.

What a pity that the details from the bailiff's records are now missing, for they might have told us so much more about the work carried out on the old building. For Smythe says: 'The accompts of all this lords receipts and disbursments were ingrossed yearly in parchment with singular exactnes . . . The profits of his three hundreds of Bedminster Portbury and Hareclive [Hartcliffe] were allwayes cast up in one roll togeather. . . .' His statement that Maurice, 'the third of that name', had rebuilt the priory for 'fryers' on the island has been for many years an enigma to historians, some of whom, in the absence of other confirmatory documents, were doubtful whether the project was ever carried out. But the archaeological work of 1979 showed that a certain amount of rebuilding did take place at that time. The final clue to solve the problem was revealed by the discovery of a vital reference; and in the meantime the excavations provided confirmation that the bailiff's accounts were concerned with 'new' building for secular, not religious, purposes.

In 1315 Maurice had not yet inherited the Berkeley estates or title from his father, Lord Thomas, and he was then living with his wife and family at the Manor of Portbury, hereditary home of the heirs to the title. Why should he have any interest in the repair of the old priory buildings on Steep Holm? There was in fact a very good reason: he wished to provide accommodation for warreners.

The Normans had introduced conies, or rabbits, into this country – animals so greatly prized for their meat and fur that at first it was only the wealthy who could afford to import and keep them. For this reason it is unlikely to have been the canons of St Michael's Priory (a comparatively poor foundation) who were responsible for introducing conies to Steep Holm.

The Berkeley archives show that before 1154 King Stephen had granted free warren rights to Roger Berkeley, Lord of Dursley, in his manor there – a privilege renewed from time to time by later kings. But this hunting warren was somewhat different from one kept for domestic and marketing purposes. For a wealthy landowner, where better to confine the conies than on islands where they could burrow as they wished without straying to another's land; where they could readily be rounded up when needed; and where they could be protected from poachers?

As an offshore warren for these animals Steep Holm was far from being unique. Suitable islands around the coast were sought after as places on which conies could be kept under the guardianship of paid keepers, who were accommodated on the premises. Often, either set apart from or even incorporated into the warreners' house, a watchtower was built so that an eye could be kept on the animals, and any prospective raider instantly challenged.

From recent research and fieldwork it is clear that Lord Maurice's renovation of the former priory building was for use by his warreners. The island was an obvious choice for a Berkeley coney warren. The family had owned certain fishing rights in the 'Seaverne' since at least the mid-twelfth century; and a hundred years afterwards Maurice, the 5th baron, and his son Thomas (subsequently father of Maurice 'the third of that name' who rebuilt the priory) both stipulated when granting leases for 'rockes or fishings in Seaverne' that 'all the fish that should be taken upon Fridays' should be reserved as their rents – which must have tempted lessees to resort to occasional cheating. No record exists of the former priory being granted fishing rights, although one might assume that this formality would have been observed.

The Warreners' Quarters

Of Robert de Berkeley's motive for leasing Steep Holm from Thomas de Bec there is no documentary evidence; and we can only surmise that he could have been responsible for establishing the first warren not many years after the closure of the priory of St Michael, when the old building should still have been in reasonable condition for the housing of warreners.

West end of priory site, showing east/west warreners' wall (centre) within priory walls, overlaid at right angles by remains of Victorian walling

By 1315 Lord Maurice found it necessary to approve plans for the adaption and repair of the structure which had become dilapidated over the fifty-five years since the departure of the canons; and in the south-west corner of the priory foundations our excavations revealed the remains of two interior walls, at right angles to one another, forming an oblong room, approximately 15 ft by 7 ft 6 in (4.8 m x 2.4 m). An interior doorway, with two large stones still remaining at ground level to act as the base for a sill, is approximately 34 in (0.85 m) wide. It is flanked on one side by the original west wall of the priory, and on the other by blocks of blue lias stone. Some of these have been reshaped, and appear to be broken grave slabs or even altar stones, reused as building material. Smaller offcuts of lias have been noted incorporated into other parts of these interior walls, which are generally no more than a single course or so high.

There is ample evidence of warreners' activities in this part of the old priory. A thick build-up of midden, or rubbish material, was excavated from the area in and more particularly around their room or workshop. Quantities of rabbit bones have been found in these deposits, with many thousands of limpet shells, some of which may have been residue of pig food; but limpets also would have provided none too palatable nutrition for the warreners. Numerous pottery sherds in deposits associated with the Steep Holm warreners' room can be dated principally to the fourteenth and fifteenth centuries. The general impression gained is of a poor diet of limpet and vegetable stew, enlivened with rabbit, bird, fish, or (less often) joints of sheep or pig. It must have been an unpleasant environment with discarded and rotting debris in and around the room. Complete and broken pennant sandstone tiles from the original priory roof occurred at frequent intervals spread throughout the various levels of waste, almost as though placed in an irregular and uneven pattern of 'stepping stones' as the rubbish accumulated. One puzzling feature of these deposits is the presence of many crudely fashioned flints; none having the distinctive forms of the prehistoric tools which have been found on the island. That this flint 'industry' accompanied by waste flakes seems to fit into a medieval context is remarkable, and has prompted much thought. It could be conjectured that the warreners occasionally ran out of their standard tools when supply vessels failed to arrive, and had to improvise with flint material – for a few edges are capable of cutting or scraping. Some flints may have been used for 'strike-a-lights', a practice which continued from early times until the advent of modern friction and chemical methods of ignition in the last century. Much of the source material is of poor quality for tool making, and some of the fragments are very similar to another enigmatic assemblage found on the Mendip Hills. On Lundy, too, crude flints which fit into no known culture have puzzled archaeologists.

From the excavation evidence it is obvious that the warreners lived and worked here – and one of the rarer finds, from just outside the old north wall of the priory, was a tiny worn and clipped silver farthing from this era. First minted during the reign of Edward I, this new coinage, along with the halfpenny, was introduced to

Farthing of Edward I excavated from priory site in 1989, with new penny for scale

avoid the tedious necessity of having literally to cut a penny coin into halves or quarters to obtain the lower values. The 'warrener's' farthing was minted in London and portrays the king's full face head outlined with shoulder length curls, the reverse retaining the established long cross design with three pellets in each angle. This design was to continue in circulation with minimal variations through the next two reigns; and indeed (with many debasing changes) the farthing was to remain legal currency until as late as 1961, when inflation finally led to its demise. Clipping was a major problem with the high silver content of coinage during medieval reigns, and severe penalties were introduced in 1290 to try to stop the practice, but without much success. Did a warrener search diligently for his lost coin, only to be forced to give up the quest? Such a small object would be easily lost among the debris of limpet shells, bones and broken pottery from cooking vessels and lead-glazed jugs which littered the area in and around the west end of the building. But there is more to a medieval warren than a sordid dwelling place and workshop for the keepers.

Setting up a Warren

To establish any warren was an expensive speculation, and good management was essential if the undertaking was to succeed. Island warrens were obviously more difficult to keep well supplied, and the export of meat or skins was unpredictable. But balanced against these disadvantages was the confinement of conies within rigidly defined boundaries from which they could not escape – or be easily stolen. On Steep Holm flat topped shallow banks across the plateau were plotted during the 1977 survey of the island, and these low ridges were also remarked upon by Skinner, who was deceived into thinking them the remains of a 'Danish Fort'. Other nineteenth-century writers thought them to be prehistoric. These may indeed have been outliers of ancient fortifications, but ones which were at least partially adapted to become desirable residences for the coney population. Such low banks are commonly recognized by archaeologists, and often called 'pillow mounds'. More traditionally they are known by the old name 'buries'.

Adequate grassland was essential for a healthy warren, so for the hundred or more years when the warren was being managed we can picture an island very different from its present appearance of rough scrubland with a few welcome patches of grass now being regenerated. Gone were the earlier 'fields' and farm animals cared for by the canons. Instead, a grassy sward had to be protected from hostile salt winds by using the island's native privet and elder bushes as partial shelter and windbreaks.

Often a coney warren included the introduction of other game animals, usually deer, which were a valuable source of winter meat. Steep Holm could not have supported the larger deer, but 'many bones of deer' were said to have been found near the priory in Victorian times, and the recovery of the occasional fragment of roe deer antler during excavations might indicate that a herd of this species was kept in the island warren. Certainly roe deer herds figure in the Berkeley records, and the successful present day introductions of Muntjac prove that the smaller deer can thrive on the island.

Once established, conies soon increase dramatically in numbers, having, in ideal conditions, several litters in a year, and being capable of breeding when six months old. Periodically the animals were culled to prevent the warren from becoming overstocked, and the grass overcropped. 'Ferrettes and dogges' were used to drive the conies from their burrows, or feeding grounds, into 'nettes'.

Two types of nets were used to round up conies. Many early warreners favoured long nets held by staves, which were erected a little distance from the burrows, so that when the animals emerged to feed, dogs drove them into the nets from which they were easily extracted. There were also purse nets, which were fastened over exits from the burrow from which the warreners hoped the conies would flee when a muzzled ferret was let loose among them.

Berkeley records and inventories provide intriguing glimpses of the uses of the end product. The fur is itemized as trimming for the under-servants' livery 'of cloth and furred with coney, lambskinne and budge [lambskin with the wool outwards]', each a degree under the other. More illustrious members of the three hundred strong Berkeley household of Lord Maurice III and his successors were clothed in 'cloth of gray and scarlet and furred with miniver [Siberian squirrel] of the best'. Expensive white ermine tipped with black was reserved for the robes of the lord and his immediate family.

Steep Holm suffers from National Politics

Lord Maurice III, 7th Baron, who rebuilt the priory, was greatly favoured by Edward II, and in 1319 was known as 'the King's beloved kinsman'; but he was an impulsive character, who was able to keep out of trouble only as long as his father Lord Thomas was alive to caution him against dangerous intrigues. As soon as he inherited the Berkeley title in 1321, political ambitions led to his rapid downfall – and contributed to the deterioration of Steep Holm as an asset to the family estates. Lord Maurice became involved in private feuding, and a raid against the property of the king's favourite, Hugh le Despenser, led to his capture and imprisonment in Wallingford Castle – within six months of his acquisition of the Berkeley title. A failed rescue attempt by his son Sir Thomas placed the lives and inheritances of both men in jeopardy; but Lord Maurice remained in close custody in Wallingford until his death at the end of May 1326. His escapades had resulted in the Berkeley lands being committed into the care of constables, on behalf of the king, with the family jewels, money, plate and other goods being confiscated, together with hereditary lands in the possession of his sons. These included Portbury, with its attendant warren on Steep Holm.

Family Fortunes Restored

Edward II was deposed in January 1326 and later imprisoned in Berkeley Castle during what was to become the darkest time of the family's history. The evil death of the king at the castle in 1327 need not be dealt with here, save to say that Lord Thomas was suspected of complicity in his murder, but acquitted when a perfunctory trial was held in 1330. Most of his property had been restored to him by Queen Isabella, acting on behalf of her fourteen-year-old son, King Edward III, who had been crowned within days of his father being deprived of the throne; but when Lord Thomas returned to his inheritance he found the estate much decayed and his Portbury property in ruins. On Steep Holm the management of the warren was also adversely affected by this sequence of events.

While all this political activity was taking place the old de Burci name briefly reappeared on the scene for the last time. John de Burcy had acquired some of the attainted Berkeley properties, including the advowson of Brean; and in 1322 he was named as patron when presenting a new incumbent. Ten years later, with the Berkeley fortunes restored, Walter de Burcy formally quit claimed to Lord Thomas 'all his right in the island of Stepelholme and all lands which the said Walter holds in Upphall [Uphill] and Churcheston [Christon] as well as in the church of Broen [Brean]'. There seems little doubt that the reason for this legal transaction was to clear up Lord Thomas's title to the remaining Berkeley lands which had been attainted by King Edward II.

When Lord Thomas died in 1361 his Inquisition post mortem listed Portbury under his Somerset properties, but Steep Holm, which was attached to that Somerset manor, was included with his Gloucestershire lands. His heir, Lord Maurice IV, the 9th baron, during an adventurous youth in the service of his king, had built up his possessions by the purchase of additional lands in Christon and Uphill, while he still lived at the hereditary manor of Portbury with his family. He was married to Elizabeth, daughter of Hugh, Lord Spencer, when they were both only eight years old; and Portbury church still displays the crossed arms of these two families in its fourteenth-century north aisle. But there is irony here, for their grandfathers, Maurice III and Hugh, had been avowed enemies; and on Maurice's imprisonment in 1321, much of his property had been given by the king to Hugh le Despenser.

Maurice IV became Lord of Berkeley when he was thirty years of age, but he enjoyed his inheritance for only seven years before he succumbed to a fatal illness in 1368, having been 'never cured of his wounds' sustained in battle for the king. Smythe relates a rather odd episode. Lord Maurice's wife Elizabeth 'the year of her husband's sickness, made a newe gowne for her selfe, of cloth furred throughout with coney skins out of the kitchen'. That she should have made her own gown seems strange; and for it to be of coney fur, usually reserved for the under-servants, seems out of keeping with the rich ermine normally worn by the family. As the fur was retrieved from the kitchen, the animals were probably from the home park, rather than from Steep Holm's warren.

The overlordship rights had by now been acquired by the Earl of Devon as recorded in the Inquisition post mortem of Maurice's Somerset properties: 'Portbury: Two thirds of the manor . . . held of the Earl of Devon . . . includes two gardens with vines and fishponds in them, a fishery in the Severne, a rabbit warren called "le Holmes".' This entry confirms that the long-standing fishing rights were still held by the Lords Berkeley in return for some form of service to the earl; and that the warren on Steep Holm was still considered viable.

Similarly in another Inquisition, of 1377, Hugh de Courtney, Earl of Devon, possessed Portbury: '2 knights' fees held by heirs of Maurice de Berkeley.' On the death of her husband, the Lady Elizabeth was assigned the manor of Portbury with its attached island warren as a dower property for her own use. Her eldest son Thomas, being only sixteen years old, was made a king's ward under the guardianship of Lord de L'isle – to whose daughter Margaret he was already married.   Elizabeth did not marry again, and it was not until 1388 that she leased the manor to her son Lord Thomas. His direct inheritance on his father's death had included Berkeley Castle, numerous manors, and 'The Isle of Stepholmes in Seavern', so technically it was his property; but he had to wait a long time before coming into possession of the island and its warren.

After surviving her husband by twenty-one years, Elizabeth died in 1389; and Steep Holm again appeared in an Inquisition post mortem, this time as part of the estates held by her. The island was still attached to Portbury Manor, and Lord Thomas at last 'entered upon the lands which she [had] held in Joynture & [widow's] dower' – not as her marriage settlement, as has sometimes been assumed. All that now remains of this formerly magnificent fortified manor house, occupied by the Berkeley family for centuries, are a few vestiges of walls within private woods on a hill above Portbury village. Thomas IV, 10th baron, died in 1417 'possessed of Ye Isle of Stepilholms in Ye Severn in which is a cony warren & messuage' – the final clue that throughout all the vicissitudes of politics and family fortunes over more than 100 years, the island was still credited with having a viable warren, with a small tenement for the keepers – the site of which has now been discovered within the old priory precincts and excavated to provide additional evidence of how the keepers lived and worked.

Chapter Nine

PROPERTY DISPUTES AND NEGLECT

Feuding Families

The Lords Berkeley, with their hereditary separate manor at Portbury for the eldest son, were in a sense near neighbours as well as owners of Steep Holm, but this situation was to change drastically. The death of Thomas, Lord Berkeley in 1417 marked the beginning of a family feud which was to last several generations, eventually to end in bloodshed and to affect the history of the island. His numerous possessions were divided between Elizabeth, his only child, and James, his nephew and male heir to the title. The castle and Barony of Berkeley with the other baronage properties, including the manor of Portbury, therefore went to James.

All the remaining properties were inherited by Elizabeth, and these included Steep Holm and the advowson of Brean. In this way the previously linked Portbury Manor and island warren were separated. With so vast a personal estate, Lord Thomas might perhaps have hoped that his daughter and nephew would both have been content with this division of his great wealth, but they were not. Elizabeth not unreasonably felt that as the only child the whole estate should have descended to herself and her family; while James considered that the barony should have had more of his uncle's other properties to support it. This quarrel began what Smythe called 'the greatest sutes in lawe and of longest continuance that were in those times or since' – perhaps because of the ample funds available to pay the lawyers! James certainly had other substantial possessions which he had inherited from his parents. Elizabeth's husband, Richard Beauchamp, Earl of Warwick, enjoyed his own rich estates.

Elizabeth's personal quarrel was not to last for long. She died young, only five years after her father, having borne her husband three daughters. For a son and heir to his earldom he had to marry again, and it was to the son by his second wife that the Warwick properties were to descend. Elizabeth's estate went to her daughters: Margaret, Countess of Shrewsbury; Ellenor, Duchess of Somerset; and Elizabeth, Lady Latimer – all titled ladies with lands elsewhere.

Again the overlordship of Steep Holm had changed – this time from the hands of the Earls of Devon to the 4th Earl of Ormonde, Lord Lieutenant of Ireland; both

Steep Holm and the advowson of Brean appearing in an Inquisition post mortem taken after his death in 1453. There it is confirmed that they were held by the 4th earl, although Strachey says 'not of ye King'. The fact that the earl's family (the le Botillers) already had a long standing interest in the separate Manor of Brean had probably encouraged him to acquire the advowson as well.

For a while the history of the later medieval ownership of the island becomes a little obscure. Certainly the possession of both the island and the advowson of Brean passed to the 4th earl's son, who in 1449 for his fidelity to Lancastrian interests had been made Earl of Wiltshire by King Henry VI. On his father's death he became the holder of both titles (Ormonde and Wiltshire); but once more those were troubled times. The long and bitter Wars of the Roses were about to begin, and the 5th earl was one of the combatants. In 1461, the Lancastrians having been defeated, he met his death by execution in the Tower of London – and yet again the properties of a recalcitrant nobleman connected with Steep Holm were attainted by a king, this time the newly-crowned Edward IV.

On 5 May of the previous year the advowson of Brean had been exercised, not by the earl but by Margaret, Countess of Shrewsbury, and Ellenor, Duchess of Somerset, the two elder daughters of Elizabeth Beauchamp (née Berkeley). In 1462 they again presented a new rector to the parish.

Norton Beauchamp joins Steep Holm

Margaret, who was the second wife of John Talbot, Earl of Shrewsbury, had been named after her maternal grandmother, Margaret de L'isle, wife of Thomas of the disputed Berkeley will; so when their son John Talbot Junior was to be given a title it was natural that Viscount de L'isle was the name chosen. He married into the de Cheddre family, and through Joan his wife obtained numerous properties which formerly had belonged to her grandfather, Robert de Cheddre, a wealthy burgess of Bristol. Included were the advowsons of Uphill and Christon, and also the Manor of Norton Beauchamp, a few miles farther north along the coast. So, once again, an ownership link was being forged between Steep Holm and the church of Uphill; while for the first time a bond between Steep Holm and the Manor of Norton Beauchamp was being formed. This renewed relationship with Uphill church was not to last for long, but the connection between Steep Holm and Norton Beauchamp would exist for over three hundred years.

More Family Quarrels

Title rights to the new acquisition of Norton Beauchamp had been a subject of dispute for many years before the marriage of John and Joan; while the feud between the descendants of Elizabeth and James was still festering.

The quarrel over the Norton Beauchamp holdings had originated in 1389, when a member of the Gamage family had disposed of the property to a Cheddre representative 'for 300 marcs of silver'. Later generations of Gamages bitterly resented the transaction, and in 1439 a descendant decided to take the law into his own hands. In the resulting court case the jury found that:

Thomas Chedder [Lady de L'isle's father] was for a long time lawfully and peacefully possessed in his demesne . . . the Manor of Norton Beauchamp . . . until Thomas Gamage [and named persons, including William, Prior of Worspring] . . . with many other unknown men, by the strong hand and arrayed in warlike manner, by force and arms . . . on the Thursday next before the Feast of St Clement the Pope, the 17th year of the reign of King Henry VI, entered the Manor of Norton Beauchamp [and other properties] . . . and held, kept and occupied them from the same Friday until Monday next after the Feast of St Andrew the Apostle . . . to the disturbance of the King's peace. . . .

The feud was not settled, and twenty-three years later tempers erupted again when the families were involved in another serious incident. By then Norton Beauchamp was in the possession of Lady de L'isle. The proceedings for the king's bench court for 1463 record:

Thomas Gamage, late of Lanyhangell in South Wales, Esquire [with other known and] unknown malefactors and disturbers of the King's Peace, armed and arrayed in warlike manner, viz. with swords, lances, glayvys, [cutting edges fixed to poles] breast-plates, bows, arrows and other defensive arms, on September the 19th, the second year of Edward IV [1462], entered upon the possession of the Manor of the said Lady by main force and ejected her . . . out of the possession of the premises in contempt of the Lord the King and to no small damage of the said Lady and against the Peace of the Lord the King, from the said 19th day to the day of this Inquisition.

From these court cases there is no doubt that Lady de L'isle (who died less than a year after this second attack) was the lawful owner of the manor, as well as of Steep Holm, which had by her marriage become attached to that property. By Lady Joan, (née Cheddre), the Viscount de L'isle had three children; and it was Thomas, their eldest child and only son who in 1471 became involved in a notorious conflict with his relation William, Lord Berkeley, son of that James who had inherited his uncle's baronage in place of Thomas's own great-grandmother, Elizabeth. As Dugdale expresses it, 'Thirsting for the Castle of Berkeley', Thomas schemed with various persons 'to betray it into his hands'. The plot being discovered, the hot-headed young Viscount then sent Lord Berkeley (by now a forty-five-year-old veteran) a challenge: 'to appoint a day and meet him half-way, to try their quarrel and title, to eschew the shedding of Christian blood, or to bring the same day the utmost of his power'. The challenge being accepted, the two met:

on the morrow at Nybley Green by eight or nine of the clock . . . and the Viscount's vizor being up, he was slain by an arrow shot through his head. After which [the same day] the Lord Berkeley advanced to Wotton, and rifling the house, took thence many writings and evidences of the said Viscount's own lands, with a suit of arras hangings [set of wall tapestries], wherein his arms, and the arms of Lady Joan, his mother were wrought, and brought them to Berkeley Castle. To this skirmish came divers from Bristol, Thornbury, the Forest of Deane, and other places, to the number of about a thousand, which exceeded what the Viscount brought.

This account vividly pictures the two noblemen each enlisting their many supporters to engage in private battle and pillage, solely to settle a personal property dispute which ended in tragedy. Viscount de L'isle had no children, and the descent of his family had eventually to rely on his youngest sister. Although the lineage can be traced in devious ways through several generations, the ownership link with Steep Holm disappears.

Connections with Royalty

The combined holding of the island and Norton Beauchamp with that of other properties is found next in a Deed of Attorney dated 1533, the year in which King Henry VIII married the ill-fated Ann Boleyn, and in which the future Queen Elizabeth I was born. But the king, disappointed in not having a male heir and tiring of Ann very quickly, fell in love with one of her ladies-in-waiting, Jane Seymour, and it was Jane's capable and ambitious brother, Sir Edward Seymour, who was to become the future owner of Steep Holm, Norton Beauchamp, and the advowson of Brean, along with his many other estates.

King Henry and Jane Seymour were married in 1536, the year in which all small monastic houses were dissolved – including Studley in Warwickshire to which the brethren of St Michael of Steep Holm had been transferred almost three hundred years earlier. In that same year Queen Jane's brother was created Viscount Beauchamp, and in 1537 he became Earl of Hertford. It is as Edward, Earl of Hertford, Viscount Beauchamp, that we find him presenting a new rector to the church at Brean in 1547. This was shortly after the death of King Henry VIII but, as uncle and Protector of the young King Edward VI, the earl was rapidly advanced in the nobility to become the first Seymour Duke of Somerset. Only four years afterwards (1551) he was found guilty of plotting against the king, convicted of treason and duly executed. His various titles were put in abeyance, and his properties were attainted, with the ownership of Steep Holm being retained by the monarchs until it was returned to his son (also Edward) by Queen Elizabeth I, soon after she acceded to the throne in 1558. The titles of Baron Beauchamp and Earl of Hertford were also regained by the late duke's son, but the dukedom itself was to be left in abeyance for another hundred years.

Some of Steep Holm's Plants Achieve Fame

In the interval Steep Holm seems to have become thoroughly neglected. William Turner, after surviving the displeasure of King Henry and later that of his daughter, Queen Mary, by temporarily fleeing the country, became Dean of Wells. Despite ill-health, he apparently undertook the hazardous sea voyage to Steep Holm some time before 1562 – when the second volume of his *Herball* was published. His famous note constitutes the first 'official' British record of alexanders (*smyrnium olusatrum*) growing 'in a certain Ilande betwene the far parte of Somerset Shere and Wales'. Earlier, in more general terms, the 'Feate of Gardening' written about 1440 had listed alexanders as a herb widely grown in England. Perhaps by Turner's time they were already regarded as less palatable, and their habitat was consequently more localized. By the seventeenth century they were virtually replaced in the kitchen by celery, and their roots were far less popular as a stewing vegetable. An early record of the wild leek is found in Camden's *Britannia*, first published in 1586: 'Great round-headed garlic on the Holms found growing plentifully by Mr Newton.' This is assumed to mean Steep Holm, although the wild leek still grows even more abundantly on the sister island of Flat Holm. Towards the end of the next century botanist John Ray also refers back to D. Newton's discovery of this plant on the islands. The more descriptive (but not strictly correct) name 'great round-headed garlic' continued in use until recent years.

Early Maps

The rather negative evidence of a pictorial map showing 'The Coste [coast] of England uppon Severne' in the time of Henry VIII indicates some landmarks along the coastline, southwards from the mouth of the Bristol Avon to beyond Porlock, including several proposed fortlets. But there is no hint that Steep Holm and Flat Holm were then anything other than featureless mounds, and certainly there is no indication of any existing or intended fortification works – although in later times the construction of defences was to alter the islands' contours drastically.

A more recognizable 1583 navigation map, although still having some prominent inaccuracies, was drawn by Dutch cartographer L.J. Waghenaer. 'Stepeholmes' and 'Slech [or] Flatholmes' are shown curiously up-ended, unlike the other islands. He calls the estuary 'De Canael Van Brostv' which shows that already the more picturesque old name 'Severn Sea', was becoming replaced by the prosaic title 'Bristol Channel' – an indication of the increasing prominence of the city as an international port.

By 1607 Saxton's map showed distorted outlines for 'Stepeholms Insul' and 'Flatholms Insul'. Even in 1648 navigators would have had major problems if following J. Blaen's map too precisely. He had more variations on the theme of spelling, with 'Shepholme' and 'Flatholmes'. It was Eman Bowen, in 1750, who at last had more accurate outlines for 'Steepholmes' and 'Flatholmes'.

A Forsaken Island

The great storm of 1606 may have contributed a little to the demise of the island, and more particularly of the manor of Norton Beauchamp, as assets to the great estates which had by then been returned to the descendants of the executed Edward Seymour, Duke of Somerset. Severe damage on both sides of the estuary was recorded in great detail by the writers of contemporary tracts. For a considerable distance inland, large areas of flat low-lying fields were flooded by a tidal surge. The lower fields at Norton were under water, and at Kingston Seymour, a few miles to the north, a tablet in the church porch is still preserved, which records that, like its Welsh counterpart of St Bride's across the channel, it was inundated to the depth of 5 ft. St Bridget's at Brean also suffered as the sea defences failed. Norton itself, little more than a hamlet, did not possess its own church, but relied on that of Kewstoke, out of harm's way on the lower slopes of Worlebury Hill. Steep Holm was beyond the notice of the reporters of the day, and it is doubtful whether the absentee owners were even concerned about any damage to the island.

With Steep Holm in the continuing ownership of the Seymour family, it came within the responsibilities of the bailiff for the Manor of Norton Beauchamp, who in 1625 wrote a graphic description of a run-down little island, hardly worthy of attention. Although the bailiff's estimates of area and height are inaccurate, this report is of vital importance to the historian, being the earliest known eye-witness account of Steep Holm: 'There is belongeinge to this Manour one little Iland called Stipe Holmes, beinge West from Norton Beauchamp 7 or 8 Miles into the Sea called Seaverne; the which cont. [contains] by estimacon xxiiij acres [24 acres is but half of the true extent of the island!].' The bailiff also comments on the difficulty of access: 'There is to the same noe Entrance in but in two places onlie, the other parts be a hundred faddum [fathom] of height & more, and unpossible to enter unto it. . . . [600 ft is far in excess of the true height]'. Any kind of farming on the island plateau had long since stopped, for '. . . groweth nothinge but a certen kinde of small fuell, called Privett, Elder, & a Kinde of wilde garlicke, estemed to be of noe more value then the cuttinge or carrieinge awaie, not yet that . . .'. The warren had ceased to be managed, and the 'graie Coinies [rabbits] to the number of XX or XXX coples [20 or 30 pairs] by estimac. [estimation] . . . of noe value, because by experience had of them, they be so fedd with garlicke, privet & Elder (grass lackeinge) that they do saver of the garlicke and privet in eating'. Over a long period of neglect the grass cover had been denuded, and scrub had largely taken over. If the bailiff's count was correct the remaining rabbits had decreased drastically in numbers, as well as their flesh being tainted with the strong flavour of the vegetation which they were forced to eat in order to survive. It is an interesting modern parallel that in the 1930s rabbits taken from the bleak north end of Lundy, where little grass was available, were considered by the islanders to be of poor texture and bitter flavour – because of the thrift and other vegetation with which they had to supplement their diet.

Back in 1625 Steep Holm does not appear to have been inhabited for a long time, for there is no mention of a building worthy of the bailiff's notice. Yet cut into the west wall of the old priory is a doorway which, by its insets for wooden door posts, is not likely to be earlier than the sixteenth century. This doorway is flanked by a puzzling piece of curved walling built into the original medieval south-west corner, but itself on very poor foundations. To the west and adjoining the opening are the remains of a substantial east/west wall which deviates slightly southwards. Running almost parallel to this wall, and 2 m 50 cm away to the south, are the mere remnants of another wall – and at the present stage of excavation, one can only speculate whether these form two sides of a room, or whether they continue westwards to create terracing in association with other very faint indications of similarly aligned walling. Some time after the earlier rebuilding of the priory for the warrener's quarters, someone went to the trouble of modifying the old west wall and erecting these new features.

The bailiff, in considering the worth of Steep Holm per year, says: '. . . there breedeth yerelie within the said Ilande Gulls and some Pewetts and some other kinde of sea Fowles, but of small nomber and value; but there breedeth & cometh to good comonlie of Gulls 16 or 20 dozen, sometymes more and sometymes lesse . . .'. In his view the island was profitable only in the short fowling season. Summing up the possible income from the island he concludes: 'The same to be rented may be

Herring gull guarding two chicks in nest among tree mallow and alexanders

worthe a yere the comoditie of the Gulls, valued at 20 [d?] a dozen, as the plentie or the scantie is. But the chardges must be taken out of that monie for the Watchemen.' His final comment is that the '. . . Pewetts is of noe value, because there be few or none at all to be accounted of'. Although peewit is now an alternative name for the lapwing, in the seventeenth century it could refer to a black headed gull.

This itemized account seems to have been written in response to an order to look into the viability of leasing the island to a tenant; but why was it needed at that time – and why had Steep Holm been abandoned? The answer has been found by studying the fortunes of the Seymour family.

Royal Wrath

In 1560, only two years after he had been favoured by Elizabeth, Edward Seymour brought the queen's anger upon himself when he secretly married Lady Catherine Grey – younger sister of the tragic Queen Jane and a possible contender for the throne. When it was discovered that she was pregnant, she and her husband were committed to the Tower, and he was fined £15,000 for having 'vitiated a maid of the Royal blood'. Nine years later, after his wife had died in the Tower, he was released, to marry twice more and live to the age of eighty-three years. His grandson, William, followed the family habit of risking royal displeasure. King James I was so fearful of Lady Arabella Stuart's claim to the succession that he kept her at Court, and forbade her to marry. Even so, William eloped with her. Yet again a Seymour bride was dispatched to the Tower, where she died five years later. The young nobleman fled the country to remain in exile until the end of the reign of King James – in 1625. During his enforced absence abroad both his father and grandfather died, and he acceded to the earldom and baronage. So, on his return to England he wished to check on his inherited properties. His Lordship's steward could hardly have been encouraged by the Norton Beauchamp bailiff's account!

Fishers and Gullers

The bailiff does not mention fishing rights – privileges which were much prized and jealously guarded in the Severn Sea. Apart from the Berkeley family's centuries-old rights of fishing on 'rockes and illands' in the upper part of the Estuary, Weston-super-Mare's own 'little yland, commonly called Ankers Head' (now known as Birnbeck, and terminus of the Victorian pier) had been let for the profits of both fowling and fishing for hundreds of years. The sheltered side of Birnbeck island is sometimes the Steep Holm ferry's return landfall when south westerlies prevent a low water landing on the mainland shore.

In 1572 a lease of 'Ankers Head' provided for the erection of a tiny cabin nearby 'for such as shall wache or kepe the fowle that shall brede in the said yland'; and similarly, the Norton Beauchamp bailiff, when writing about Steep Holm added that

Lesser black-backed gull nesting on priory site

the gulls must be 'watched from th'end of Julie to th'end of August by 2 men'. This is curious, as these are months when the young birds are already fledged, and when most have dispersed. We have often wondered whether a tripod pitcher dating from about 1650, of which we have found many matching fragments in our Steep Holm excavations may perhaps have belonged to gull watchers. The pieces were all found in a small area enclosed by the former coney warreners' room within the old priory walls; and in the upper medieval layers of the same area we found a bronze sailmaker's needle in excellent condition, which we can be reasonably certain was used by island fishermen.

For many years both before and after the bailiff's account of 1625 Steep Holm was inhabited only periodically by gull watchers in the summer and fishermen in the winter; and probably the old warreners' quarters were renovated more than once to shelter these seasonal occupiers; for the pottery sherds which can be dated to centuries before and beyond the Tudor period indicate that the island was seldom completely abandoned. The evidence suggests that either it was let from time to time, or at least that local opportunists profited from nature's bounty on Steep Holm.

In 1660, in recognition of his services to royalty during the Civil War, William Seymour regained his distinguished Tudor ancestor's most important honour and became the 2nd Seymour Duke of Somerset. When he died, little more than a month afterwards, both the title and his landholdings passed to his eleven-year-old grandson – also called William.

As a relief from the difficulties of tracing the inheritances, and more obscure records of great estates, of which tiny Steep Holm was a very minor speck on the map, it was rewarding to find a snippet of direct local interest. This was a brief item in the bailiff's account roll to William, 3rd Seymour Duke of Somerset: 'The rent of Steep Holm payable by Russell of South Brent Village for one year ending Michaelmas 1671 10/- and 20 Burrow Ducks [shelduck, so called because they sometimes use rabbit burrows or holes in a cliffside as nesting sites].'

Another Change of Ownership

The 3rd duke died in that same year, when he was only twenty-two years old; and because he was unmarried his nineteen-year-old sister Elizabeth inherited, becoming one of the wealthiest heiresses of those times. Within five years she was the wife of Thomas, Lord Bruce, 2nd Earl of Ailesbury; and at that stage the control and effective ownership of her various properties passed into his hands.

Lord Bruce soon decided to sell parts of his wife's property, and although research has not found any separate sale details for Steep Holm, there are details of a contract relating to the Manor of Norton Beauchamp, of which the island was an appendage. From this we learn that 'by an indenture dated 14 July 1684 made between the Right Honourable Thomas, Earl of Ailesbury, by the name of Thomas Lord Bruce, of the first part [vendor]; Edward Ryder of Marlborough, gent, and Godfrey Harcourt, of the second part [purchasers]; and Faith Heneage of the third part [mortgagee] in consideration of £3,200 paid to the said Earl by the said Faith Heneage the said Earl did grant unto the said Faith Heneage all that the Manor of Norton Beauchamp, Somerset by way of mortgage'. This information confirms brief comments by Richard Locke and the Revd John Collinson, eighteenth-century historians, that Norton Beauchamp and other local manors had been sold by Thomas Bruce to the Ryder family in the 1680s; but the transaction also introduced Godfrey Harcourt into the picture, as well as a mortgage. We find both included in a curious episode which took place between 1695 and 1696.

A Rigged Auction

A small advertisement in the *London Gazette* for the four days Monday 10 June to Thursday 13 June 1695 sets the scene:

The Manor of Norton Beauchamp lying between Bristol and Bridgewater in Somersetshire, and also the Capital Messuage called St John's near Clerkenwell in Middlesex, are to be sold by virtue of a decree in the High Court of Chancery, on Tuesday the 25th instant at 4 after noon before Dr. Edisbury, one of the Masters of the said Court, at his chambers in Symonds Inn in Church Lane, when he that bids most is to be allowed the purchaser.

If the advertisement is simple and straightforward, the intended auction sale of Norton Beauchamp was not! The heiress Elizabeth, Lady Bruce died in 1696, and in October of that year a letter was sent by C. Becher from London to her mother (then Duchess of Beaufort by a second marriage). This tells us more of the circumstances: 'I desire the Duchess of Beaufort may know w't [what] ye Master of the Rolls directed after hearing Counsell on both sides many hours. . . . It was in substance that ye Estate should beare its owne burthen – vis. Interest [on mortgage], ye Charge of Sea Banks, & Costs of Suite etc. And that ye Estate should be sold to ye best Purchaser.'

Apart from outstanding interest on the mortgage, the reference to 'Charge of Sea Banks' is a clue to an additional reason for the property holders' financial problems. Owners of land along the Channel seaboard had a responsibility enforceable in law to maintain specially built banks along the coast and beside rivers as defences against high tides; and this obligation ceased only within living memory. The lengths of banks to be kept in repair by each landowner were delineated in multiples of archaic measurements of 'lugs' (5 yds) and/or 'ropes' (20 ft), the individual limits being designated by marker stones. For centuries the lords of Norton, and the priors of Worspring, with their tenants, had been obliged to build and maintain defensive banks to protect their low-lying land from flooding. In the early years of the fifteenth century this involved the Vicar of Locking (responsible for one stretch of defences) in disputes which led to violence when his well-maintained river banks were topped by a stockade to protect them from being worn away by the hoofs of cattle and horses. This angered local farmers, as it prevented them from using the drier banks as droveways or bridle paths when moving their animals. Philip Webbe of Norton (and others) 'with a great company with force of arms . . . broke and destroyed the said stowk [stockade] and flung [it] into the common [water] course . . .'. When the unfortunate vicar was compelled by a local court to repair the stockade, the same persons tore it down again, trampling and damaging the defensive bank to such an extent that sea water flooded into the countryside.

No such furore occurred in 1695, but income from the Norton Beauchamp property had become inadequate to keep up the mortgage repayments, and to meet the heavy cost of necessary work on the sea defences. In informing the Duchess of Beaufort that the Court had ordered the property to be sold to clear its debts, C. Becher was seeking to protect his own vested interest as current owner of the mortgage (acquired from Faith Heneage). But the auction had been a farce. His long letter continues:

It was accordingly putt·into ye Gazett, and the Day fixed; I attended, at which time a Grocer in ye Citty, or Dry Salter, came and bid £3,000, [for] whome I know not, or whether it was for himselfe. No body appeared else; so at my request ye Master shutt up ye bookes, and ordered another Day (and accordingly It was putt into ye Gazett againe) at which ye Cittizen was angry, & no doubt in Strictnesse he ought to have had it. Before ye Second day came,

I desired Sr. John Foche to bid up by his Agent so farr as he saw Occasion, That ye Cittizen might not have it at an under Price; The 2d. [second] Day no body appeared as a purchaser; A Third Day was appointed, and another Scrivener by my desire bid upon Sr. John to encourage Purchasers; The Scrivener bid to £3,600 and Sr. John's Agent, who knew nothing, had Authority to bid on, and offering £50 more, ye other desisted; No one appeared at ye 3 meetings but ye Grocer, who had [would have] bought It for £3,000 but for me, and must have had it in Spight of us all; And this is the substance of all ye Proceedings, which was carried on with all ye Candor imaginable . . .

One might disagree with the reference to 'candour', but in any case the rigged auction had failed. In fact the property did not sell until a few years later; and meanwhile Mr Becher was anxious for the mortgage and other charges to be repaid as soon as possible. He requested that the Duchess of Beaufort would give Mr Harcourt some appropriate 'Directions'. Mr Becher explains by referring back to the Court case:

The Day after ye Hearing Mr. Harcourt seemed uneasie, and said he cou'd not sitt downe with this without Order, which I thought strange, since all disputes must be decided by ye Law. This was carried on by Consent on both sides; At last he came to this; That I should take £500 upon the whole, besides £3,200 Principall, for Sea Banks etc. for Interest he could not submitt to; I thought this a strange proceeding to be above the Law, yet for Quietnesse sake I submitted; and the Decretall ord'r passed upon it by Consent of Mr. Price and my Counsell. . . . All I desire is to have ye Deed signed by Mr. Harcourt as he settled It and all ye sums therein menconed [mentioned].

The actual disposal of the property by Mr Ryder and his associates took place in 1699. From historian Richard Locke's notes we learn that the new purchaser was Bristol merchant Captain Philip Freke. Separately, a documents schedule prepared by a firm of family solicitors as late as 1822, to record which documents had been extracted from a client's deed box for sending to another town by carrier, revealed details of an indenture between Edward Ryder and others, selling to Philip Freke. Historian Locke had indicated that the Manor of Norton Beauchamp had been largely dismembered at about that time, with parts being acquired by individual freeholders, and the schedule shows that in December 1699 a number of separate transactions did take place – which included the sale of Steep Holm, as part of that manor.

Untangling the elusive succession of owners since the time of Lord Thomas Berkeley's death and disputed will set us on the trail of some of the most baffling problems to be resolved in the island's history. There were battles over inheritances and dubious methods of trying to dispose of the property. Steep Holm had been owned by and linked to the rise and fall of some of the most powerful aristocrats in the country. It had become much neglected and almost forgotten; even so, our excavations have shown that it was scarcely ever completely abandoned.

But at the very end of the seventeenth century, Steep Holm, Norton Beauchamp and the advowson of Brean together entered into a new era under the ownership of the Freke merchant family, whose descendants were to hold it for 130 years.

Chapter Ten

MARITIME MATTERS AND MERCHANTS

Storms, Wrecks, Piracy and Smuggling

The new century began ferociously, with what John Strachey called 'ye great storm of 1702', which, he noted, washed away a stone door jamb from above one of Steep Holm's two landing beaches. He may have intended to write 1703, for in November of that year one of the worst storms recorded in southern England swept away the first Eddystone Lighthouse. High tidal waters were pushed up rivers; the Severn seaboard was inundated causing severe flooding as far as Bristol; while at Wells the west window of the cathedral was blown in by the strength of the wind, and Bishop Richard Kidder and his wife were killed in their bed when a chimney of the bishop's palace collapsed. These were but a few of the incidents recalled, and loss of life and property at sea could not be fully recorded. Crews of sailing ships entering the Severn Estuary and unable to reach shelter faced a frightening ordeal as the gale roared about them. Men struggled to keep a foot- or hand-hold on vessels which rolled and pitched as great waves broke over the decks, while furled sails and rigging slammed about murderously. Having to rely entirely on sailpower, the horror of shipwreck was for many the inevitable result.

Local folk were ever on the lookout for ships in trouble during storms – often with the intention of salvaging anything they could for their own profit. As long ago as 1374 it is recorded that:

a ship of Spain was driven by a storm to the King's lordship between the islands called 'Stipholmes' and 'Flotholm' in the County of Bristol and there anchored . . . having goods (described and valued) on board. The ship itself with all its gear was worth 20L [£20]. On the Sunday John & Laurence ap Rees and John Morgan . . . and others unknown . . . by force of arms took away the ship, not being wrecked but sound and whole, with the goods to the Lordship of Sir Edward le Despenser at Kerdif [Cardiff] where the ship and goods are kept by the persons named and others of their company.

Lawlessness in the estuary was not just restricted to such instances of piracy. A Commission from Westminster dated 23 February 1387 ordered the Mayor of Bristol and certain merchants to enquire by jury 'as to the unloading by English merchants within "les Floteholmes" and the water of Severn of goods which are taken to Chepstowe in Wales and elsewhere by water and there exposed for sale and removed from Chepstowe without payment of customs and other dues'. The Commission further ordered Bristol's prominent citizens to '. . . make proclamation forbidding the practice under pain of forfeiture of the goods'. By 1421 the city was the first to have a customs vessel. Battle had commenced in what was to become centuries of tactical manoeuvres between authority and the 'gentlemen' who traditionally flouted import regulations. Ill-equipped customs men along the Severn shores could seldom compete with well-organized gangs bringing in an increasing variety of contraband – not just liquor, but many other commodities such as salt, soap and tobacco which came under crippling taxation.

Steep Holm, Flat Holm and Lundy were all notorious as smuggling haunts through the centuries, with many futile attempts being made to prevent the illegal trade. There are eighteenth-century records of (perhaps reluctant) local boatmen being hired at a daily rate of 1s 6d to take officials to Flat Holm, but being 'unable to reach the island'. In 1735 the London Customs House, acting on information received, ordered an Excise vessel 'frequently to visit this iseland [where] goods are run' in an attempt to 'prevent frauds being committed there'. By 1782 despairing Welsh customs officers were justifying the unauthorized purchase of a telescope which was 'thought very necessary as we can see every vessel that goes to the Flat Holmes, an iseland where smugglers at present run a great deal of goods and cannot just now be prevented as our Boat is too old to go into any sea'. Steep Holm, sitting in the middle of the Channel and often uninhabited apart from seasonal gullers and fishers, was even more difficult to keep under surveillance.

There may have been little respect for customs rules, or for property in the form of ships storm-driven, or even lured ashore, but there are many examples of local parishes having pity on shipwrecked mariners. The churchwardens' accounts of Puxton are among several which record alms being given to sailors. This ancient church, with its leaning tower forming a well-known landmark on the moors, was one of those damaged by flooding in the great inundation of 1606. In 1688 the accounts state: 'Gave to two poore seamen which was cast away at the Homeses, 6d.' They were perhaps the lucky ones. When bodies of drowned sailors were found on Flat Holm they were interred in shallow graves dug into ground above the shoreline. As late as 1817 between thirty and forty persons, passengers and crew of the *William and Mary* were lost when she was wrecked on the Wolves rocks near the island – where those washed ashore were buried in a communal grave. On beaches such as that at Brean victims of shipwreck were buried in the sand above the high water mark; for unless it was certain that they were Christian, they could not qualify for burial in consecrated ground. It was not until much later that this practice was discontinued, when part of the north side of the village churchyard was set aside for such interments, an empty haybarn if necessary serving as a temporary mortuary.

Captain Philip Freke

Despite the inevitable losses of ships, Bristol merchants of the eighteenth century were amassing considerable wealth, and many had the foresight to speculate in the purchase of land. Captain Philip Freke, who had invested surplus capital by purchasing Norton Beauchamp and its appendages in 1699, does not otherwise play a prominent part in the story of Steep Holm, but some of his transactions and activities can be traced. In 1704, five years after he had become the new owner of Steep Holm and Norton Beauchamp, he presented a rector to Brean Church, maintaining the centuries-old link between that advowson patronage and the island. Brean's thirteenth-century church of St Bridget had by then lost some of its medieval fabric, the rood and screen having been removed in the reformation, and the Early English windows revamped in Tudor style. A new Jacobean pulpit had been installed, and the nave floor improved by a novel paving of pebbles, collected from the beach below the southern Brean Down cliffs.

As a much respected citizen of Bristol, and a prominent and wealthy trader, it is unlikely that Captain Freke would have had any active involvement in smuggling on Steep Holm; but the tremendous upsurge of contraband movements through the Bristol Channel during the eighteenth and nineteenth centuries certainly involved both Holms as convenient hideaways for goods later transferred to mainland dispersal points. There is no doubt that smuggling activities were far from being confined to local river pilots and fishermen seeking to augment a meagre income by transporting illicit cargoes. The 'trade' was well organized and financed, and many of the great West Indiamen vessels had cunningly contrived hiding places for barrels of spirits, sugar and tobacco which were slipped past the waiting customs men.

Philip Freke died in 1729; another stormy year, when Brean church was struck by lightning. So much masonry was dislodged that the tower was greatly reduced in height, the truncated remains being capped with the unusual saddleback roof which distinguishes the building today.

An Historian's Description of Steep Holm

At about this time, John Strachey visited the obviously uninhabited island and made his invaluable observations. Among other notes already incorporated into this story, he wrote: '. . . Holms signifyes a grassy isle but it untowardly happens yt [that] ye Stepholms hath no grass expanse, scarce any earth, what is covered with Privet, Dwarf Elder, Elisandor [alexanders] & on ye rocks near ye water Sampire – There is also found Great Round headed Garlick [wild leek] . . . Inhabited only by Rabbits, vast No. [numbers] of Gulls, Cormorants, Sea Pigs [seals], Barrow Ducks [shelduck] etc. . . . .'

For many years there had been no attempt to cultivate Steep Holm, and indeed its early eighteenth-century ecology must have been very similar to that of the present day.

Another Controversial Will

On the death of Philip Freke the ownership of the advowson of Brean, Steep Holm and the Manor of Norton Beauchamp, along with many other possessions, passed to his nephew, Thomas Freke. Thomas seems to be a name linked with controversy in the history of the island. Back in 1417 Lord Thomas Berkeley initiated a family feud by his will. In 1730, on acquiring his considerable inheritance, Thomas Freke made a will which could have had far reaching effects. He already had two children, Frances and – predictably – Thomas, and his wife was again pregnant. She was to be handsomely provided for on his death, as long as she remained a widow, with the main estate eventually going to his son, including his coach and horses, plate and household goods. For his daughter Frances he decreed that she should inherit her mother's jewellery and personal possessions, and be paid the sum of £3,000 on marriage, or when attaining the age of twenty-one. But, should the child yet to be born be male, the legacy was to be reduced to £2,000, with generous provision to be made to the new child. Fortunately for family harmony the baby was a girl, named Ann, and under a codicil of 1731 the higher sum of £3,000 originally intended for Frances was reinstated. The author of this will died aged only thirty-eight years, in 1732, leaving a gift to St Stephen's church, Bristol '50L [£50] the interest thereof to the poor of this parish yearly for ever'. His little daughter who had been the innocent cause of potential family dispute, never came of age to inherit her father's intended legacy, as she died aged ten, in 1741.

It was also in 1741 that the Freke records show a deposit of 1s received from Messrs Wright and Chambers 'in earnest for the Steep Holmes'. This was obviously a payment to confirm an agreement, but as no further entries could be found naming the island, the transaction – probably to lease the fishing or fowling rights – may never have reached any conclusion.

A Lighthouse for the Estuary

Passage up and down the River Severn was both difficult and dangerous for sailing ships. The deep water channel flows between the islands of Steep and Flat Holm, and in the eighteenth century the estuary was particularly busy, with coasting and overseas traffic being augmented by ships carrying emigrants to America. Others were transporting petty criminals to the West Indies, Virginia and Maryland; while the slavers operating the triangular Bristol/Africa/West Indies route with their miserable human cargoes were returning home loaded with sugar, rum and tobacco. Having carried these goods safely over the Atlantic, the ships were often in greatest danger in the narrowing estuary with its fierce tidal currents, submerged rocks and shifting sandbanks. Merchants anxiously awaited news of their returning cargoes which were sometimes sighted entering the Channel, only to be lost within a few miles of their home port. Losses of ships and lives increased, protests mounted, and following the wreck of a vessel in which sixty soldiers drowned in 1736, petitions finally resulted in the grant of a licence permitting Bristol merchant William Crispe

Flat Holm's lighthouse tower, built 1737 and first lit in March 1738

to risk his and his partner's capital by erecting and operating a private lighthouse on the highest point of Flat Holm's cliffs. This was built in 1737 and first kindled on 25 March 1738 – being for many years coal-fired, consuming half a ton of fuel every night, and often making as much smoke as flame. After a fascinating history of human endeavour, failure and success, the same lighthouse tower, now relying on electricity and fully automatic, is still in use today.

Stranded on Steep Holm!

In April 1750 when five young men took a boat from Bristol 'to have some diversion on the Steep Holmes' the island was uninhabited. Their adventure lasted longer than they anticipated, for a gale sprang up shortly after they landed, wrecking their boat on the beach and leaving them stranded. It was nearly three days before they were able to draw attention to their plight 'when they were discovered by the keeper of the lighthouse on Flat Holme with a glass [telescope], who went and brought them off'. The rescuer was Thomas Biss, responsible for tending the light after the first keeper (Thomas Gilpin) was drowned when returning from the Welsh mainland in 1746. Although Gilpin's widow kept the light for a while, her assistant Biss was appointed keeper-in-charge following her dismissal for scandalous ill-treatment of a young apprentice.

A New Building

Thomas Freke, son of the merchant of the controversial will, pre-deceased his sister Frances, who had so nearly lost part of her legacy. She became sole heiress of the estate, and the Freke inheritance effectively entered into new ownership when in 1754 she married John Willes of an equally wealthy Northamptonshire family.

The bridegroom's father was Sir John Willes of Astrop, Chief Justice of Common Pleas; and his uncle was Edward Willes, Bishop of Bath and Wells. The island having passed into the hands of this distinguished household, the connection between property and owners again became rather remote.

Nevertheless, during this era there was a spurt of activity when the first new building for centuries was erected on Steep Holm. The old priory had been totally ruinous for many years, and if there was to be any chance of income from leasing the island, something had to be done to improve the lot of fishermen or fowlers who wished to profit from seasonal occupations. A new cottage, or tenement, was built. Writing in 1791, Collinson places the date for construction of the tenement at 1776,

East fireplace wall of 1776 tenement in the 1930s

and John Rutter, in 1829, adds the information that it was for the benefit of fishermen when attending their nets pitched on the shore line. The stones used, and the occasional pennant sandstone roofing tile tucked in between them, came from the long-derelict priory building. The new structure had no proper foundations but was robust enough to withstand lengthy periods of neglect. A corbelled alcove and a bread oven at its west end, and another fireplace between the windows in its east wall provided basic necessities. In general design the tenement was very similar to a typical eighteenth-century Mendip cottage. For a simple fisherman's lodging it was spacious enough, and its position, just north-west of the old priory remains, was the most convenient from the point of view of being near a 'quarry' of ready dressed stones available from the ruins. Like the former priory it was in the most sheltered part of the island plateau, and above the steep path which led straight down to the beach and fishing nets.

The first resident fisherman was probably Thomas Yateman, mentioned as the occupier of the island in a legal deed of 1786. This appears to be the same Thomas Yateman who at about this time was renting a fishery at Brean; perhaps even the same one who on 27 September 1780 was ordered to pay £50 to the overseers of the poor at neighbouring Berrow for the keep of a baby boy born to Betty Vincent, a single woman of that parish.

Island Fishing Methods

In the estuary the centuries-old technique for shore fishing was to fix rows of stow net stalls on gently sloping beaches or mud flats. Consisting of stout upright poles with bag-shaped nets between, these stalls were set in lines across the flow of the current to trap the fish on the ebb – a very successful method of fishing made possible by the exceptionally high rise and fall of the upper Bristol Channel tides. Winter was the principal fishing season, when big catches could be expected; on Steep Holm fish nets and basketwork salmon traps were set on the shingle spit projecting into the sea from East Beach. Facing up Channel the long nets opened out as the tide ebbed, so that fish swimming past might be swept into them to be trapped in the narrow tail section until, at low water, the fisherman undid the end of the net to tip them into a basket. But to obtain large catches required the use of many stalls, with the line of poles stretching farther and farther into the sea; so visiting and emptying the nets each tide became a long, cold and tiring process, the tails having to be re-tied each time, with the fisherman retreating shoreward step by step as the tide came in. At the height of the fishing season, several men were needed for this task, remaining for some weeks on the island to tend the fishing gear and collect each tide's haul into baskets ready to be taken up Channel to market.

Apart from needs imposed by the volume of work in setting out and emptying the many fish nets, to have men available on the island to load catches quickly into the fishermen's boats was essential. It was also important to get the fish to market without delay so that it should arrive fresh, and be ahead of other fishermen's catches. With the boats being dependent on wind and tide, or oars, the round trip could take several hours.

Thomas Yateman leased Steep Holm for some years, but probably occupied the tenement only intermittently. His tenure made little impact on the island, for to the members of the Geological Society who visited Steep Holm in 1824, the cottage was no more than 'ruins of a small hovel'; while William Withering, in 1826, commented that no inhabitant had dwelt on the island in the memory of man 'save the solitary fisherman who makes the crazy hut his cheerless abode, and that only through the dreary season of winter'. Little effort had been made to keep the comparatively new building in repair.

John Freke Willes Inherits

John Willes had died in 1784 and his son, John Freke Willes of Astrop House, Northamptonshire, inherited. A complicated deed of 1786 sets out the many properties acquired by this young man; the extensive Somerset estates, the advowson of Brean, the Manor of Norton Beauchamp, and the island of Steep Holm. Ownership of some of the Somerset properties, relating back to the 1754 marriage settlement of his parents, had been disputed, and the deed indicates that all the properties were held in trusteeship by Thomas Nutt, of Lyons Inn, Middlesex; with the Revd John Deacle, of Astrop, another trustee, being empowered to demand them on behalf of John Freke Willes – a typical legal process of the day. John Freke Willes had no direct descendants when he died in 1802, and the Manor of Norton Beauchamp was disposed of by the family in 1804. Steep Holm was retained until 1830 when it was sold by his second cousin William Willes.

Beating the Water Bounds

For a moment we must again step back in time to clarify a common misunderstanding about the ownership of Steep Holm. In 1373 King Edward III was grateful for the part played by Bristol in restoring his depleted coffers with the massive sum of 600 marks, and providing twenty-three ships and 608 sailors for his campaigns in France. He signed a unique royal charter which granted city and county status to the former town 'in consideration of the good behaviour of the Burgesses towards us, and of their good service in times past by their shipping'. The privilege was jealously guarded, and as the city and county boundaries were gradually expanded over the centuries it became customary to beat the bounds in more and more elaborate fashion to mark and preserve their exact positions. By the eighteenth century the traditional walking of the land boundary was extended to include the water limits.

As part of a special ceremony which took place on Friday 26 May 1727, a large party, led by the Lord Mayor, aldermen and other members of Bristol City Council set sail down the River Avon and the Channel. The sword-bearer's diary lists a few provisions which sustained the adventurers: '120 lbs beef; 2 sides lamb; Sallating [salads] and Coucumbers; 1 cask ale, 1 cask cyder; 4 dozen bottles White wine; 2 dozen bottles French wine; 2 dozen bottles Port wine; 2 quarts Brandy; 15 bottles Hotwell water.' Apart from sampling the refreshments, council members were justifying expenses of £32 7s 10d by the serious business of beating the water bounds of the County of Bristol, of which the two Holms formed the south and west extremities.

The tradition continued, and as one nineteenth-century guide book writer expressed it: 'The Holmes lying within the jurisdiction of Bristol, the Corporation occasionally visit it to assert their right, when they spend a convivial day, combined with a delightful aquatic excursion.' The famous P. & A. Campbell paddle steamer *Britannia* was chartered in 1900 to beat the water bounds of Bristol. This time the total expedition costs had risen to £712, for a week's perambulation of the entire boundary; and the trip down Channel took place, perhaps unwisely, in September. The *Bristol Times & Mirror* carried a graphic description of the scene:

> Only one boatload could be landed on the bleak and dreary Steep Holm and the envious left behind watched the unpleasant tossing of the well-laden craft and said they hoped no accident would mar the day's proceedings. Even with the help of a Corporal and some gunners from the Fort [to be described in a later chapter] there was a good deal of trouble in finding a landing place. It transpired that there were 6 or 7 captains aboard the boat and their conflicting orders threatened to produce mutiny amongst the crew. Meanwhile the boat kept pecking at different parts along the shore like a huge drowning bird. Finally the passengers were dragged out and an iron stake inscribed CB 1897 was driven into the rocks at high water mark.

After this difficult landing for the ceremonial marking of the water boundary by somewhat ruffled officials, Flat Holm proved easier. A large party was able to explore the island and place a boundary marker there also, afterwards enjoying an excellent meal on board ship during the return journey. The significance of the inscription 'CB 1897' is that the land boundaries of Bristol were extended in that year. On Steep Holm, until steps were constructed by Kenneth Allsop Trust workers a few years ago to improve access from East Beach to the zig-zag path leading to the plateau, a stone marker with exactly the same inscription could be seen, but it is now buried beneath concrete.

Because of these regular excursions, and the boundary markers which were placed on Steep Holm's East Beach against the base of the cliff, a myth gained credence in the late nineteenth century, connecting the ownership of the island with Bristol Corporation. Although the same ceremonies took place on Flat Holm's north-east beach, no such fable could be attached to that island, as it was clearly Welsh, its alternative name being Ynys Hafren, and was attached to the parish of St Mary, Cardiff. Indeed in 1793 Mrs Taylor, the lighthouse keeper, described as 'a careful woman who kept a good light', and who also farmed the land, was terrified by the vicar of that parish, when he threatened her with ex-communication for not paying tithes on her corn and other island produce.

An additional explanation for the Corporation of Bristol being incorrectly credited with the ownership of Steep Holm was that for ecclesiastical purposes the island was formerly attached to the parish of St Stephen, on the old waterfront in the city centre. This church was closely associated with Bristol merchants trading up and down the Channel and to the West Indies, who donated generous gifts to the poor of the parish. Some of these wealthy traders were interred within its vaults, including members of the Freke family, the eighteenth-century owners of Steep Holm.

Since December 1966, after a long period of being ex-parochial, Steep Holm has been incorporated into the ecclesiastical parish of Brean; but it was never the property of the Corporation of Bristol – merely a boundary point, with the beach being used as a marker because the true position against the sheer north cliffs was inaccessible.

Chapter Eleven

STEEP HOLM COMMERCIALIZED

The Beginnings of a Seaside Resort

The early part of the nineteenth century ushered in a period during which Steep Holm was to undergo great changes. The conversion of small fishing villages on the south coast of England into seaside resorts for health and leisure pursuits had already begun in the mid-1700s with the convalescence of members of the royal family leading to people of fashion seeking the invigoration of sea breezes and bathing. Gradually the formerly popular spa towns lost favour to coastal beaches, and a new craze gathered momentum around Britain's shores – soon spreading to the Bristol Channel.

Although Steep Holm was considered an unwelcoming grim rock, to be visited only in the most favourable weather by intrepid botanists seeking the rare plants which had been isolated there, Flat Holm's lighthouse was still privately owned, and something of a novelty to the enquiring explorer looking for an excuse for a short but adventurous sea voyage and a stroll around the island. Its keepers farmed the land as well as being in charge of the light; and this placed them in an excellent position to encourage visitors to stay in simple accommodation at the farmhouse, and enjoy fresh home-produced fare.

In 1789 there was some concern that the head keeper was becoming too prosperous. On 4 September Thomas Rothley (agent and part owner of the coal-fired light) wrote a letter to William Dickinson, his fellow proprietor: '. . . Taylor [the keeper] wants to have a Dairy House. I am told it would be convenient for him, and enlarge his kitchen. . . . I am informed several persons who had lost their appetites & were apprehensive they were consumptive have lately been greatly relieved by living on the island a month or 6 weeks & Lord Cardiff [owner of Flat Holm] told me that he thought Taylor should pay the Proprietors [of the lighthouse] for residing there, instead of our allowing him a salary.'

Less than eight years later advertisements started to appear in a Bristol newspaper signifying that the Biss family (Jane, related to Thomas, the former keeper and rescuer of those stranded on Steep Holm in 1750; and her son John, later himself to become keeper of the Flat Holm light) were anxious to offer superior accommodation to visitors to Uphill, with the added attraction of boat trips to 'the Holmes'. A young medical student, Thomas Turner (later to become a distinguished surgeon), was holidaying at Weston in 1815 when he unexpectedly experienced the hospitality offered at the Flat Holm farmhouse. He was lucky enough to obtain a passage in a skiff taking a mason to measure for some work on the island, but intended to return the same evening. Arriving soaked by the waves which swept over the frail craft, Turner dried out by the farmhouse fire and enjoyed a satisfying dinner; but after tea, also prepared by the farmer's wife, sea conditions made it impossible for the boatman to return to the mainland. Reluctantly Turner asked if he could be accommodated overnight, and was taken to see 'some bedrooms. . . . On entering the chambers I was not a little surprised to find they were so good. . . . There was a neatness about them which one would scarcely expect to find. . . . After making a hearty supper of bread and milk I went to bed, and slept very soundly. . .'. He was so impressed with the island and the attention he had enjoyed that on departure next morning he asked what would be charged for board and lodgings for a week, and was told 'Twenty-five shillings, sir.' Needing to return to Weston he found that during his enforced overnight absence his landlady had re-let his lodgings; so he collected his luggage and hastened back to the boat to return to Flat Holm – there to spend one of the happiest weeks of his life, and to write a unique diary account of his observations.

Solicitor and local historian, George Bennett, from the hamlet of Rolstone, had written in 1805 of the village of Weston-super-Mare that in summer and autumn the place was becoming much frequented by visitors seeking to benefit from the sea air and bathing, with several good lodging houses being erected for their use. In 1810 these houses were augmented by Weston's first hotel – now the Royal Hotel – and in 1821–2 medicinal baths were built on the tiny offshore islet of Knightstone.

Lessee Atwell and Smuggling Tales

It was Benjamin Atwell who first rented Knightstone's medicinal baths, and at this time was also tenant of the fishing rights at Steep Holm – carrying on one trade in the summer and the other in the winter. Since 1824 there has been a causeway joining Knightstone to Weston's promenade, but before then the connection was a shingle bank, usable only at low tide. At other times visitors had to be ferried across by rowing boat. In winter the same boatmen were occupied with fishing at Steep Holm. One of them was Aaron Fisher, appropriately named, as by 1840 he was in business as a fishmonger, selling his own catches. By 1850 he had become the proud owner of the *Katie*, a new locally-built boat.

As a weather-beaten old man, living in his little cottage, Fisher recalled to historian Ernest Baker his younger days, when he had been an exciseman for about seven years. There was a great deal of smuggling at that time, but he never captured any cargo and never had any fights with the smugglers – for he said they were too sharp and clever to be caught; although one Brean man was sentenced to six months' imprisonment when a keg of brandy was found under the floor of his cottage. Aaron Fisher said that stray kegs of spirits could be picked up every now and then on the beach, from smugglers' cargoes which had been buoyed ready for recovery, but often some broke loose, and drifted ashore. Once, when returning home from Brean with his fish-pots, he noticed disturbed sand, and dug with his hands until he came to a rope. By the time he had finished exploring, he had recovered two tubs of brandy. Placing one in his fish-pot and covering it with fish, he hid the other until it could be safely carried home, with the help of a friend. When burning the incriminating empty tub 'flames went up 10 ft above his [friend's] chimney. . . . The spirit, you know, was very strong, a long way above proof; why, a teaspoonful would, when mixed, make a pint of ordinary spirit'!

Not quite smuggling, but partaking of illegal bounty, was the episode of the *Rebecca* which the *Bristol Mirror* of 28 September 1811, reported as 'Lost . . . from Jamaica to Bristol, near Cardiff; crew saved.' Casks of rum from her cargo drifted across the Channel to be scattered along Weston sands, where outnumbered (and not very enthusiastic) customs officials could not prevent the local populace from helping themselves to an unexpected bonanza. Everyone from the lord of the manor (who claimed the right to retrieve wreck from his land) to the humblest labourer had a cask, or brought buckets, jugs, and saucepans to be filled. Enterprising farmers arrived with churns, and drove away after filling them with rum – which must have improved the flavour of the milk for the next few days – and the tapped casks were left to drain, so that the road was 'ankle deep in mud and rum'.

As Aaron Fisher talked to Ernest Baker he remembered his Steep Holm experiences:

> In the winter when the bathing was over, I went down to the Steep Holm to fish: Atwell rented the fishery there too. One season, while it was blowing very hard, I, with some others, was down there five days without any food; it was so very rough no boat could land. A boat did put off to us about the third day, but it missed the island, and was blown to Newport. We were taken off at last by a pilot boat, and landed at Sand Point, and mighty hard work we had to walk home to Weston, we were all so weak and feeble from want of food.

By contrast with this stormy memory, Aaron also recalled times when the sea was so calm and the air so quiet and still that from the fishery at Birnbeck Island he could hear Benjamin Atwell hammering nails on Steep Holm! Some years later Birnbeck was to be joined to the mainland by Weston's first pier. This illustration of the sharp hearing of Fisher must have occurred when Benjamin was living on the island, being described in a local parish register (on the birth of his son, Samuel in 1836) as a carpenter, residing on Steep Holm. At that time he still retained the fishing rights.

Island for Sale

On 9 June 1827 an announcement appeared in the *Bristol Mirror*:

THE STEEP HOLMES.
Property to be sold or let – The Steep Holmes and Fishery in the Bristol
Channel. The island has long been celebrated for rabbits and an extensive
Salmon and Sprat industry. The Bristol market is mostly supplied with fish
caught at this island. For particulars apply to Mr A. Murray, Surveyor and
Land Agent, 61 St Martin's Lane, London.

This is useful confirmation of the commercial viability of the fishing which was
taking place at Steep Holm at that time, but in fact the island was not sold, and for a
few more years it was to remain in the ownership of the Northamptonshire Willes
family.

Meanwhile Weston-super-Mare continued to grow at a phenomenal rate.
Numbers of visitors increased rapidly, many more lodging houses were built, and
the first section of promenade was completed.

John Baker, New Owner

If it was the passing of the Weston-super-Mare Inclosure Act which had begun the
development of the town, the Baker family of Aldwick Court, near Blagdon, may take
some of the credit as the solicitors mainly responsible for advising and acting in much
of the legal work involved. It is a member of this family who next appears in the Steep
Holm story, as purchaser of the island in 1830. At long last Steep Holm stood alone as
an individual property, the large Somerset estates of the Willes family having been split
up by separate sales transactions. Proving a point can sometimes be difficult, and when
our discovery that John Baker owned the island for a short time in the 1830s was first
published in 1977, it was frankly disbelieved – because of the long established, much
publicized (and now firmly discredited) myth that Bristol Corporation had been the
owner, from whom a Colonel Tynte had purchased Steep Holm at about that time. But
in our early research work we were still faced with trying to prove exactly what had
happened in the 1830s. Having listened to members of the Baker family, who stated
that John Baker had indeed purchased the island – for his own purposes, and not
merely as an agent acting for someone else – we took note of what local researcher and
historian Kingston James had written in the early years of this century; and also of a
comment by Ernest Baker, prominent Weston solicitor and writer of local history, who
confirmed that his grandfather had bought Steep Holm. Skinner, when he visited Steep
Holm in 1832, wrote that the island had been recently purchased for £700 by a Mr
Baker: 'a very cheap bargain, if it be true that he lets the fishery for £40 a year'. When
observing features of archaeological interest, he further commented: 'as Mr Baker, the
proprietor of the Holm, is I find, fond of antiquities, he will, I daresay, keep a good

lookout'. Thomas Clark, who provided another valuable account, with the description of his visit to the island in 1831, was effectively able to confirm the recent purchase price of £700, although his boatman was not sure whether it was £700 or £7,000!

But all these comments needed to be substantiated with more formal evidence if possible. It was particularly gratifying when, in 1978, the original conveyances were received by Somerset Record Office, and proved beyond any possible doubt that William Willes (of the family which had owned the island since the marriage of Frances Freke to John Willes in 1754) had indeed sold Steep Holm to John Baker on 24 June 1830. For the stated figure of £700 he had acquired Steep Holm with its 'messuage or tenement' – the one which had been built in 1776, and which had been occupied formerly by fisherman Thomas Yateman.

John Baker had plans for developing the island as a tourist attraction to complement the growing resort of Weston-super-Mare. By 16 August 1831, when Thomas Clark visited Steep Holm, the improvements were well under way. He observed that the proprietor was about to construct a pier for fishing boats, and that several men were employed in cutting a winding road from the little pebbly beach to the top of the island. This 'road' is still the path from East Beach to the plateau, and it replaced the ancient steep and difficult ascent, which soon fell into disuse. The old tenement for fishermen, at the top near the eastern end, Clark noted, had been in part repaired to provide accommodation for the workmen. There he and his friend, Dr Gapper, happily ate sandwiches and tarts in a room reminiscent of 'the romance descriptions of a cave of banditti' containing 'three or four small beds, and the pots, frying pans and other cooking apparatus of the whole inhabitants of the island'. He returned to Weston so thrilled with the adventure that he remembered this simple meal as tasting much better than the grand fare served on his return to his lodgings. In conversation he learned that in the previous season '£500 worth of sprats' had been caught around Steep Holm. Slightly less than twelve months later, the occasionally irascible John Skinner complained of the boatmen: 'Owing to the carelessness of the man at the helm [of the hired sailing boat] we ran on the shingly bank outside the little harbour, and were obliged to go on shore in the small boat. Had it blown hard, the sailing boat we quitted would have been in great danger, as the surf sometimes breaks from 15 to 20 feet high, as we learned afterwards.' The unfortunate boatman said that 'it had never occurred to him before to ground on approaching the Island, as he knows every inch of the shore having been occupied in fishing on it from his youth . . .'. That same shingle bank, stretching out to sea from East Beach and only visible at low tide, still gives headaches to the unwary sailor; tidal conditions often move the pebbles quite dramatically to bank up upon the 'gooseneck', or to scour the beach into totally different contours.

The Steep Holm Inn

At the time of the Revd Mr Skinner's visit, the new owner was building a house to be used as an inn. The situation chosen was on levelled rocks just above and to the

'House on the Steep Holms': a sketch made in 1832 by an unknown artist, showing the newly-completed inn with walled front garden, sheerlegs on the newly-cut path, cliffs almost bare of vegetation, fishing stakes on beach, and Flat Holm with lighthouse tower distant

north of East Beach. It was quite an imposing structure, built of island stone, rendered, and three storeys high, with a decorative castellated roof balustrade. Its sea-facing frontage looked out upon a small walled garden area, and the lower floor was built directly against the rock face with a flight of steps leading up to the newly-cut 'road' at the rear. Against the north wall was a large water catchment tank. One small detail in the construction of the building was of particular interest, for the drip stones around the windows were actually reused pennant sandstone tiles from the medieval priory roof!

Inside the building the lower floors were of flagstones, and the walls were plastered and whitewashed. Some of the rooms had large cupboard recesses, and there was at least one range-type fireplace of ornate design. The inhabitants of the inn will be discussed later, when the chequered history of the building is told.

A Short-lived Harbour

Like Thomas Clark, Skinner noticed that 'In order to render the little harbour more secure a number of men are now actually engaged in building a pier under the new inn . . .' and from the safety of a projecting ridge he witnessed 'the blasting of the rock above the Pier, with an explosion as loud as a Cannon'. An 1858 watercolour by M.A. Sweeting shows the 'pier for fishing boats' constructed by John Baker in 1831–2, as well as the inn. This substantial harbour wall was within a few decades destroyed by sea action, and an occasionally visible curved erratic line of large sea-worn blocks now forms the only remaining trace of the structure.

Mysterious Cliff Cottage

A further observation by John Skinner was that 'There are two small huts [cottages] on the rock [island], besides this more extensive habitation [the inn], both appear to have been recently erected.' One of these was in fact the renovated 1776 tenement on the plateau, where Thomas Clark had enjoyed his picnic; the other was a new cottage which John Baker had built part way up the 'winding road' above the inn. When the workmen had made this habitable they moved down from the old tenement to be nearer the harbour and inn work; and a talkative old soldier was brought to the island to live in the tenement while he cleared and cultivated the soil.

The new cottage, in general design very similar to the inn, being rendered and battlemented, with drip-stones above the windows, was a well-built and artfully planned structure. It was apparently intended as additional servant/fisherman accommodation – but this was something more than just a simple dwelling, and

Cliff Cottage in the 1930s, showing the original door and window of the end wall with drip stones to match those of the 1832 inn

evidently adapted with a very different sideline in view; something more sinister, judging from a later account written in 1913 when the cottage had fallen into partial disrepair, and was being restored: 'Secret hiding chambers for men and goods abounded. A space was contrived between the staircase and the cliff, there were secret cupboards in the walls, and the chimney stack was half a sham, one side forming a roomy niche where a man could lurk unsuspected.'

Across the top of the island plateau, Skinner followed the rough track of a narrow footpath 'worn through the dwarf privet by the feet of pilots who land here to have a good lookout on the channel' – yet another reminder of the dangers and difficulties facing ships as they reached the narrowing and shoal-ridden estuary; and of potential smugglers, for most of the Bristol Channel pilot cutters at that time were suspected of running contraband.

A Profitable Sale

John Baker, with his comfortable home at Aldwick Court and his prosperous mainland solicitors' practice, never planned to reside on Steep Holm. His purchase was purely a commercial speculation – and despite the firmly held opinion in some circles that the inn was initially built as a 'gentleman's residence' this was not the intention, either of John Baker or of the person who bought the island from him. For, after three years of intensive building, resulting in a harbour pier and improvements to access from the beach, and with the inn and its attendant cottage sparkling new, John Baker sold the island which in 1830 had cost him £700.

On 1 October 1833, for £2,500, Colonel Charles Kemeys Kemeys-Tynte of Halswell House (with its seventy-one rooms) near Bridgwater, and of Cefn Mably, Glamorgan, country gentleman and member of parliament, became the new owner of Steep Holm – by normal business transaction and not, as has been said, by winning it when playing cards! Steep Holm was to remain in this family's ownership for over 140 years, and in that period was to be leased to many different tenants. Despite what has been written in the past, Colonel Kemeys Kemeys-Tynte did not buy the island for his personal residence, intending to use the inn as his permanent home. Communications and access to Steep Holm were both difficult and uncertain, and the inn with its small rooms and tiny garden was unsuitable for a gentleman's house. He probably bought the island as an investment, and perhaps at first as a fashionable curiosity – somewhere to take guests on a novel excursion, midway between his two main residences; for wealthy families at that time competed to provide 'diversions' of entertainment for their visitors – which may be why, in his first enthusiasm, he tried to improve the vegetation.

A newspaper story concerning Steep Holm's new owner appeared in the *Bristol Mirror* of 16 August 1834:

This island, hitherto considered as barren rock and mere warren for wild rabbits, was lately purchased by Col. Tynte, MP. At present it bears three patches of wheat and one of barley in good state. Also in healthy growth are mangel-worsel, carrots, potatoes, turnips, etc., besides a profusion of wild strawberries, myrtles, and geranium, etc. The worthy Col. sent over in the spring a large assortment of wild and hedge flowers which are at present in bloom. In a small garden are very fine dahlias and other rich flowers.

Before the colonel had bought the island, Skinner noticed in July 1832 'patches of wild strawberries still bearing fruit' among the dominant privet. As late as April 1913, visitors commented that 'strawberries ripen precociously'. Since then, like the new plants introduced by Colonel Kemeys Kemeys-Tynte, they seem to have given up the battle for survival. The potato patch was probably that referred to by Skinner two years previously, during John Baker's ownership. His diary then mentioned 'an old man – who inhabits the hut [tenement] at the summit of the rock and had resided here 7 months [from the beginning of 1832] for the purpose of clearing away the privet, and wild carrot [alexanders] which now wholly occupy the surface, and planting the soil with potatoes and garden stuff'. While this ex-soldier was working on the island during John Baker's ownership he also had predictable difficulties with the cultivation of 'Cucumbers and Cauliflowers in his garden, but complains of the trouble of watering them, as there is only one Spring on the Island, and that a small one near the base of the rock . . .'. What he did not complain of was the depredations of the rabbits – for he had brought with him a dog and cat; and according to Skinner these two animals had 'almost destroyed' the resident population. The gardener was surprised by the many broken pieces of ancient pottery which he dug up when tending his plot. As he observed to Skinner: 'People must have been very careless of their ware to break so many pots and pans.' With the patches of wheat and barley, vegetables and garden flowers, these seem to have been the first real attempts to cultivate the island since monastic times. More serious farming had to wait for a few more years.

The Steep Holm Peony

One plant which was certainly not introduced by Colonel Tynte was the famous *paeonia mascula*. Francis Bowcher Wright is officially credited with having been the first to notice it growing on Steep Holm, in August 1803, although according to the memories of local fisherman it had been known on the island for at least sixty to seventy years before his visit.

Were earlier visiting botanists there at the wrong time of year to notice these plants, perhaps growing in the least accessible places? Trips to Steep Holm were usually taken in the months of July and August, when the peony was in its less noticeable intermediate stage. Flowering in April or May, depending upon the severity of the winter and early spring weather, this beautiful plant retains its single row of brilliant cerise petals for only seven to ten days. Until the spectacular red and black seed head bursts open, usually in October, the plant could easily be

The Steep Holm peony in bloom – note the very broad leaves

overlooked, with its broad leaves and gradually ripening seed pods blending with and overshadowed by the foliage of surrounding alexanders. Who exactly introduced the peony remains a mystery, but it seems unlikely that it was first planted by warreners, fishers or gullers. Far more credible is that the peony was introduced when its medicinal and magical properties were better appreciated – either in Roman or medieval times.

Once publicized, of course, a long succession of botanists competed to 'collect specimens', to such an extent that the plant was several times threatened with extinction. Steep Holm is said to be the only place in this country where the peony grows in its wild state, and there is just one situation on the island where that could be said to be true. Other plants have been carefully nurtured and specially planted in positions where pilgrims can readily see and appreciate them.

The Revd John Ashley and Bristol Channel Missions

One day in 1835 a clergyman, on holiday before taking up a new appointment, was walking with his young son at Clevedon – or perhaps Weston, no one is quite sure which – when the boy noticed light reflected from windows of buildings on the Holms. He asked his father how the people living there could go to church. What sprang from this question is a story in itself, for it prompted John Ashley to hire a local fishing boat to take himself and his son to the two islands to meet with the isolated communities living there. He at once recognized the desperate need for someone to talk to and care for these lonely people. He also learned that often the crews of the many sailing ships in the Severn were becalmed or forced to ride out unfavourable winds sometimes for several days, causing hardship and great frustration to crews so near, and yet so far, from home ports.

That boat trip was to have far-reaching effects, for Ashley decided not to take up his new appointment, but instead to devote his time and energy to the people of the Channel. For the first few years his visits were by open hired boat, until he used his private income from a West Indian plantation to pay for a cutter to be built at the River Avon port of Pill. The new vessel, fitted with below deck cabins, was completed in 1839 and named *Eirene* (Greek for 'Peace'). From her he constantly visited the islanders of Lundy and the two Holms, as well as the sailing and lightship crews. To read his surviving journals is an inspiration, for he abandoned an easy and lucrative living to drive himself (and, one suspects, the crew of the *Eirene*) to the limits of endurance. In one typical entry, for 26 November 1841, he writes that in twenty-seven hours he visited twenty sailing ships, both of the Holms and a lightship!

From these early visits, and by the sheer determination of this devoted clergyman, evolved the Bristol Channel Missions to Seamen, later to become the worldwide Missions to Seamen, with its famous 'Flying Angel' symbol. Ashley's diaries detail many of his visits both to Flat Holm, where he talked to the lighthouse keepers, the farmer and his family, and a succession of craftsmen brought in for building or repair work; and to neighbouring Steep Holm. Here he was less likely to find large numbers of people, for the fortunes of this island ebbed and flowed like the tide. In fact it is the diary of a friend who accompanied him in 1841 which gives a clue to what had happened to Steep Holm during the early years of Colonel Kemeys Kemeys-Tynte's ownership: 'On this island formerly, when the chaplain's attention was first drawn to the Channel with its islands and extensive roadsteads, there were 16 inhabitants, and the chaplain's congregation here, with the addition of pilots, used to amount to upwards of 20 persons. But the man who rented the island having failed, and the families to whom he gave employment having left the island, the chaplain on a recent visit found but one solitary individual who had charge of the fishing nets, and dwelt upon the island alone.' There is little doubt that the tenant who had 'failed' was Benjamin Atwell, who had held the fishery since before the island had come into the ownership of John Baker, and until several years after Colonel Kemeys Kemeys-Tynte bought it. Although he had abandoned the island before the chaplain's visit, he was not with his wife Harriet and four-year-old son Samuel at Centre Farm, Hutton, when the census for that parish was taken in 1841, and he disappears completely from the scene. The diarist who accompanied Ashley on his mission to Steep Holm, wrote: '. . . there is only a narrow pathway [from the landing place] . . . part of which having been washed away by the sea its place is supplied by a bridge of planks laid across'. Above the beach, the 'very good house which used to be used for an inn' was in 1841 unoccupied, simply a net store; and the 'solitary individual' who had charge of the nets was Horsington – a dour character, who did his best to avoid the chaplain, and who lived in Cliff Cottage beside the path from East Beach.

Eye-Witness Description of Cliff Cottage

The diary continues:

> At the time of our present visit [30 August 1841] he [Horsington] had a boy about 9 years of age with him who was sent to assist him with preparing the nets for the fishing season. The boy met us at the landing place and said he would go and look for the man. . . . When we reached the cottage we found it open, but the man was not there. We went in. Although it is a good cottage it looked extremely wretched. In the middle of the room was a rude block for a table. At one side of the fireplace a stool with a piece of worn and dirty sheepskin on it by way of a cushion. In the centre, over the fireplace, hung a coloured print which seemed to be a Chartist production, for it represented an engagement between the people and the military and there was an inscription underneath about the 'rights of the people', but it was all much defaced. On each side hung fishing tackle, knives and nondescripts of various sorts. The floor was strewn with feathers and bits of decayed fish, and the whole was thick with dirt. I wondered how any human being could live in such a place, and worse still in solitude!

This description is reminiscent of the conditions in which the warreners had lived and worked within the former priory, all those centuries before. The fisherman, apart from looking after the nets and cooking some of the catch for himself and the boy, obviously augmented his diet, and perhaps his income, by taking rabbits and birds – not being at all fussy where he left the scraps. Ashley and his friend waited for Horsington to return, but not liking to sit down in the cottage, they talked to the stubborn old man on the wider pathway above the abandoned inn. Outside, in total contrast with the squalidness of the room, 'the scene was lovely' overlooking Weston Bay, with the sun sparkling on the sea; the *Cambria* pleasure steamer plying her way across the water; and the *Eirene* 'looking beautiful' as she awaited their return.

Gull Trapping and Egging

For many centuries profits from seasonal collecting of eggs had attracted those brave, foolhardy or desperate enough to clamber down the cliffs in search of Nature's bounty. River Pilot Cullimore was one who fell to his death while bird nesting on Steep Holm in 1775, and his remains were interred at Easton-in-Gordano churchyard. Methods of trapping the island birds were brutal, as an early nineteenth-century account by the Revd H.F. Yeatman shows:

On the Steep Holmes, in the middle of the Channel . . . these birds, of every species, build their nests in the summer months; the fishermen at this time, with a long pole armed with a noose at the end, climb to the edge of the cliff where they are sitting, and having uttered a peculiar cry to excite the bird's attention, and which causes it to thrust out its neck, throws the loop with great dexterity over the bird's neck, and with one twitch jerks it into the boat beneath, where his family are waiting to strip it in a moment of its feathers, and to commit its body to the deep. The eggs are sold by boatloads to the Bristol merchants for the purpose of refining sugar.

Lundy islanders also carried on the dangerous pursuit of 'egging'; with a man being let down the much higher and more precipitous cliffs on the end of a rope, to collect a variety of seabirds' eggs, leaving his hands free by storing the booty in his open-necked shirt, or in a bag tied to his waist – and many were the disputes between the islanders and fishermen or Channel pilots who also considered the nesting birds fair game for additional profit.

Quite apart from local consumption of the gulls' eggs, thousands were sent to Ascot each year, and refiners at Bristol used the whites as the setting agent in light syrup with which they mixed the tiny crystals of sugar when making the cone-shaped sugar blocks for the cooks of that period. The down and feathers were used in various ways, as stuffing for pillows or, more fashionably, in the millinery trade, to decorate ladies' hats.

Despite the depredations of the gullers over many centuries, the birds still continued to breed in great, if fluctuating numbers on the islands every year, but at the inn newcomers were due to take their turn in trying their fortunes on Steep Holm.

Chapter Twelve

MIXED FORTUNES

John and Betty Harse

New permanent tenants arrived on Steep Holm after Horsington, the old fisherman, gave up his temporary 'caretakership', moved out of Cliff Cottage, and returned to the mainland. In January 1842 John Harse came to live at the inn, his wife following before the end of February to make it their home.

John was another Weston 'character' – an opportunist, ready to switch employments and take up new ventures to avail himself of the wealth which could come to enterprising local people during the early years of the town's prosperity as a growing resort. He came to Weston from Badgworth as a young teenager in the early 1800s, and his first job was as a farmer's boy, working for James Capell of Ashcombe Manor Farm for low wages plus keep; but the companionship of the serving maid proved a compensating bonus. Betty Coles was seventeen years older than John, but attractive and still in her early thirties. Following their marriage in 1809, John bought a horse and cart and ventured into the carrier business. Weston at that time had no shops and no public house, and the villagers obtained all their supplies from Worle, two miles inland.

As an example of the difficulties, around 1802 an invalid lady had been recommended to stay at Weston. She arrived expecting to find a resort geared to supply the comforts which she needed. To her dismay she discovered that there were no more than six houses 'of mean appearance and chiefly occupied by the fishermen . . . it was with great difficulty that she could procure eatables of any description . . . they were so badly off for provisions that frequently they were obliged to eat bread which was completely turned mouldy, and their substitute for butter was generally liquefied bacon fat . . .'.

John Harse's twice weekly delivery service to Bristol, bringing back goods to retail in Weston, was an instant success. By 1815 the fishermen's few cottages had become linked to a small village of some thirty newly-built houses and an inn; even so, visitors still had 'considerable difficulty in obtaining lodgings'. As demand increased, John changed his cart for a two-horse fly wagon and began carrying passengers. Perhaps he was too successful, for a disgruntled provision dealer from Worle drew attention to the fact that John had no licence, with the result that he was stopped from trading and fined. But the carrier had influential friends, who had been grateful for his reliable service to Bristol, and their representations resulted in a licence being obtained, the penalty reduced, and the resumption of his trade.

A coach and four horses replaced Harse's former vehicle, and by 1818 he was entrusted with the mails. His boast was that his horses were never passed on the road, but as Weston increased rapidly in size competition also grew, and his venture became less profitable. He diversified to farming, renting a large part of the Smythe Pigott estate, but this was not as lucrative as the coaching business which had started him on the road to fame. New horizons were beckoning, and he and Betty tried their luck on Steep Holm, where they rented the fishing and attempted to farm the plateau. They may have hoped that their efforts would be rewarded by similar success as that already enjoyed by the tenant of Flat Holm.

More than twenty years earlier the Elder Brethren of Trinity House had taken over the formerly privately owned lighthouse and established their own keepers. William Yeatman had no responsibilities to keep the light, so he and his wife and family were able to concentrate on running a thriving inn, and exporting farming produce, rabbits and, of course, fish to the Welsh mainland. Did John and Betty Harse have similar ideas of prosperity? Were there also prospects of a share in another less scrupulous but profitable sideline?

John Ashley visited the ageing couple on 24 March 1843, and his diary entry highlights some of the hazards of travelling to the island. Although delayed, he was determined to complete his schedule of calls to be made that day:

> [from Flat Holm] we reached across to Steep Holm, and coming under the island at half past 7 in the evening after it had become dark, we parted from the vessel [*Eirene*] taking with us a signal lantern in the [small] boat that we might be able to show our position to be picked up again by the vessel on our return. It was very dismal as we pulled in around the steep cliffs of the island in the dark and heard the sea roaring like thunder in the caverns in the rocks as we skirted them around. A party of the coastguard at this moment might well have suspected our purpose approaching the island in this manner under cover of night – especially as a landing of brandy was effected on the island a short time since, advantage being taken of its lonely situation to introduce and keep it in the rocks there till opportunity admitted of its being conveyed to the mainland.
>
> The [winter] fishermen are now gone from this island and the only inhabitants are a poor old couple . . . and two very young grandchildren. I ascended the rocks unperceived, my approach to the island of course not being known, and as no friendly visitor ever lands there – except it may be on a morning on a fine day – no wonder the little party started as my hand was laid on the latch of their always unbarred door.

We know how eerie Steep Holm can be on a dark night, with the peculiar noises made by birds, by the sea in the rocks, and by the wind blowing through vegetation or around a creaking building. When no other person should be on the island, even familiar sounds can be very unnerving! For John Harse and his family, sitting around their table talking quietly in the candlelight, and believing themselves to be entirely alone, the unexpected footstep and a hand rattling the doorknob terrified them almost out of their wits; but it was old Betty who snatched the light from the table and came forward to protect her family from the intruder. Ashley managed to calm them before re-embarking on the *Eirene*, but there is no further record of his returning to Steep Holm after dark! Flat Holm was different. There were more people living there, with a long established farmhouse capable of providing lodging for visitors; and although that island has its own approach problems and dangerous rocks to avoid, it is generally the more accessible of the two islands. Ashley landed there before daybreak and after nightfall on several occasions.

Conditions for farming on Steep Holm were far less amenable. The old tenement had again become ruinous, and the inn/farmhouse was at beach level, with the fields and animals on the plateau, nearly 200 ft above. By the time John Harse leased the island he was over fifty, and Betty just into her seventies – if the record of her date of birth is correct. The harsh conditions and enforced steep climb made husbandry difficult to cope with, and shore fishing was mainly a winter occupation. Within five years John and Betty Harse left the island to return to the mainland. For a while they turned their talents in yet another direction, by carrying on a wheelchair business in Union Street, Weston, before enjoying well-earned retirement. After Betty's death, John himself died, in 1874.

Parsons' Cave

Ashley's diary entry of his visit to John and Betty shows that he was very well aware of the movements of the local smugglers. He was concerned that his late arrival on Steep Holm might be misconstrued by the customs men – and he knew that brandy had been hidden on the island until it could be conveyed safely to the mainland. The consignment had been kept 'in the rocks'. There are dozens of handy little fissures and natural caves, the entrances of which could be easily concealed; and of course Cliff Cottage was specially adapted for hiding contraband.

There was also another place where the brandy and other smuggled goods could have been hidden. In 1985 Tony Parsons, the Kenneth Allsop Trust's Natural History Advisor, was trying to get close to a group of butterflies which he had noticed on a cliffside, when to his amazement he realized that he was standing by a well-concealed pair of caves. These had not been noted by explorers during (now banned) caving expeditions, being in a quite different location from those already mapped. Although the smaller of the two caves was still in its natural state, the larger one had been at some stage cleverly disguised by a rough limestone wall being built across its mouth. The stones had been mortared into position, leaving a narrow gap as an entrance way which could be quickly blocked when necessary. Even with the wall in ruinous condition the cave is virtually invisible from even a short distance away; and with the wall complete, and plants growing profusely in front, a customs officer would have had the greatest difficulty in finding it. Both caves are of phreatic origin, being formed by the action of swirling sea water during one of the far distant eras of much higher sea levels, although they are now some 150 ft above the tide line. Before cliff erosion in more recent times, the two caves, although so well hidden, were within easy reach of the old winding path which used to lead up the south slopes to the plateau. We feel they would have provided an excellent hiding place for smuggled goods, as an alternative to Cliff Cottage and the small fissures above East Beach, which would have been the more obvious places to suspect. South Landing's tiny pebble beach is exposed only at low tide, with the added advantage of being tucked behind the large outcropping Calf Rock, which looms from the water as the tide recedes, shielding any daytime activities from direct view through telescopes on the English mainland; whereas East Beach, directly visible from Weston, was a safer landing place at dusk, or in misty weather.

We had to name these two new caves, and immediately dubbed the larger one Parsons' Cave, in honour of its discoverer, with its secondary connotation of

Parsons' Cave, just after discovery, showing roughly built walling mortared into cave mouth, and phreatic tunnels at the rear

'Brandy for the Parson' – a well-worn phrase in connection with smuggling. Less imaginatively, the smaller cave was named Little Cave. Neither is accessible to the public.

The Revd John Ashley's Adventures

Flicking through the pages of Ashley's diary, we read that on 14 December 1842 he left Steep Holm about 4.30 p.m. and decided to anchor for the night to the north of the sister island, having promised to visit the men there before they started work for the day. He spent the evening in his cabin writing up his records, and held a service for the crew. By midnight, when he finally threw himself upon his bunk, he was exhausted and unwell – but there was little rest:

> The angry elements conspired to drive [all sleep] from our vessel. As the wind increased and the sea rose . . . our vessel began to drift; the deep rumbling noise of the anchor dragging, with the horrible undescribable sound of jarring from the chain, causing our wooden walls to quiver and shake all round us. . . . About 2 in the morning we thought of getting under way, but just about this time our vessel brought up and we held on for the remainder of the morning.

Despite all this he was up, dressed and breakfasted in time to be ashore by 6 a.m. while it was still dark, to conduct yet another service before the island workforce started the daily routine.

In January there was a terrible storm at sea. Ashley's vessel was moored near the mouth of the River Avon while he attended to some business in Bristol, and he writes:

> Throughout the whole of yesterday it blew a tremendous gale. . . . The cutter that sailed last Saturday is just returned, having carried away her main boom gaff and trisail gaff. Her mainsail and trisail gone, her ballast all adrift and her cabin knocked to pieces by it. Two men killed and lying dead on board; seven severely wounded, one with his arm and thigh broken, and having had two men washed overboard. . . . On all sides we are hearing of damage done through the gale, and lives lost. A vessel is rolling about in the channel bottom up, not yet known what she is. Two vessels, the *Union* [owned by William Dickinson, former joint proprietor of the Flat Holm lighthouse] & *Worcester*, which I visited the day before yesterday in Portishead roads . . . have been driven on shore, having sailed soon after I visited them. The *Worcester* is reported to have had her bottom torn out. A boy and two men have perished from the *Union*. . . . The boy that was lost was one of those I used to examine on the Steep Holm island, and in whose hands I placed a New Testament on first going to the island. . . .

After a very wet day on one of the islands, Ashley describes his appearance: '. . . wrapped neither in silk or satin but in broad coarse oilcloth in which I had just been contending with the rains, and which was still dripping from its nocturnal bath, I stood . . . a shawl rather than a handkerchief wrapped around my neck in fullest style, and copious folds took the place of bands, whilst a weather beaten glazed hat – such as might have . . . covered the head of a cab driver through many a winter's night – surmounted the whole figure'. During one bitterly cold spell Ashley tells of breakfasting in his cabin on the *Eirene* by eating his frozen milk with a fork!

After fifteen years of such experiences, worn out by his exertions on behalf of the Channel folk, enduring great hardship – and having to cope with near mutiny from his crew on occasion – John Ashley's health broke down and his Jamaican source of revenue failed. The *Eirene* was laid up in 1850, and he faced enforced retirement on crutches. He never went to sea again, but toured the country to address meetings, raising funds so that others could carry on his work.

A Fishing Dispute

In the interval between John Harse's departure from Steep Holm and the arrival of new permanent tenants, it was a Mr Hill who had the fishing rights. He was the subject of a court case in December 1847, when he was sued by a Weston boatman, Mr Hazel, whom he had engaged to bring fish from the Steep Holm fishery at £1 per week, with an additional 6s per week for hire of the boat. The judge heard that the defendant refused to pay the extra 6s per week because Hazel had neglected to go out on a particular day to collect a boatload of fish, which was spoiled by the delay. The boatman contended that it had been impossible to set out then owing to the state of the weather. Hill admitted that a boat had been driven on shore that day, but nevertheless managed to find two witnesses to show that it was not too rough to sail to the Holms. After some argument about the direction of the wind and its effect on being able to land on the island, the judge ruled that Hazel must deduct 5s from his total claim of £16 arrears owing for fishing and boat hire – which meant that Hill had to pay the balance of fifteen guineas.

Harris Family Enterprises

About a year after the Hazel versus Hill court case, the Harris family came to Steep Holm. The new tenant, Fred, was an ambitious young man in his early thirties, his wife Mary a couple of years younger; and their three children, all under the age of ten, included a son, also called Frederick.

Fred Harris was the proud owner of the *Victoria*, with which he had won regatta prizes in 1845 and 1846, including the Knightstone Cup. Not long after he arrived on Steep Holm he had the misfortune to lose this boat, wrecked at the island on 3 July 1848. Like most boatmen of that time Harris had no insurance, and the financial loss was devastating; but local people rallied round with donations. One exceptional gift, made to him and his Weston boatman associate Jim Jones, was a replacement yacht – a 16-ton vessel called *Sisters of Charity*. This was presented to them by Mr F. Crawshaw, of Cardiff. There must have been some business connection, perhaps with one of the principal fish dealers of that city market, who would have been sorely out of pocket without his regular supply.

Some time later, Fred Harris was to sell his half share in the *Sisters of Charity* to Dennis Jones, brother of Jim, to become the sole owner of the fast yacht *Mystery* which he used both for fishing and ferrying – even for pleasure trips down Channel from Weston. The sailing performances of the two boats were roughly equal, and in local regattas in the mid-1850s there was keen competition between them.

On the island Harris had need of all his skills, both as farmer and boatman. The cleared land on the plateau was by no means easy to cultivate, or to graze – and there was still no farmhouse, except the inn at beach level, which was also being run as a hostelry. Even when the small harbour was in existence it could be difficult for sailing ships to enter, and running a boat on to the rocky beach was never without hazard.

For nearly forty years Steep Holm was to remain the focus of activities for the Harris family, while Weston was rapidly developing into a busy resort; and when it was anticipated that the island's popularity would grow with the town.

The enterprising family specialized in fresh fish dishes for tourists who ventured to land there – with excise-free drinks being sold at appropriate prices, and a complete absence of licensing rules at the inn. Prosperity for Steep Holm seemed assured. On the sister island in 1850 several hundred people arrived on no less than five steamers and numerous small boats, with the sole aim of having a grandstand view of Newport's sailing regatta. Never had there been so many people on Flat Holm. Towards evening the food supplies ran out, and the entire stocks of wines, spirits, beer and cider were exhausted. Would there be similar invasions of Steep Holm to the profit of the inn there?

During the summer months of mid-Channel regattas around the two islands, Fred Harris's yacht *Mystery* invariably raced well; but this was not just a pleasure boat. It was the mainstay for bringing supplies to Steep Holm, and for taking the fish to market. Her speed was essential to get the catches to Bristol or Cardiff more quickly than the Weston boatmen could by road or rail. When the *Mystery* carried visitors to the island, flatners (small flat-bottomed boats) often assisted in ferrying passengers to and from shore.

In June 1851 there was an exceptional private charter when a Bristol debtor sought to escape the country by boarding an outward bound emigration ship in mid-channel. Suspicious debt collection officers on board a steam tug saw the Harris sailing boat just below the Holms, as though about to put someone aboard a passing vessel. The waiting passenger, Tom Locock, was a young and fit man, and as the steam tug came alongside the Harris boat he jumped into a small punt and rapidly sculled away towards the approaching emigration ship. A small punt in mid-channel had little chance against a powerful tug, but as it was caught the debtor escaped by wielding an oar to keep the officers away. Despite all the odds he succeeded in reaching the passenger ship and was pulled aboard. Meanwhile Fred Harris had sailed out of trouble – not that he had any idea that his passenger was trying to leave the country unlawfully! One wonders, did he ever retrieve his missing punt?

When one of the children became seriously ill while on Steep Holm, the intrepid father set off to sail single-handed across a dangerous, storm-swept sea to summon help. With their unconventional lifestyle the family had to overcome many crises – sometimes with unscrupulous methods.

A Terrifying Ordeal for Miss Besozzi

A young Italian lady whose family had fallen upon hard times had taken a position as governess to a family in Clifton, Bristol. Wishing to spend a free day in adventurous voyaging, Ann Caroline Besozzi took an excursion by steam packet down river to Steep Holm on 17 September 1857. With her were four other ladies; and on the steamer she met the Gully family, already known to her. On landing safely, the rest of the visitors made their way to the top of the island while Miss Besozzi and Mr Gully entered the inn to request dinner for their party. Having taken the order, one of the Harris girls pointed the way out through a door – and as they left, a large bear, chained to a 'kennel', struck the lady a ferocious blow in the back, knocking her to the floor before mauling her. Hearing her screams, another visitor, Mr Hazard, dashed to the rescue, armed with his umbrella, which was broken into pieces as he belaboured the beast, until at last Charles Gully was able to pull Miss Besozzi free. She suffered grievous injuries, and what had promised to be a happy day ended miserably.

The Resulting Court Case

After her frightening experience Miss Besozzi was unable to continue teaching, and had to undergo painful and expensive medical treatment. Even so it was feared that she would suffer permanent disability. She and her friends considered the innkeeper to be responsible for her misfortune, and wrote to Frederick Harris, requesting that he at least pay the doctor's bill, amounting to £20, and some compensation; but he failed to answer any of the letters. At last her friends brought a civil action heard at Bristol Assizes in April 1858, to recover damages from Harris. In court Mr Greig, the surgeon, described the wounds which the bear had inflicted, the operations which Miss Besozzi had undergone, and the lameness which would probably remain for life. But the defending lawyer pleaded that Harris, who was 'of very humble station', was paying Colonel Tynte rent of £60 a year, farming the land, eking out a living by fishing, and having a very hard struggle to provide for his family.

In evidence Fred Harris maintained that the bear, which he had had for three years, was 'like a dog, playing with the children, running in and out of the house, going about the island with the men, and behaving in the most playful and docile manner'. It was suggested that Mr Gully should be blamed for taking Miss Besozzi too close to the bear; but the result of the case was that Harris was ordered to pay £50 compensation for damages, and costs, amounting to £141 in total.

A Remarkable Sequel

That was by no means the end of the affair. Frederick Harris had no intention of obeying the court order, and went to extraordinary lengths to avoid paying his debt. When he was called before the Taunton Assize in June 1858 he was described as 'late of Steep Holm'– for the very simple reason that he was at that time in debtors' prison; not for failing to comply with the court order, but because he had arranged the 'friendly' arrest of himself on 27 May, by a fellow fisherman to whom he 'owed' a 'debt' of £30. Even before the first trial, Harris had gone to a great deal of trouble to dispose of his assets. One of his vessels (the *Roebuck*) had been mortgaged with an IOU to Mr Gwillim, an innkeeper of Newport, with whom the family often stayed, and from whom he also claimed he had borrowed money to pay his attorney. It also transpired that on the Saturday before that trial the yacht *Mystery*, which he had owned for about two years, had been 'sold' for £30 to a fisherman named Watts who rented the Weston fisheries, 'to pay for supplies for the island'. Sometimes there were seven men in his employ, each at 12s per week, but he could not tell how much he had paid out in wages as it varied with each month, becoming more during the winter. How he managed to keep his fishing contracts without his boats was not explained; but when Miss Besozzi and her friends wrote to him, he 'had nothing at all', nor did he have any assets at the time of the trial.

By the time the second trial was held, only two months later, the rent to Colonel Tynte was stated to be £70 per year for the island. Harris's circumstances were described by his defence counsel: '. . . it [the island] was not good for much, and the land would not pay for cultivation. His furniture was taken for [a year's] arrears of rent [but remained on the island]. . . . The things were made over to Colonel Tynte, and he allowed his [Harris's] family to use them. They were now subsisting on the rent received for the sheep, and depending for a home on the sufferance of Colonel Tynte.' The sheep and lambs had been 'sold' to a butcher but were being kept on Steep Holm for 5s a week until he needed them!

Prosecuting counsel pointed out that Harris had spent at least £72 in paying his defence attorney, but had refused to compensate in any way for the injuries of the unfortunate lady who had visited Steep Holm. Under cross-examination at the second hearing, wily Harris said that the previous summer had been 'nearly the worst season he knew; there might have been a great number of excursionists, but most of them brought their own provisions, went on the hill and away again without so much as coming into his house'. Adroitly avoiding the more awkward questions, and being described by the prosecution as a 'cunning' witness who had conducted a 'wicked and fraudulent transaction', Harris's defence was that the young lady had 'brought it all on herself'. Somehow he gained the sympathy of the judge, who ruled that he was insolvent, and discharged him.

An artfully worded advertisement appeared in a local newspaper at about this time: 'The Holms. Frederick Harris returns his sincere thanks to the Visitors and Inhabitants of Weston-super-Mare for the support extended to him for the last ten years, and begs to assure parties about to visit the Steep Holms that every accommodation can be supplied to them on moderate terms, under the superintendence of Mrs Harris. Day parties provided with dinners, teas, etc. The Steep Holms commands the most magnificent views that can be obtained in any part of the Bristol Channel.' To anyone not knowing the circumstances it was innocent enough; but 'debtor' Harris was careful to place his wife, not himself, in charge of the island, and there was no mention of his yachts.

The co-operation of compatriots on both sides of the Channel in helping Fred Harris to wriggle out of any payment to Miss Besozzi is remarkable, and one is tempted to speculate whether this was more than friendship; perhaps something connected with the 'brotherhood' surrounding contraband activities. The case also provides an explanation for the persistent story that a Steep Holm innkeeper stayed on the island for seven years to avoid bankruptcy, returning to the mainland only on Sundays when it was believed that he could not be arrested. Obviously the time-scale is greatly exaggerated and the details incorrect; but, living on the island, Harris was able to defy the law officers in their utmost efforts to serve him with a writ. He deliberately remained on Steep Holm for a few months while the cases were pending, spending the time in arranging his affairs until the time was right for his planned arrest for debt.

The *Mystery* Returns

Little more than a year after the trial, in October 1859, virtually all boatmen in the West Country suffered losses, and both the *Mystery* and the *Sisters of Charity* were among the many local boats badly damaged in one of the severest storms recorded at Weston. Fourteen others were totally wrecked, the tumultuous seas snapping ropes and anchor chains, and dragging vessels from their moorings. One of the first to break away was a boat laden with timber, called the *Palace*, followed quickly by the *Sisters* and the *Affo* – a coal sloop which, when scrubbed up, was used to take excursionists and a band to both Steep Holm and Flat Holm. In the storm all three boats were driven ashore. The *Mystery* was moored in the River Axe, where she had been kept at the time of the Harris trials and where she should have been safe, but the yacht and several coal sloops moored nearby failed to escape the fury of the sea. The sloops went aground and the *Mystery*, dragging her anchor, was thrown heavily against the solid landing stage. At the opposite end of the bay, on the horse road at Birnbeck, the waves reached well beyond the anticipated level to pluck at boats drawn high up on the shore for safety. Set adrift they were quickly smashed to pieces on the nearby rocks. Two of them, the *Cygnet* and the *Lily*, belonged to fisherman John Watts, ancestor of our present boatman – but it is not surprising that the *Mystery* was no longer 'owned' by this family, now being described as the property of Fred Harris! Once again the local population rallied to help its boatmen, most of whom would otherwise have been deprived of their livelihood; and a committee was appointed to administer the relief fund which was immediately started.

It was probably this storm which swept away the harbour wall built by John Baker below Steep Holm's inn: it is prominently featured in an 1858 watercolour, but missing from 1861 engravings. This loss must have added considerably to the difficulties of the islanders, for they were left with no safe anchorage for their boats. The harbour was never rebuilt. Instead a small boathouse was constructed on sloping rock at the head of the beach. Later, this in turn was to disappear.

Undeterred by all his recent adventures, and narrow escapes from justice, Fred Harris once more expressed thanks to his customers – by indulging in rather differently worded advertising in a local newspaper of 1861: 'The Holms. Fred'k Harris, occupier of the Steep Holms, and proprietor of the fast sailing yacht

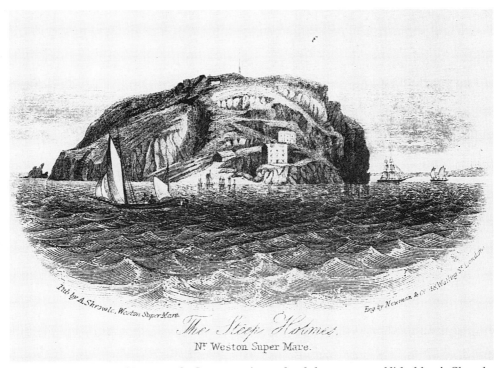

The Steep Holmes.
Nr Weston Super Mare.

'The Steep Holmes' by Newman & Co., engraving on headed notepaper published by A. Shrowle, 1861. The annexe to the 1832 inn has not yet been built, but Cliff Cottage is just above. The harbour wall has disappeared and there is a boathouse at the head of the beach. The 1776 tenement can be seen above the zig-zag path, and a flagstaff stands on the plateau

Mystery, returns his sincere thanks to the visitors and inhabitants of Weston-super-Mare for support to him during the last 13 years. Day parties provided with dinners, teas, etc. Rabbit shooting by permission.' To encourage rabbit shooting was one way of trying to keep these energetic little nibblers from his crops, and at the same time add to his profits by charging a fee.

So the Harris's island lifestyle continued; with not all their visitors coming to spend a pleasant summer day feasting and exploring the island. Smuggling continued during their sojourn, adding both to their income and to the risks which they took. Then one person landed for a much more serious purpose which must have caused them to feel a few qualms. For this military gentleman was there to assess the possibility of changes so drastic that they could never again enjoy the same isolated freedom as before. Yet what was to take place in the 1860s was to bring, along with greater restriction, far more prosperity to the innkeeper. So, for the moment, we have to leave the Harris story.

Chapter Thirteen

BUILDING FORTRESS STEEP HOLM

Letters are Written

In 1803 artist and antiquarian George Cumberland, who lived near Axbridge for several years, wrote to his more famous namesake, the Duke of Cumberland, to suggest the establishment of a defensive mortar battery on Steep Holm; pointing to the risk of both that island and Flat Holm becoming possible invasion bases if held by an enemy. This was no idle worry. Centuries earlier the islands had been used by the Vikings for a similar purpose; and, as late as the 1600s, Lundy had been used as a base for French privateers. Now the potential threat came from Napoleon Bonaparte.

At the close of the eighteenth century, with the breaking up and defeat of the former alliance against France, and the return from the Low Countries of remnants of the British Army, the shores of Britain itself were in great danger. Several times invasion threatened, and indeed in 1797 a small French unit with a group of Irish rebels had landed in the West Country with the specific aim of burning Bristol. In north Somerset fears were widespread that Weston Bay might become a landing place for the French; and local philanthropist and authoress Hannah More offered her spacious home at Barley Wood, Wrington, as a military post for army officers. This did not become necessary as the attack never came. Napoleon's armies were defeated, and in 1813 he was forced into abdication, and exiled to the Isle of Elba. Again Hannah More wrote to the authorities, this time to state her opinion that the 'barren rock of Steep Holm' would be a safer prison for the former emperor. She was probably right, for in February 1815 he escaped from Elba and returned to the mainland to make his way in triumph to Paris, from thence to prepare for renewed battle – only to be routed finally at Waterloo.

But if Steep Holm was ignored by the authorities at the beginning of the nineteenth century, its military value was not entirely forgotten. A letter dated 17 August 1860, from the Royal Engineers' Office, Exeter, signalled advance warning of traumatic changes which were to take place within the next six or seven years: 'Dear Sir, I have to inform you that I was instructed by the Secretary of State for War to prepare plans of the sites selected on that island [Steep Holm] for two

Batteries which I am given to understand may at some future day (more or less remote) be constructed, when the defences of the Bristol Channel and Severn now under consideration are authorised. [signed] (Col.) G. Bent.' This letter was typical of many being sent at about that time to landowners around the coast of southern England, and was a direct outcome of the report of a Royal Commission set up by Lord Palmerston in August 1859 to enquire into the adequacy of the country's defences against any possible invader. This country was not at war, nor was it actually threatened by war. But France was becoming increasingly aggressive, building up her military and naval forces and beginning the construction of ironclad warships, capable of making the Royal Navy's wooden-walled ships and armament obsolete. From an entry in the private diary of Queen Victoria, it is apparent that the attitude of Napoleon III (nephew of the late Napoleon I) towards Britain had alarmed both the queen and Prince Albert, as well as the Government.

In 1858 the *La Gloire* had been laid down as a wooden warship, to be sheathed with iron at completion stage. British response to this latest threat by the French was unusually prompt. The construction of an advanced naval vessel, the *Warrior*, having an iron framework clad with iron plates, lined with 18 in thick teak and an extra interior sheath of metal, was begun in May 1859. So quickly was the ship built that she was launched in 1860 – before the *La Gloire* – making her the first fully armoured ship in the world. But this did little to reduce the fear of war.

By February 1860, the Royal Commission had done its work, and the expenditure of millions of pounds for new fortifications was subsequently authorized by Parliament, although not without the inevitable opposition. A debate took place in March 1862, during which the MP for Swansea argued (without success) that the Severn defences were unnecessary, as a telegram would bring one of the men-of-war from the ports at Falmouth or Milford Haven to speedily intercept any 'privateer' long before she reached Steep Holm. Despite this, the proposal for a barrier of defences across the upper reaches of the Bristol Channel was approved. However, this part of the overall plan was low on the list of military priorities when Colonel Bent wrote his letter to Colonel Kemeys Kemeys-Tynte. Several years elapsed before work commenced to create the chain of gun batteries which included Steep Holm and Flat Holm, and reached from Brean Down in Somerset to Lavernock Point on the Welsh coast. Meanwhile changes were made in the number of batteries proposed and in the type of armament.

It was to be October 1865 before proposals crystallized sufficiently for a provisional arrangement to be entered into between the military and the owners of the island. Colonel Charles Kemeys Kemeys-Tynte had died in 1860, and the agreement was between his executors and the War Office. Terms were set out for the requisitioning by the Crown of very precisely measured areas of Steep Holm 'as sites for the purposes of constructing Batteries, Fortifications, or other Military Works of public defence . . . and of erecting Magazines, Storehouses and other buildings thereon, and for the construction of a pier and landing place, and for roads or other communication works in connection with the said defences and buildings . . .'. The total area needed covered exactly 4 acres, 2 roods, 4 square poles, and 23¼ square yards in seven separate parcels of land; and the rent was determined at £6 17s 6d per annum, payable half-yearly. Amazingly, nearly all the numbered concrete markers designating the limits of the various Victorian military areas are still in position, despite later building and military works dating from the Second World War, and the tendency on all islands to reuse any available materials.

The Navvies Move In

By February 1866 final decisions had been taken, and the construction gangs which were to make such dramatic changes to the appearance of the island set up their temporary quarters on Steep Holm. They were under the control of local agent John Perry, who in July of that year changed his sailing boat for a powerful steam packet, which was also available for excursion trips to the Holms. The initial labour force was made up of local men together with Irish navvies who had been working all over the country during the construction boom; they had moved from canal works to new railway lines and stations, and in still rapidly expanding Weston were building Birnbeck pier, starting an ambitious new harbour project on Brean Down (which was never completed), and were engaged on sewerage works. These tough men needed little machinery to help them, relying principally on muscle-power to complete their tasks, while living in the poorest conditions.

At the tip of Brean Down, apart from the civilian harbour scheme, gangs of navvies had already started work on the construction of the new military fort with its accompanying gun batteries. The Down was swarming with workers and those members of their families who travelled with them, living in simple dwellings, huts or even sheds, which were hastily erected as soon as a new gang arrived. The men worked in most weathers, for the rule was 'No work, no pay'; and if the conditions were so bad that work had to stop, the men and their families suffered hardship. Nevertheless, in an extraordinary incident on 15 September 1866, men stopped work on Brean, disgusted by the 'constant building up and pulling down' when the contractor was unable to carry out the impossible views of the Government representative. Many of the navvies were illiterate, and there were no schooling arrangements for children continually on the move. In the spring of 1866 many of the men were transferred out to the islands to work. John Pelgrave was one of these, leaving his wife and eight children on the Down. Shortly afterwards his wife was able to move to Uphill, and for a while their four eldest children attended school in the village. Another labourer was Joseph Sweeting, of Banwell, who was then about twenty-five years old, and who had previously helped to build the Taunton/Barnstaple railway line. The experience of working on Steep Holm did him no harm, as he lived to become 'Britain's oldest working farmer' at West Brinsea Farm, Congresbury – and to reach the age of 105 years.

On the island one of the navvies' first tasks was to excavate a 'roadway' almost all round the upper perimeter of the island by explosive, pickaxe and shovel, to provide easy access to gun batteries and barracks yet to be built on newly levelled and built up areas. In this way the natural curve of the plateau to the cliff tops was cut into, and the contours of the island changed for ever. Instead of the tentative suggestion by Colonel Bent that two batteries might be needed, six were in fact constructed, with their attendant ammunition stores. To make room for the barracks buildings an enormous volume of rock had to be gouged out to make a sufficiently large platform, with tons more rock being excavated for an underground water tank to the rear.

Where the Navvies Lived

Some of the navvies were lodged at the inn and in Cliff Cottage, to bring steady income and extra trade at the bar for Fred and Mary Harris. Others occupied temporary homes in several 'huts', two of which were built over the few remaining foundations of the long defunct priory building, using stones left on the site or from cutting the roadway. As told in an earlier chapter, the foreman decided to have the 1776 cottage renovated yet again, as accommodation for himself and his wife. When human skeletons were found within the old cottage walls he had them lifted and re-buried in a heap inside the south wall of the priory – directly beneath the floor of one of the navvies' huts instead!

It was the archaeological work of 1980 that first alerted us to the Victorian re-use of the ancient priory site. At the beginning of the project stratification was 'upside down', with obvious infill material being used to level the space within the old ruins. Hundreds of discarded stones and chunks of rock were mingled with soil; artefacts from many centuries were mixed together; and some matching fragments were spread over a wide area. Roman pottery and tiles were recorded above medieval material and alongside Victorian sherds. The whole site was an archaeologist's nightmare.

As some poorly constructed walls were gradually revealed some very odd details became apparent. Close examination showed that these walls had been hastily erected above the sturdy medieval foundations. On the lower remains of the old south wall the Victorians had built upwards, with a much narrower wall; then had cut across the site, not bothering with foundations, but placing their west wall directly upon a heap of loose stones and the warreners' midden. Another wall was similarly built across the site, without foundation. Others, like the south wall, were constructed more or less upon the priory foundations, but using quite different techniques and mortar. The infilling and levelling of the enclosed spaces with soil, stones and debris made us at first wonder whether this area could have been used as a temporary storage compound. Further study of the interior treatment of the thin walls, however, made us discount this theory, for they had been plastered and limewashed – quite unnecessary for an open compound. The Victorian walls formed two adjoining rectangles, in an L shape, an outline which seems to have deceived some archaeologists and indeed the later Ordnance Survey mappers, who assumed it to be the shape of the priory.

Careful analysis of records showed, however, that the priory walls had 'grown' since the 1830s. At that time visitors saw nothing which could be identified as a priory building; only the 1776 tenement was still standing. Yet F.A. Knight in his 1902 account commented that 'priory' walls stood 7 ft high; and photographs taken during the 1930s clearly show remnants of walls with limewashed plaster adhering, several feet above ground level. What the later observers saw were the remains of the Victorian navvies' homes, with the foundations of the priory itself having disappeared below ground level.

Saving the Souls of the Navvies

A clue to the use of these two buildings was found in a small booklet printed in 1879 to raise funds for the Somerset Branch of the Navvy Mission. This was an almost daily record kept by Missioner Thomas Steevens, who, for a salary of £65 per year, trudged from one building site to another, preaching to various groups of labourers working on the fortifications on Brean Down, as well as at other major construction sites (including the new Birnbeck Pier) in the rapidly expanding town of Weston. Not always did he have an encouraging welcome. One labourer, digging in a trench, snapped: 'Master, the parsons and men like you have the best on't, but poor fellows like we have to work like hosses. I should like to see some of the rich ones come here and try this a bit, and we to take their place for a time.' He received a sharp answer, not from the missioner, but from a philosophical fellow worker: 'Bill, thee bist a fool big enough now, and if thee'st had money thee'st soon kill theeself; thee doesn't know much now, and thee'st know less then. If thee and I had money what think we should do with much on't?' The agent, John Perry, offered the scripture reader free passage to the Holms for as long as the work was in progress, and Steevens took advantage of the invitation to sail across to Flat Holm to minister to the large workforce there; but it was on 27 April 1866 that he first mentions going to Steep Holm, where he 'visited the men's wives who live in the huts'. He was kindly received and invited to come again. Considering what must have been observed on these visits, the diary is a disappointment, for Steevens's over-riding concern was to tell of his missionary work. He detailed sermons preached and tracts distributed, but little else was recorded by him, with absolutely no descriptive passages. It was from asides that we were able to piece together something about the tenants of the temporary stone huts.

On his second visit to Steep Holm, Steevens met a ganger named Burgess and his wife 'who appear to be decent persons', and discovering (like John Ashley almost exactly thirty years earlier) that these people could not attend church, he redoubled his efforts to spend some weekends with them, and others with the Flat Holm community, to conduct services on their free Sundays. It is probable that Burgess was the foreman who ordered the renovation of the 1776 tenement, and had such an unpleasant surprise when the new wooden floor was being fitted.

Steevens mentions 'four huts' in which lived people connected with 'the Works'.

He gives no hint as to where these huts were situated; but, remembering that nineteenth-century writers called any small or substandard dwelling a 'hut', whether timber or stone-built, we concluded from the archaeological evidence that at least two were built upon the site of the former priory. Although they seemed rather large for the purpose, they may have been lightly partitioned; for Thomas Steevens does mention that he held a service in 'one of the large huts' when over fifty persons were present. A fortnight later, when he again spent a weekend on the island and held another service, the number of men employed there had risen to sixty or more.

Steevens was permitted to talk to the navvies as they worked, as well as in their free time; and occasionally, when he was marooned for an extra day, they were called together after work for an additional Monday evening service as well!

Mrs Pugsley and Mrs Vile were living on the island, caring for their households of husbands and lodgers. One hut is reported to have housed ten men and 'the man and his wife belonging to the hut with three children'. A man, his wife and twelve lodgers were in another hut. 'Seven lodgers with the man, his wife and two children' were present in the third. The wife in the fourth hut was fortunate: she had only her husband and four lodgers to look after.

One navvy, Jonah Daws, aged a surprising seventy years, became seriously ill, and the cause of special concern and care from Steevens, as he was nursed back to health by two of the women on the island. Mrs Mary Harris, who ran the inn, welcomed the missioner, and sent one of her lodgers to offer her kitchen for a service if he could find nowhere else. She also subscribed 10s for prayer books to be kept on the island for the use of the men. Few could read, but by helping one another the majority of men and their wives were able to understand at least parts of the booklets and tracts which Steevens left for them.

During his last recorded visit to Steep Holm, on 16 October 1866, Steevens gave reading lessons to two of the children – something he frequently did when visiting the workforce on Brean Down. One navvy was drunk and had fallen and hit his nose. He was apologetic for being caught in that state by the missioner, and meekly received a lecture, which seems to sum up the attitude of the men and their families on the island. Steevens was always listened to with respect and attention; there were virtually 100 per cent attendances at his services, and his evident concern and kindness, mingled with a stern approach to what he believed to be wrong, was appreciated by his flock – which appears to have added up to nearly forty men living in the huts, and at least four women and five children, in addition to those lodged in Cliff Cottage and the inn – which had to be enlarged by the building of a three storey annexe.

The former priory site was not included in the final requisition by the military, and as soon as the navvies had finished their tasks, they abandoned their temporary quarters to go to other building works.

Tantalizing Clues to Daily Routine

From many pieces of broken Victorian pottery, such as tableware, storage and bread bowls, and other artefacts – including bottle glass – recorded on the site, we have intriguing glimpses of life in the huts. That the men spent much of their hard-earned wages on tobacco is obvious from the many fragments of discarded clay pipes found. One of these told a different story for it was complete, with the tobacco ash still in the bowl, which was marked by burns along one side. We can imagine the frustration of a certain mason of nearly 130 years ago, working on stones for the huts. He filled and lit his clay pipe to enjoy a quiet smoke, then put it aside for a moment. Perhaps he was called away, and the pipe fell or was knocked to the ground, to be covered by a large stone, leaving the puzzled mason to search in vain while the tobacco gradually burned out in the bowl, and the stone itself became buried under several inches of soil. In 1981 this was lifted during archaeological work, and the lost pipe was revealed, resting on earlier midden material. This incident must have caused the same sort of agitation as the loss of a shiny 1864 sixpence, which was found in 1979.

A bone mustard spoon and butchered domestic animal bones, together with the ubiquitous limpet shells, rabbit, bird and fish bones, afford clues to the meals served by the ladies for their families and lodgers. Alexanders, no longer a popular vegetable as they had been in previous centuries, were gathered for a different purpose – to be dried and bundled for kindling the fires. To quote Skinner, writing of the island plants more than thirty years earlier: 'Alexander[s]: the stalk grows to the height of two or three feet, and bears abundance of seed, the roots of some being nearly the size of my wrist, for want of better fuel I perceive they bind the stalks of this herb into bundles to burn.'

Bedrock to the north-west had been chipped away to form a gully with what appears to be the remains of a hatch – possibly connected with a not very hygienically situated latrine.

So, gradually, some pieces from several different jigsaws have been interlinked to show at least part of a still incomplete picture. As well as cracking the puzzle of the correct location of the foreman's hut, yet another occupation of the medieval priory site has been identified; and we have even learned of occasional religious services being held there – of a very different character from those of more than 600 years earlier.

The Fortifications

The cutting of a road around the perimeter of Steep Holm was familiar work for the labourers. Techniques were similar to those used in railway construction, and in some ways the task was easier – for much of the unwanted earth and rock removed could be heaved over the cliff edge. Circular concrete platforms were erected for the gun batteries, each with a low protective parapet; four batteries were to have two guns each, with two others being designed for single guns. To meet with stringent regulations, all had well-ventilated underground ammunition stores containing separate brick-lined, barrel-vaulted chambers for cartridges and for shells. Above several of the entrance doorways it is still possible to read the legend: 'Cartridge Store for 7 in. gun' or, 'Shell Store for 7 in. gun'. For each store an antechamber had to be provided, incorporating a recess for a bulls-eye lantern and space for a small seat and a workbench, with a clothes rack screwed to the wall. In some of these antechambers the clothes racks with their large wooden coat pegs can still be seen.

For the double gun batteries the ammunition stores were immediately below the raised gun mountings, with flights of steps leading up to the guns and down to the stores. By contrast, the underground ammunition magazines for the single gun batteries were positioned at the rear of each; and it was when the navvies were digging out an area for magazines at one of these sites that they made a remarkable discovery.

A Thirteenth-Century Tombstone

What the labourers said when they struck the large blue lias stone, with its moulded edge and carving of an incised floreated cross, has not been recorded – perhaps fortunately – but someone recognized that it was something which should be preserved. Whether the stone was then intact or whether it was still marking an

Fragment of thirteenth-century tombstone carved with words 'Excavated near this spot 1867', set into stonework below the aperture in the side-arms store at Victorian Tombstone single gun battery, and still in position in the 1930s

actual grave is not known; but what survived the workmen's pickaxes was treated in a novel way. Each gun battery was supplied with a stone-built side-arms store constructed in a convenient place just to the rear of the gun mounting; and, like the barracks, having a slate roof. Most of them were capped with black-glazed locally made ridge tiles. When the store for this particular battery was erected, the remnant of tombstone or graveslab had the words 'EXCAVATED NEAR THIS SPOT 1867' carved into it, before being built into the end wall below a small aperture.

There it stayed for many years – until the Second World War, when the Victorian side-arms store was partly demolished. The remnant of tombstone was badly damaged and the Victorian lettering was lost. Mr Edmund (Ted) Mason, and other members of the Steep Holm Trust, a collective body leasing the island from 1953 until 1974, found the stone in its sad state, and prised the surviving piece from its perilous position before staggering along to the barracks with their burden. The relic remained on a specially constructed shelf until a few years ago, when it was moved into the main barracks room where it can be more readily admired by visitors.

Rudder Rock

An even more ancient feature was disturbed when building the ammunition stores at the rear of the Rudder Rock gun battery. The nearby enclosed area within the oval ridge of stones – which we believe to be the site of an Iron Age compound or Roman signal station – was used as a convenient hollow space in which to build the separate shell and cartridge stores needed for the single 7-ton gun. Rubble, deliberately heaped high above the ammunition chambers, created an artificial hillock to hide and protect the stores, but at the same time disguising the east part of the earlier feature – so much so that another author in 1978 (commenting on Skinner's 1832 sketches of the oval, and taking his wrong compass bearings literally) wrote that it no longer existed. Our own field studies on the island in 1977 had revealed the existence of two remaining segments of the old stone walling, and close examination of the abutment of Victorian stonework against the centuries-old ridge clearly showed the quite different styles of construction.

The Gun Batteries

Following the Victorian custom of naming gun batteries, more usually after topographical features, the single gun battery where the thirteenth-century stone was found became, predictably, Tombstone Battery. The others were Rudder Rock Battery (single), after the jutting rudder-shaped sea worn rock near which it stands at the western extremity of the island; Garden Battery (double), as its position was thought to have been the site of the former priory garden; Split Rock Battery (double), from the almost vertically fissured rock formation below the battery; Summit Battery (double), although not on the summit, standing in a prominent position high above the north-west cliffs; Laboratory Battery (double), which is the exception to the rule, being where tests were carried out to determine the various effects of differing weights and types of propellant explosive. An additional small building constructed at this battery was used as a workshop. The positioning of the gun batteries was determined by the arcs of fire required to achieve the most effective defensive screen, but from an archaeologist's point of view it is unfortunate that one battery had to be so close to the site of the medieval priory, and the underground stores of another on the remains of an ancient enclosure at Rudder Rock.

To the rear of Summit Battery the immense defensive bank which was constructed by digging a deep ditch has obliterated a centuries-old rampart. The Victorian bank is an interesting and rather awkwardly placed survival of 'ditch and bank' techniques of defence which were still in vogue even as late as the 1860s. On neighbouring Flat Holm the whole of Lighthouse Point (which includes the barracks square and a three-gun battery) is virtually cut off from the rest of the island by a deep dry moat. The tip of Brean Down is similarly isolated, all with the intention of enabling the garrison, in dire necessity, to make a 'last ditch stand' against an overland attacker. Although Steep Holm's batteries, housing a total of ten guns, were almost 200 ft above sea level, each barbette was provided with a protective semicircular stone parapet 3 ft high and 2 ft thick, with an inner diameter of 19 ft 6 in. On the seaward side of each were sloping earth banks which, when grassed over, formed a perfect disguise and additional protection for the gun emplacements.

On the low-lying sister island of Flat Holm such a system would not have been as safe for either guns or gunners, but those installations were just in time to benefit from an ingenious new invention. Concealed below ground in deep circular pits and mounted on Moncrieff lifting carriages, the guns were brought into the firing position by use of counterweights; the recoil on firing providing the force necessary to lift the weights and lower the weapons back into safety for reloading. Four batteries were built, two with three guns each, one having two guns, and another having only one – a total of nine. Here too the sites were named after topographical features: Lighthouse Battery (three guns); Castle Rock Battery (three guns); Farm Battery (two guns); Well Battery (one gun). As with Steep Holm, there had been tentative plans to build yet another battery, but these ideas were abandoned.

Steep Holm's Barracks

From a superb position on the south facing side of the plateau many tons of rock had to be blasted away to form a level platform on which to construct the barracks. A deeply excavated cavity between the newly-cut cliff face and the rear of the two buildings accommodated a large brick-built tank capable of holding 49,000 gallons of catchment water collected from the roofs and filtered through beds of charcoal and pebbles. The slate-tiled barracks were built of stone with brick interior facings, and included the Master Gunner's quarters, stores, and the soldiers' accommodation. For the actual building work skilled masons were brought to Steep Holm, and pre-dressed facing stones for the barracks, the parapet walls and the

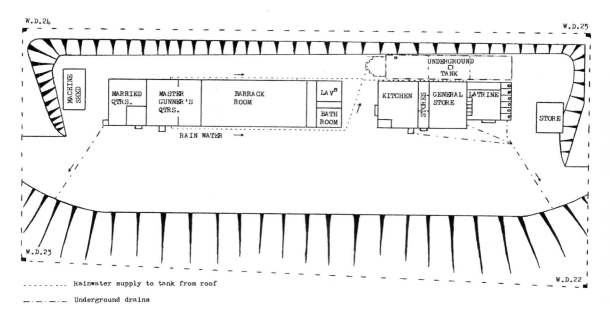

W.D.24

W.D.25

MACHINE SHED

MARRIED QTRS.

MASTER GUNNER'S QTRS.

BARRACK ROOM

LAV^B

BATH ROOM

RAIN WATER →

UNDERGROUND TANK

KITCHEN

STORES

GENERAL STORE

LATRINE

STORE

W.D.23

W.D.22

.... Rainwater supply to tank from roof

_._._._ Underground drains

Plan of Barracks, 1867

ammunition stores were specially imported to the island from Wales. A keystone above one of the barracks doors neatly dates the work to 1867, Flat Holm's barracks being dated in similar style to 1869.

Shipwreck of the *Lucy Sarah*

One of the sailing ships contracted to transport the faceted square-cut stones for the island fortifications, set out on yet another journey to the Holms. A newspaper account of 3 November 1866 takes up the story:

About 10 a.m. on Tuesday, the smack *Lucy Sarah* of Cardiff, John Powell Master, laden with limestone intended for the works on Steep Holme, went ashore on the rocks at Anchor Head and became a total wreck. It appears that she anchored off the Holmes on the previous night, and was driven from thence by the fury of the gale, dragging her anchor and being totally unmanageable, and was wrecked. . . . She belonged to Mr Taplin of Cardiff, and as far as we can learn she was not insured. The casualty created no little excitement, and thousands of people visited the scene of the disaster in the course of the day.

When consignments of stone reached Steep Holm, ships and barges offloaded at South Landing, in the shelter of Calf Rock. Platforms provided stacking space from which materials landed with the help of davits and sheerlegs could be winched up a steep straight track to the perimeter roadway. This incline is shown on the 1886 and 1903 Ordnance Survey maps, and in 1938 Leo Harrison Matthews recorded that 'A recess beside the [perimeter] path above [the incline] accommodated the winch.' The remains of what seems to have been a later winch still standing in that position suggests that the army in the Second World War had a similar arrangement, even if it was not greatly used at that time. Indeed, the soldiers also laid a narrow gauge rail track down the steep incline to South Landing. But the present winch frame is a relatively light structure, unlike the powerful equipment which army personnel in the Second World War installed on the route up from the main landing beach. We think they relocated Steep Holm's old marine winch, which for many years had stood just above East Beach ready to haul small boats above the water line. In the new situation it may have been used occasionally to bring light loads up the incline. There are no aids today up the steep track which is an alternative (and strenuous) route to the plateau when sea conditions prevent a landing on East Beach.

Lime Kilns

A well-preserved lime kiln stands on a platform at the foot of the incline. This was used for making lime mortar for the fortification work, the South Landing beach providing a plentiful supply of broken-up rock as raw material for burning, with coal being brought across from Wales for fuel, and island vegetation usually available for kindling. As marked on old Ordnance Survey maps, another lime kiln formerly stood to the east of the head of the incline path from South Landing. This was thought to have been completely destroyed when a Second World War generator hut was built, but it has been possible to identify the few remaining remnants of the rear of the lime-burning bowl, with traces of ash deposit in front of it. Again, a ready supply of limestone was to hand, this time from the cutting of the perimeter roadway and excavation of rock for the barracks and gun batteries.

Pier Charges for 'the Holms'

Birnbeck Pier opened on 5 June 1867, and examination of the entries in an account book covering the first six months of 1868 shows that already the pier was involved in transporting supplies to the islands. A few items from the list provide examples:

TOLL CHARGES:
For Severn Defences:

29.2.1868 Earthenware	0s 8d
12.3.1868 Sundries (6d per cart)	1s 0d
9.5.1868 Sundries (1s. 0d. per waggon)	3s 0d
11.5.1868 Passengers' Luggage	0s 2d
18.5.1868 Passengers' Luggage	0s 8d

Split Rock Victorian double gun site when manned, 1871–1902

Drowned during Fog

Throughout the building work on the two islands the surrounding sea continued to create hazards. Ironically it was a French sloop which picked up a very fatigued Weston boatman at the end of December 1867, and put him ashore at Pill. He had been rescued from a small open sailing boat drifting out of control down Channel, forty miles below the islands. Read, the sailor concerned, and John Dunstan, another Weston boatman, had been employed carrying messages and providing other services for the officials in charge of the fortification work at Steep Holm. Dunstan in particular was well accustomed to the locality, having worked for many years on the island fishery, but on this occasion, shortly after he and Read had set out for the mainland, dense fog came down and they lost their course. Eventually striking a sandbank they found themselves among breakers, and in trying to steady the boat they broke an oar. When reaching for the broken part Dunstan fell overboard and was drowned. Still in fog, the boat drifted back into deep water and for forty-eight hours floated up and down Channel with the changing tides until at last it was seen by a lookout on the sloop, and the exhausted boatman was saved.

With such difficulties and dangers, and some loss of life, the building of fortress Steep Holm progressed until it was sufficiently advanced to allow the next stage to be undertaken.

Chapter Fourteen

THE MILITARY TAKES OVER

The Guns

Installing the guns and their carriages was a military matter, although some preliminary work was necessary at the battery construction stage to provide a central pivot for each gun mount. An ingenious solution was to use earlier, obsolete George III cannons mounted vertically, with some 8 ft of the barrels in the ground, and muzzle uppermost to help support and locate the rotating gun platform. In the past, smaller obsolete guns were sometimes reused as bollards for ships mooring at ports and harbours. On Steep Holm, use of the 24-pounders manufactured about 1800 was a particularly appropriate method of providing the strength and rigidity needed to withstand the enormous shock of a 7-ton gun recoiling when firing. For the same reason the 'racer' – a circular rail or track 11 ft in diameter, supporting the flanged wheels of the gun carriage which rotated around the central pivot – was anchored with great iron 'claws' set deep into the concrete platform, to prevent it from being wrenched from position when the gun was fired. As always, the design of armaments had developed rapidly with the threat of war; and although still muzzle-loading, the massive new weapons were not only bigger, heavier and stronger but also far more accurate and efficient than earlier guns. The increased accuracy, range and fire power was achieved partly by 'rifling', and partly by a new and stronger method of 'built-up' construction developed by Sir William Armstrong, Superintendent of the Royal Gun Foundry at Woolwich.

'Rifling' – the cutting of long spiralling grooves inside the gun barrel – gave the projectile stability in flight by making it spin, so that there was no longer the risk of it tumbling in the air. With this breakthrough the traditional spherical cannon ball could at last be replaced with a bullet-shaped shell packed with explosive. The strengthening of the guns to take a more powerful propellant charge had been achieved by adding hoops of wrought iron to the rear section.. The resulting bulbous gun became extremely strong – but at the same time very heavy and cumbersome. The range and combined fire power of the ten new-style Woolwich Mark III 7-in bore, 7-ton rifled muzzle-loading cannons to be installed in Steep Holm's six batteries could annihilate any wooden vessels that ventured up the

Channel. Using a 30 lb propellant charge of gunpowder, and travelling at 1,560 ft per second, a 112 lb shell could penetrate up to 8 in of iron at a range of 1,000 yds, or could crash through decking, causing havoc within an enemy ship.

On rugged Steep Holm – the most difficult of all the sites chosen for the new Bristol Channel defences – the weight and size of the guns created tremendous problems of transport and installation. Visitors to the island often cannot imagine how these secret weapons of the 1860s could ever have reached the top of the cliffs, for the eventual practical difficulties of removing them has meant that most can be seen still lying in or near their original batteries. Techniques now long forgotten were used; relying on muscle and man power, with ropes, pulleys, levers, wedges, skids, sheerleg poles, and the simple windlass and winch. Parbuckling a gun, for example, meant wrapping ropes around the muzzle and around the rear, to roll it sideways along raised beams into the required position. A sling wagon was a simple arrangement of oak frame, strong enough to take the weight of the gun, and mounted above large diameter wheels so that the weapon could be slung beneath. A fixed windlass above the stub axles lifted the load into position. On the mainland the more substantial 'drug', incorporating a heavy oak platform on which the weapon was loaded, was used to move guns longer distances. But on Steep Holm the solution probably lay in the simple sleigh – two heavy skids linked by an

Garden Battery, Victorian double gun site: ramp and east barbette, central ammunition stores with ventilator shaft above and sloping roof of side arms store – seen from the priory site where H.W. Maxwell is excavating, 1938. The walls (foreground) which were believed to be from the medieval priory are now proved to have been those of navvies' huts, erected on the priory ruins while the fortifications were under construction

arrangement of cross beams capable of taking the full weight of a 7-ton cannon. Sections of 6 in diameter tree trunk made effective rollers where the gradient was not too steep; while the main motive force was provided by draught animals aided by a considerable number of men working in unison, with levers and wedges, and making vociferous use of lung power. Sheerlegs – which were used where guns needed lifting more than a few feet, or had to be swung ashore from a barge – were themselves heavy and difficult to handle. To lift 7 tons the two sheers, or fir poles, forming the inverted 'V' support from which pulleys and tackle were suspended, had each to be over 40 ft long, so that the angle at the top of the triangle remained narrow. To hoist these poles into position – especially in a location such as South Landing – was in itself arduous and dangerous. The task of unloading the guns on to the island from barges, dragging them up the steep incline, or along the equally difficult old south zig-zag path (now long out of use) was daunting. Having achieved this, the guns had to be manoeuvred to the batteries before being mounted on their carriages.

It was indeed fortunate that the feared invasion never took place, for the first guns to be mounted were not even available until 1868, and most not until 1869. The defences erected with such labour and careful workmanship were never tested by war, and for that reason they have often been classed, rather unfairly, as Lord Palmerston's Follies. But the prime minister died in 1865, when many of the batteries still had to be armed, or even started, and no one at that time saw any reason to countermand the fortification orders.

Most of Steep Holm's 7-ton cannons, with their splendid royal cyphers, are still in good condition; and the majority may be dated accurately from their left trunnions (or horizontal pivots), where the 'R.G.F.' (Royal Gun Foundry) incised stamp is accompanied by the individual gun number and its date of proving after manufacture:

Split Rock Battery	(2 guns)	No. 86 (1868)
"		No. 67 (1869)
Rudder Rock Battery	(1 gun)	No. 79 (1869)
Summit Battery	(2 guns)	No. 87 (1868)
"		No. 97 (1869)
Laboratory Battery	(2 guns)	No. 72 (1869)
"		No. 81 (1869)
Tombstone Battery	(1 gun)	No. 85 (1869)
Garden Battery	(2 guns)	One gun missing;
		markings on 2nd gun illegible.

It should perhaps be noted that in the relevant text and illustrations of *Steep Holm – a case history* (1978) the positions of Tombstone and Laboratory batteries were transposed, and an island souvenir postcard also misnamed Laboratory Battery as Tombstone. There is no doubt that Tombstone is the single battery north of the

Victorian Laboratory double gun battery showing ventilator shaft above ammunition stores (left) with lifting davit, 7-ton gun on eastern barbette, side arms store and additional building for testing explosives – photographed in the 1930s

priory site, so named because the thirteenth-century incised grave slab was found nearby and built into its side-arms store. Laboratory, above the north cliffs, is the double battery which was provided with an extra small building for use as a workshop.

While Government officials may have intended originally that all defences should be completed within four years of the Royal Commission report of 1860, the enormity of the task was such that it was to be 3 September 1870 before local newspapers reported that fortifications on Brean Down were nearly complete – needing only the installation of the seven guns to be finished, with the island guns due to be positioned by 1871; and during all this time the threat of war had receded even as the batteries were being constructed.

A Lease is Signed

At this stage of the work, with all the batteries constructed and only awaiting their cannons, an indenture was signed on 26 February 1871 between Dame Anne Cooper, who had also signed the initial agreement of 1865 (and who was by now the only surviving trustee of the estate of Colonel Charles Kemeys Kemeys-Tynte) and the Principal Secretary of State for the War Department. But this confirmation of the land leased by the army for a provisional 999 years brings in another complication: two mortgagees also signed. More than ten years had elapsed since the colonel's death, and after the signing of the 1865 agreement a £3,900 mortgage had been entered into, on 11 May 1868, to provide the trustees with additional funds without having to sell the island.

Apart from designating the land which the War Office was entitled to use, the lease made allowance for compensation in the event of the tenant's buildings being damaged, or even removed in case of need, and also to pay the occupier for any 'lands which shall be used or entered upon or fired across'. Mineral and mining rights were retained by the owners; and the solicitor was careful to make provision for 'full liberty for the reversionaries and their lessees, or assigns, friends, gamekeepers and servants at all seasonable times in the year to hunt, course, fowl, and sport in over and around . . . the said Island . . . [except over the specific areas leased by the army] and also to shoot fowl and fish around the said Island in the same way as might have been the case if this demise had not been made . . .'. With this lengthy document duly signed and witnessed, all was ready for the final stage of fortification.

The Garrison

The Times reported on 6 August 1872 that officers and men of the 12th Brigade, Royal Artillery, were leaving Plymouth to be employed in arming the forts of the Severn defences. This announcement was followed by the local newspaper of 28 September 1872, stating that Flat Holm's Royal Artillery consisted of thirty-eight gunners, two full bombardiers, two acting bombardiers, three corporals, two sergeants, one sergeant-major, one lieutenant, one major, and one medical officer – fifty-one men in all. 'As on the Steep Holmes, the men are partly under canvas, and appear to enjoy the life, especially when they can get over to Weston-super-Mare.' Steep Holm's complement was fifty-seven gunners, one bombardier, five acting bombardiers, two corporals, one sergeant, and two lieutenants – sixty-eight men in all. There may have been more men in total on Steep Holm, but the commanding officer of the sister island was of higher rank. Colonel Palmer, who eventually retired to Burnham-on-Sea, was proud to recall that he started his career as a raw recruit at the newly erected Steep Holm fort.

With such a large force engaged on both islands, and 'the fine battery, barracks, and officers' quarters' on Brean Down reported to be 'for the present quiet', it seems that the installation of the guns on the Down had been completed; but on the islands the work was taking longer than anticipated.

A Brave Rescue

Arming the Severn forts necessitated much interchange between the various bases, and Frederick Harris ran into trouble on the afternoon of 8 December 1872, when using the *Mystery* to transport an officer and eleven men from Flat Holm to the fort at Brean Down. As he left the island the wind suddenly strengthened, and with only one crewman to help he was forced to turn about and make for the shelter of the Welsh coast. Coming behind Penarth Head, the *Mystery* went aground on a submerged bank, and in the confusion her dinghy was lost. When she refloated on the incoming tide the anchor dragged, and ferocious winds carried her out to the roadsteads where she was swept across the stern of the *John Pearce*, a large schooner whose sail boom tore the yacht's mast from its seating. With her deck planking torn open, and waves sweeping aboard, the *Mystery* rapidly filled with water. The quick-thinking schooner's mate, Richard Johns, launched a small boat and rowed single-handed to the sinking yacht. With the aid of a rope the *Mystery* was pulled alongside the larger ship, and her passengers scrambled to safety – except for two soldiers who slipped between the two vessels. Without thought for his own life, Johns sculled into the narrow gap to pull them out of the water. In the lee of the schooner, Harris and his crewmate were then able to bail out their boat, and she was later taken to Cardiff for repairs, before resuming her adventurous career. For his brave conduct Richard Johns was awarded the Silver Medal of the R.N.L.I.

Reduced Task Forces

There are conflicting accounts of the number of soldiers stationed on the islands once the guns were satisfactorily installed and initial problems overcome. By 1875 the officers had left, and on Steep Holm an N.C.O. master gunner was in charge of a much reduced garrison, with a regular routine becoming established.

At about this time Master Gunner Bond was living in the barracks with his Canadian-born wife and the first children of what was later to become a family of thirteen – the last survivor of which was still alive in 1959 to recall her father as a strict disciplinarian and schoolmaster. In 1877 the forces were reported to have been 'augmented', with twenty-eight men about to be accommodated in the barracks.

Master Gunner Ware was in charge of the garrison in 1887, but only five gunners were reported to be on the island by 1889. Steep Holm, like the other Severn fortifications, was probably never fully manned once the guns had been positioned and tested. Occasionally the sound of practice firing was clearly heard in Weston, with 'smoke wreaths blowing over the rocks and floating away upon the sea breezes'.

In 1891 the Master Gunner was thirty-eight-year-old Levi Collins, a Wiltshire man, accompanied by his young wife Jane; their four-year old son, Richard, born in Gibraltar on one of his father's tours of duty; three-year old Emily, born at Plymouth, her mother's home town; and George, only eleven months old and born on Steep Holm. Collins was in charge of only four gunners: Irishman James Counley; John Hitchman, from Worcester; Robert Studd of Middlesex; and John Turner, a Devon man.

Firing Practice

The permanent garrison had dwindled to a mere caretaker force, but for a couple of weeks each summer the number of men was greatly increased by the militia soldiers arriving from the mainland for their annual artillery practice under the watchful eyes of the regular gunners. This was one answer to the moot question of how the great chain of forts across southern England was to be manned with comparatively few fully trained artillerymen. Somewhat naively, perhaps, it was thought that if war were to come, the local 'ploughboys and other volunteers' would be able to master the intricacies of servicing and manning the new cannons after a few firing sessions with the master gunners.

The scene during firing practice can readily be envisaged. Fishing boats and other vessels have been warned away from the target area; and at the Split Rock battery, with the sun glinting on the sea 170 ft below, groups of soldiers cluster around the shining barrels of the two massive guns.

Standard procedures and safety regulations are being followed strictly, and after each firing the barrels are cleaned with a sponge dipped in water. A hoist is used to lift the cartridges and heavy shells from the separate underground stores below, and after reloading and re-aligning the gun, the order to fire is shouted. A tug on the long lanyard attached to the long friction tube placed in the fuse hole of one of the weapons results in a deafening explosion accompanied by a cloud of black smoke from the muzzle, while gun and carriage recoil sharply up the mounting ramp. Afterwards, reloaded yet again, and re-aligned, the cannon is ready once more. So the practice continues, but not for long as shells are expensive and only a limited number can be used. With firing practice finished, the soldiers are employed on cleaning the guns and numerous other duties. But the, routine is not too rigid, and at the end of the day there is a distraction to which they all look forward; for on this isolated but not so lonely island they can make their way to the Steep Holm Inn, where they find a warm welcome from the Harris family, and during a convivial evening add to the prosperity of Fred and his wife. Sometimes they enjoyed too convivial an evening, and years later a member of the Harris family told of one soldier who 'got too fond of the beer'. As he staggered up the path to the top of the island, he missed his way and fell to his death over the rocks.

A Crew Member of the Ration Boat Remembers

In the early 1890s it was the cutter-rigged *Osprey*, owned by Rowland Perry, which was the main boat used for deliveries of post (carried in a red mail box), food, coal and ammunition to the military garrisons on Brean Down and the two islands. Later, the Watts family took general supplies to the Brean Down garrison via the River Axe ferry, then pushing hand trucks along the 2½-mile military road on the Down, although the *Osprey* continued to unload coal and ammunition direct to the fort at the tip of the headland. Over the years this boat had several different captains, but during school holidays her crew often included young Leonard Lott – in later life to become an optician. He never forgot his early experiences, and two years before he died he revisited the island, and afterwards wrote a letter setting out his memories.

The 17-ton *Osprey*, with its single mast, large cockpit and small hold, generally berthed at Weston's Knightstone slipway, but if the weather was bad or the boat was late on the tide, the Uphill river provided an alternative anchorage. The summer mooring by Birnbeck Pier was used only in fine weather, but on one occasion the *Osprey* was caught there in a south-westerly gale and, breaking adrift, was dismasted against the pier structure before going aground in Sand Bay. Afterwards refloated and repaired, the boat continued in service for a number of years until, in a final adventure, a gale drove her on to Brean sands. Mr Perry oversaw the salvage of the precious red mail box before the cutter was towed to Highbridge where she was left to rot.

By the 1890s the inn on Steep Holm had closed and, writing about the island at that time, Mr Lott recalled that when he was helping to crew the *Osprey* the only persons there were soldiers of the Garrison Artillery:

> . . . [the island] was well kept, and all the white [hand] railing was regularly painted all the way up the zig-zag path. There was a small garden by the Battery [barracks] and the only wreck [ruined building] was the old Inn. Lots of rabbits kept the grass closely grazed. . . . There did not seem so many birds as now [1959]. . . . At the top of the beach was an elaborate landing stage on iron wheels, and I understood it was placed there by the War Office for a V.I.P to make an inspection . . . the War Office sent regularly [for it] to be painted by an outsider [contractor]. On a Sunday in winter we had to collect General Wolsey [a famous campaigner of that time] who had been to Steep Holm for an inspection. As it was dead low water we had to land him at Birnbeck Pier, and Mr Perry met us at the gate in his red Salvation Army jersey. The General left by [horse-drawn] Cab for Weston Station. . . . Messrs Spencer Tyler [grocers of High Street, Weston] supplied the rations [for the garrisons]. These were packed in hampers so that if the weather was bad they could be thrown to the men on the beach. Coal [for which there was a large punt, the *Winnie*] and 4½ gallon casks of Beer were taken on special trips, and the 2 [Army] Donkeys had special Pannier harness to take the casks and the coal up to the Barracks. . . . The Garrison Artillery men had Pill box hats, tight trousers and white Pipe Clay Belts and Trimmings. . . . The Garrison was usually between 3 & 5 men but these were increased a great deal for seasonal Practice when training was carried out on these guns. . . . I was often in the boat towing the Target against the tide.

Under Shell Fire

New plans had been drawn up on several occasions to update the weapons and defences of the Holms, but due to changes of the military mind, and on grounds of cost, none had been implemented. There had even been a proposal in 1888 for an additional battery on Steep Holm. Meanwhile the small garrison continued to maintain the existing, technically obsolete guns and occasionally to fire them. Towards the end of the century there was a real prospect of change, and on 18 August 1898 a bombardment of Steep Holm by the Royal Navy cruiser HMS *Arrogant* presented journalists with a dramatic story, although the actual record of the captain's log was rather different from that reported in the press.

The French threat originally feared when the island fortification plans were drawn up had not materialized, but the development of weapons had continued to make progress and the teething troubles of breech-loading guns had been eliminated, making muzzle-loading guns finally obsolete. New methods of protecting guns were also under consideration, and the Rudder Rock single gun battery at the west point of the island had been selected for an experiment in defence against the weapons of a modern warship. Mr Gibson, son of the War Department contractor at that time, recalled (in a 1951 interview) helping 'to construct a large concrete emplacement . . . with a hardened, sloping surface'. The

HMS Arrogant, *the cruiser which shelled the Rudder Rock gun site in 1898*

7-in muzzle-loading cannon was removed from its carriage and rolled to one side, the carriage was dismantled, and a dummy 9.2-in breech loader was mounted on a specially built stone plinth, defended by a large curved shield of 3-in thick nickel steel.

With the island preparations completed, the navy dispatched the brand new three-funnelled cruiser HMS *Arrogant* (laid down at Devonport in May 1896) to the Bristol Channel, and she put into Portishead the day before the test to take on 9 tons of water and to re-coal. The ship's log records that a quantity of stores was also taken on board – including 614 lb of stewing beef, 312 lb of vegetables, and 1,320 lb of bread. As was usual after a re-coaling the ship had then to be cleaned down, and the main boilers re-lit and stoked before everything was ready for sailing. During the course of this hectic day, one unfortunate Marine, Private Twaddle, R.M.L.I. lost a mess kettle overboard, 'part of the cost to be met out of his pay'. Also among the ship's crew were C.P.O. W. Brookling and A/B Waite, both of whom later settled in Weston, and A.E. Stacey who, in February 1955, celebrated his golden wedding at Burnham-on-Sea.

HMS *Arrogant* was at anchor off Steep Holm by evening, with the engines stopped and fires banked. By 6.30 a.m. on the following morning she had weighed anchor, and the official test observation boat had left Weston, heading for the island, with General Sir Richard Harrison and other officers aboard; including Surgeon Col. Phelps, the medical officer, who was to have remained on Steep Holm during the experiment – but tidal conditions prevented him from landing until halfway through the proceedings. Would-be sightseers were already lining Weston sea front armed with their telescopes, but had little hope of seeing much action. Army personnel and lighthouse keepers on Flat Holm had a grandstand view, but most members of the small caretaker force on Steep Holm were moved to safe positions at the east end of the island, from where they could see nothing. From a newly-erected look-out post on the rampart behind Summit Battery, one person was detailed to signal results of the firing runs to the cruiser. To make the test more realistic, dummy soldiers were placed at the Rudder Rock gun battery.

After some delay, while small boats full of sightseers were cleared from the danger area, the *Arrogant* made her first run past the island, firing at the Rudder Rock defensive position. Her log records a smooth sea with light northerly wind, and the following details: 'Carried out 2 runs firing 5 maxims [machine guns]. Dist[ance] when abeam 800 yds. 2 runs firing all Starb'd [starboard] 12 po'rs [pounders]. Dist. when abeam 1400 & 1800 yds; 1 run firing 3 6-in Q.F. [quick-firing] guns. Dist. when abeam 1800 yds. 11.58 stopped. 2.40 weighed anchor [to resume test] 2.44 carried out 1 run firing 3 6-in Q.F. guns. Dist. when abeam 1400 yds. 3.35 finished firing.'

Although officially the *Arrogant* was equipped with four 6-in and six 4.7-in guns, plus maxims, the log shows that at the time of the Steep Holm experiment the armament used was 6-in and 3-in guns, and maxims. The 12-pounders referred to

Elder bushes growing in the Victorian Rudder Rock gun site, but showing plinth built on barbette over the racer and the displaced gun. The hardened concrete apron is to the right – photographed in 1938

in the log may be alternatively described as 3-in 12 cwt guns, and the gunnery officer's separate record confirms that this was the type of ammunition used: 4.7-in guns would have fired 45-pounder shells.

The final run with the big quick-firing guns at last shattered the shore battery's protective steel shield. The sham gun was dislodged, the dummy soldiers scattered, and some of the surrounding masonry destroyed – at a total cost of 4,437 machine-gun bullets, 253 12-pounder shells, and 79 6-in shells – a somewhat expensive method of proving a point; although at the time it was considered a valuable lesson in the vulnerability of the proposed new defences.

The *Arrogant* steamed back to Portishead, where the log shows that it was midnight before fires were banked and she was again 'ship-shape'. This was probably her most unusual assignment, although she served during the First World War, to be finally scrapped in 1923. Shrapnel from the bombardment can occasionally be found in the area, and the remains of the broken shield can still be seen within the parapet of this battery. The supporting plinth for the gun is no longer visible, but the curved 'hardened' sloping concrete apron is as solid as when it was laid down by Mr Gibson and his father.

HMS *Hercules*

At the War Office's request, a spectacular and rather similar test bombardment had taken place at Portland Bill thirteen years earlier. HMS *Hercules* was the warship then involved, and permission had been given for her to bombard a dummy 6-in gun mounted on the latest design of disappearing carriage, housed in an underground pit of the Moncrieff type. A special mechanism automatically raised the gun into the firing position at intervals throughout the test, and the discharge of a small puff of smoke each time added authenticity to the experiment. Shells and machine-gun bullets from the attacking vessel whined overhead or plunged into the ground nearby; but the dummy gun and its emplacement remained intact. In the eyes of the experts the disappearing carriage (an improvement over those already in use on Flat Holm) had proved its value.

Brean Down Catastrophe

In 1900 one of the reduced task force on Steep Holm was to attain notoriety less than a week after he had been drafted back to the mainland fort at Brean Down. Gunners Haines and Johnson who had served together on 'the Holmes', set out after duty on Tuesday 3 July to walk the eight miles to Burnham-on-Sea to collect bicycles previously left there, and to enjoy a few drinks at the Commercial Hotel. A puncture at the start of the return cycle ride was to have a dramatic sequel. Haines did not arrive back at the fort until two hours after the 10 p.m. roll call, and had a restless night worrying about disciplinary action in the morning. Shortly before 5 a.m. he left the dormitory without bothering to dress, but clutching the first carbine in the rack. Did he have suicide in mind, or was his foolhardy firing into the ventilator of No. 3 magazine, containing nearly three tons of explosive, merely an ill-tempered gesture of defiance which went wrong? The resulting blast blew Haines to pieces: two of the 7-ton guns were dislodged, masonry was tossed a considerable distance, and the fort was thrown into indescribable confusion.

Farmer Edward Champion of Brean Down was already at work when he was startled by the explosion and saw a column of thick black smoke over the fort. He immediately sent his twenty-year-old son Maurice to raise the alarm by cycling to the nearest telephone at Berrow post office. At the same time the sergeant in charge of the fort discovered that the military telephone line had been cut by the blast and also dispatched a messenger, who cycled the nine miles along country lanes to alert Surgeon Col. Phelps in Weston. Miraculously only one soldier of those sleeping in the barracks was seriously hurt. Gunner Reed, who had also served at the island forts, had two arteries severed by flying glass. After emergency treatment he was conveyed to Weston hospital by boat.

The inquest on Gunner Haines took place two days later, when Sgt. Major James Withers, who was in charge of the fort, said that he had never seen the dead man the worse for drink; and Master Gunner Brett testified that he had noticed nothing strange about the behaviour of Haines, although he had a violent temper. The coroner's jury found that deceased had caused the explosion while in a state of temporary insanity.

The end of the Fortification Era

Within months of the official enquiry into the Brean Down incident, the fort was shut down and the weapons removed, with preparations being made to close the other garrisons of the Severn Defences. A corporal and a few gunners were at the Steep Holm fort in September 1900, but in 1902 the island bases were vacated by the army. Two rare photographs from this period were given to us by Sgt Walford, who served on Steep Holm in the Second World War. One shows his father, in corporal's uniform, and Master Gunner Sgt Stepper at the Split Rock Battery with island pets. The second depicts Sgt Stepper and Cpl Walford with another soldier and several boatmen, posing outside the old boathouse at Anchor Head, Weston, with one of the army donkeys that had been brought back to the mainland at this time.

The obsolete muzzle-loading cannons and carriages were left to be sold for scrap in 1903. Carriages were dismantled and the metal taken away, but, fortunately for those interested in military history, to remove the massive guns from Steep Holm proved impractical for the scrap dealer, and nine of the original ten 7-in guns can

Master Gunner Sgt. Stepper and Cpl. Joe Walford with pets at the Split Rock gun site, c. 1902

Sgt. Stepper and Cpl. Joe Walford with boatmen and army donkey at the old boathouse, Anchor Head, Weston-super-Mare, c. 1902

still be seen there. All are intact, except that the one at Rudder Rock has lost a trunnion. The missing gun is from Garden Battery – significantly above the path down to East Beach and therefore in theory the easiest to remove. It was this gun which Dr Leo Harrison Matthews, writing shortly before the Second World War, recorded as having at some time been cut in half with an oxy-acetylene burner. Scars on the remaining 7-in cannon at Garden Battery show that an attempt was also made to cut the barrel from this gun, which was levered down from its barbette, before the scrap dealer gave up trying to salvage the metal.

Flat Holm retains three of its nine guns intact, all at the Lighthouse Battery and so the most difficult to remove; one of these still lies upon a collapsed trolley after an attempt to transport it to the mainland in more recent years. Two cannons from other batteries have been taken away, although not without considerable difficulty. The rest were cut into sections during the original salvage attempt, and the remaining pieces are still scattered around their emplacements.

The departure of the small caretaker force of soldiers from Steep Holm struck the final blow to the nineteenth-century fortunes of the island, which was then abandoned for several years, although the army continued to hold a lease on the vacant military sites. Capt. Blandy of the Royal Engineers' Office, at Pembroke Dock, eventually wrote on 10 October 1908 to give the required six months' notice to terminate the army's tenancy '. . . of the various plots of land on the above island held under a lease dated 26th Feb'y 1871'. At first the War Department was dubious about the informality of Capt. Blandy's letter, but the Rt. Hon. Charles Theodore Halswell Kemeys-Tynte (8th Baron Wharton) readily accepted the original notice, and the official solicitor agreed that the lease should end on 10 April 1909.

Years before then the military equipment and stores had been removed from Steep Holm, but one donkey had remained – later described as belonging to a previous tenant. An R.S.P.C.A. inspector was alerted and checked its condition, but concluded that although there was a shortage of water there was plenty of grass for the animal – indeed sufficient for seventy sheep if necessary.

Memories

A rare personal impression of the fortification era was provided by a master gunner's widow who in the autumn of 1934 revisited Steep Holm, and recalled to warden Harry Cox her memories of the island some forty or more years before. She had enjoyed an adventurous life, accompanying her husband to various overseas bases, including one in China, before the start of the First World War, during which he was killed in action. But Steep Holm had a special place in this frail old lady's affections, being her first home as a young bride. In particular she remembered her impression of the island as the sail was hauled down and the boat crunched into the pebbles, with half a dozen kindly soldiers anxious to lend a hand to see her safely ashore. During the next two or three years she was to make many such voyages to and from the mainland. She and her husband had occupied the separate master gunner's quarters at the west end of the main barracks building. There was heartbreak when her baby son died and was buried in a local churchyard, but otherwise her stay on the island was remembered as a happy one. At that time the great guns were polished and gleaming and the men smart and attentive; the food was excellently prepared by the army cook; and, best of all, the fortnightly supply run by the contractor's boat which brought rations and stores also carried eagerly awaited mail, sometimes with little surprise gifts from the agent or the crew. Every board in the barracks was kept scrubbed, the woodwork was clean and painted, and all was spick and span with well-stocked gardens, and paths free from weeds. It has to be admitted that Steep Holm does not look like that any more!

Chapter Fifteen

PROSPERITY AND DECLINE

The military development of the island, which began early in 1866 with an influx of navvies and army personnel, added a new dimension to the lives and prosperity of the innkeeper and his family. Since moving into the inn in 1848, only hard work, shrewd business acumen, and some dubious dealings, had made a living for the Harris family. Suddenly, almost twenty years later, there were more than fifty thirsty men on Steep Holm, with money to spend, and just the inn within easy reach. There was an immediate need for more space to house those without other lodging on the island. More supplies were required, and consequently more storage space, more staff and more household equipment. The fishing was still profitable, and extra ferrying was involved; although Mr Perry, the works contractor, used his own small steam tug for transporting men and materials for the fortifications – and sometimes to bring excursionists to Steep Holm.

It is no coincidence that the inn was enlarged at about this time, to be almost doubled in size by the addition of a three-storey annexe, with a separate door leading directly on to a sloping rock shelf just above the beach where boats could be made fast to a convenient mooring ring for the unloading of stores. The fortunes of the inn had never had such a boost. From the time when it was built just above the shore-line it had served principally as a home for several island farmer tenants – a base from which they also controlled the winter fishing and gulling in the spring and summer months. Ferrying, and supplying refreshments to tourists who came for a rabbit shoot or simply for an adventurous day out, was at first a sideline. Playing host to the crews of sailing ships at anchor off the island waiting for a favourable wind or tide provided opportunities for less innocuous occupations, especially during the Harris era.

Many years later, when it was safe to have such memories, Frank Harris told of how his grandfather was the 'boss' of smuggling on Steep Holm, with his father helping. Fred used to take rum and tobacco 'by night to a little place called Uphill, and up the Axe, where he was met a mile or so up river for barrels of spirits to change hands. It came from the West Indies, sailing ships, you know. There was two, one going and one coming. They used to race across with this stuff and of course our people knew the time they'd be up at the island, and they'd be there to meet them. French ships went past the islands and dropped barrels of spirits overboard. Little boats from the island [Steep Holm] went out to pick up the barrels from the water.' Some of the over-proofed spirit was diluted on the premises and duty-free drinks were served to customers without regard for licensing rules. To complete the hospitality offered, Mrs Harris had a well-deserved reputation for the excellent fish meals which she offered to tourists at modest prices. Goat meat was on the menu when the animals could be caught or shot, but they became very wild and adept at clambering down the steepest cliffs to avoid their hunters.

A Farmhouse is Built

Throughout the years of upheaval caused by the fortification work, farming continued on the plateau with some difficulty and disruption, taking second place to running the inn and attending to the profitable fishing. The old tenement, built in 1776, renovated in 1830 and again restored in 1866 for the construction foreman's temporary home, was used in later years as a barn, and was fated to deteriorate yet again from lack of maintenance.

Once the building of the fortifications was complete, the presence of the military in its specially demarcated areas did not restrict the Harris family's movements, nor

Looking across the priory site from Garden Battery (sloping roof of side arms store foreground). The 1870 farmhouse ruins are in the distance (left), 1776 tenement in the centre, and the 1930s excavation spoil heap in the south-east corner of the priory (lower right). Low walls (centre) are the remains of navvies' cottages

did it prevent tourists from viewing the new 'Works' – and so brought even more impetus to the innkeeper's trade. With an added demand for fresh supplies there also seemed to be prospects of higher farming profits, by controlling the island agriculture separately. For this purpose a new traditional-style farmhouse was built on the plateau, to the west of the old tenement. Island stone was used, some quarried from nearby, with the rest robbed from derelict navvies' huts, and remnants of the medieval priory. Of the four ground-floor rooms two had open fires, and another an iron stove, parts of which were still in position in the late 1970s. A catchment tank attached to the south wall provided an adequate water supply, and at the west end of the house the large adjoining brick-floored washroom was accessible only from the outside, with a water-closet cubicle in one corner, flushed by bucket. This was an improvement on the arrangements for the tenement, which had relied on a separate stone-built privy. Until rather heavy-handed restoration work on the farmhouse ruins in recent years, a change of roof-line could clearly be seen at the apex, reducing the original very steep pitch but retaining the overall height. The positions of windows and doors could also be plotted readily. Around the farmhouse was a very substantial wall, part of which incorporated one of the ancient rampart/warren banks. This wall enclosed a large relatively sheltered kitchen garden, where lines of stones marked separate beds for plants.

Dating evidence for the erection of this building is gleaned from the wording of the War Office leases. 1865 had seen the signing of the first agreement between Her Majesty's Principal Secretary of State for the War Department, and the executors of Col. Kemeys Kemeys-Tynte, who had died in November 1860. This lease, when listing the various properties on Steep Holm, specifically refers to: '. . . the Farmhouse also used as a Public House . . .' which has to be the 1832 inn above the beach. But by 1871, when the final lease was drawn up, the farmhouse and the public house were clearly identified as two separate buildings. The cost of constructing the farmhouse, as well as the earlier annexe to the inn, would have been borne by the Tynte family.

Prosperity for the islanders now seemed assured. Weston was continuing to expand, and with the railway and improved roads bringing more people to the town, a general increase in the number of visitors to the island was confidently expected – quite apart from the needs of those manning the fort. Later records suggest that a second tenant took over the farm. Perhaps this was Frederick Henry Harris and his growing family, but whoever lived here does not seem to have stayed for very long, as the building soon deteriorated. The navvies had gone, and with an unexpected decline in the numbers of military personnel stationed on Steep Holm, and fewer visitors than had been anticipated, potential sales of produce were disappointing.

Two Island Boats Wrecked

Spring 1869 again saw severe storms in the area, and at the beginning of February strong winds coincided with high tides to tear the small steamer *Industry* from anchorage in the River Axe at Uphill. Dragging her anchor, she drifted northwards across the bay to pile up on rocks at the landward end of Birnbeck Island. The mast and superstructure crashed into the supports of the newly-built pier as she swiftly broke up. Formerly engaged in the fortifications work on the two islands, the vessel had been purchased from the Government by Mr Bissicks, a Bristol man, only a day or two before the accident, and she was lying in the river without anyone aboard when the force of the tide swept her away.

The Harris family's own boating activities were not confined to fishing, ferrying and pleasure sailing. They had also acquired a sloop, the *Roebuck*, for more general work in the estuary. The son, Frederick Henry Harris, who captained this boat, was on board when the 1861 census was taken. After years of successful trading, the *Roebuck* was also lost in 1869, foundering off Portishead when carrying coal to Weston from Lydney, much higher up the River Severn and on the opposite coast. The coal had been intended for unloading at Weston's Knightstone wharf, and was consigned to the Phillips Royal Potteries. This name is familiar to us from many examples of wares still surviving around Weston, and from stamped roofing tiles we found in debris around the present remains of Steep Holm's Victorian farmhouse – which delimited its construction to a short period ending in about 1871. Although Charles Phillips had been in business since 1847, it was an Honourable Mention at the Great Exhibition of 1851 which resulted in orders to supply flowerpots to the royal parks in London, so entitling him to call his potteries 'Royal'. From 1871, when the business was sold, the name stamped on the various pottery products was changed to that of his successor.

Proprietor of the Claremont Royal Pier Hotel

As well as the opening of a pottery, the first seventy years of the nineteenth century had seen an almost unimaginable transformation of Weston, from tiny fishing community of shanty dwellings, scattered farmhouses and a church to popular seaside resort – connected by rail to Bristol, and with crescents and terraces of well-built stone houses to accommodate scores of professional and middle-class visitors, who often took lodgings for as long as a month at a time.

Among the first of the new properties were large, well-separated detached houses near the sea front, one of these being the attractive Claremont Lodge, built in an excellent position immediately above the rocky cove, pebbly beach and landing place at Anchor Head. Here the Revd John Skinner had called to visit his friend and superior, the Bishop of Bath and Wells, who was relaxing from episcopal duties in the summer of 1830. Twenty-one years later, in 1851, the Claremont Hotel was to be built near the Lodge, with the somewhat notorious Frederick Martell as its licensed beer retailer.

By 1872 the proprietor of the adjacent Claremont Royal Pier Hotel was none other than Frederick Harris, whose advertisement proudly proclaimed that he was also owner of the champion yacht *Mystery* and tenant of the hotel and fishery at 'the

WESTON-SUPER-MARE ADVERTISEMENT. 171

ROYAL CLAREMONT

PIER HOTEL,

WESTON-SUPER-MARE.

FREDERICK HARRIS, Proprietor.

THIS HOTEL is the only one in Weston-Super-Mare in close proximity to the Sea, with pleasure grounds, and walks down to the Beach.

It adjoins the new Pier, where Steamers arrive daily from all parts, and is replete with all modern improvements.

PRIVATE SEA BATHS.

COFFEE ROOMS, commanding complete Sea View.

GOOD STABLING AND COACH HOUSES.

SPACIOUS DINING ROOM, capable of Dining 200 persons, with Enclosed Grounds, *special* for large Parties visiting Weston-Super Mare.

Board & Lodgings, from £1 10s. per week.

The Champion Yacht "MYSTERY" is the property of the Proprietor, who has also rented the Steep Holmes for the last 27 years, where he has a Hotel and Fishery, offering peculiar advantages to Visitors and Tourists.

Advertising the amenities of the Royal Claremont Pier Hotel in 1872. From Morris & Co's Commercial Directory and Gazetteer of Somersetshire with Bristol

The Royal Pier Hotel, Weston-super-Mare, at the entrance to the private road to Birnbeck Pier, when Frederick Harris was proprietor, in the 1870s

Steep Holmes'. In May of that year he relinquished the licence of the Claremont Refreshment Rooms to John Martell. With his farming venture, two hotels, and extensive boating activities, former 'debtor' Frederick Harris (assisted by his hard-working family) had become an extremely busy and successful entrepreneur. The Claremont Royal Pier Hotel was close to the pleasure steamer pier connecting Birnbeck island to the shore. This had been completed in 1867 and was the gateway to Weston for thousands of day excursionists from South Wales – and Frederick Harris was there to take advantage of the new trade. In addition to board and lodgings from £1 10s per week, he offered good stabling and coach houses, a spacious dining room capable of seating 200 persons, coffee rooms commanding a complete sea view, and private sea baths. So respected did he become that a few years later a local directory lists Frederick Harris among the gentry of the town. It was his daughter-in-law, Ann, who was effectively managing the Steep Holm inn, while her husband (Capt.) Frederick Henry Harris operated the boats. By then aged thirty, Ann also had to cope with daughter Mary, aged eight, son William, aged five, and one-year-old Henry. William Urch, of 'No. 2 Steep Holme House' was helping to run the fishery. Later, his son Henry Urch was to succeed him as fishery manager.

Travelling the Hard Way

A chilly, windy day in September 1875 saw great excitement on the island, when the first swim from Weston to Steep Holm was successfully completed. Touching shore at South Landing, the powerfully built, hardy swimmer found Harris waiting for him with blankets and hot coffee; while the master gunner in charge of the fortifications greeted him with a salvo – not from the 7-ton cannons, but from a shot gun!

Led by his escort boat, *The Superior*, crewed by George Jones and his partner Albert Coles, twenty-six-year-old Henry Garrett, M.A., had started out from Birnbeck Pier at 10.26 a.m., with his body well coated in seal oil. He reached the island in two hours sixteen minutes, despite choppy sea conditions and difficult currents. Long ropes had been attached to the stern of the boat, with cork buoys carrying pink flags, so that he could grasp them in case of total exhaustion; but he swam strongly, without taking any offered stimulant. At regular intervals the boat crew encouraged him with a rousing cheer, and a sailing vessel carrying his father, the Revd Thomas Garrett, swept past the swimmer in mid-channel, on its way to warn Harris that food and hot drinks would be needed. At East Beach, the nearest point, the tide race proved too strong for Garrett to land, and he was forced instead to swim around the corner of the island to come ashore in the shelter of Calf Rock. There he was able to clamber stiffly out of the water after completing a total swimming distance estimated at 8 miles or more, when including tidal drift.

After refreshment, and wrapped in blankets, Garrett was rowed around to East Beach and taken to the inn, where a short rest, sandwiches and more coffee enabled him to recover sufficiently to climb the steep path up to the plateau, and to walk around the top of the island before returning home to Weston by boat.

The Beginning of a Decline

Soon after this exciting event the fortunes of Frederick Harris started to fade, and several misadventures overtook the family, as well as social changes which affected both Weston and Steep Holm. The number of day trippers to the town was increasing rapidly, but there were fewer long-stay visitors with the time and inclination to sail to the islands. The entertainment enjoyed by the day trippers also differed materially from that of the more leisured class of visitor. Increased bar takings at the mainland hotel did not compensate for the reduction in paying guests, while ferry work, and trade at the Steep Holm inn was reduced.

Loss of the *Mystery*

The high winds of spring 1878 caused a major crisis for the Harris family when the yacht *Mystery* was torn from her moorings off Steep Holm. Unmanned, the vessel drifted helplessly down Channel for several miles before being thrown on to rocks off Minehead, to become a total wreck. During the previous afternoon, her crew had been engaged in offloading stores which they had brought to the island from Weston, using a smaller boat to take the articles ashore. With the wind increasing, they were unable to return to the yacht to sail back to Weston; sea conditions worsened overnight, and the vessel broke away in a storm force gale to begin her final fatal journey.

With the loss of the *Mystery*, local traders who had relied on her to transport goods to the garrisons on both islands were in danger of losing their lucrative contracts to competitors in South Wales. Sympathizers setting up an appeal fund to enable Harris to replace his yacht were quick to make this point. It seems that the *Mystery* was replaced by a vessel bearing the same name as another of his wrecked boats. In 1880 the owners of Birnbeck Pier paid Frederick Henry Harris 2s 0d as part of the cost of shipping a crane to Newport – in the *Roebuck*.

By 1881 Frederick Harris, then stating his age as sixty-four, was back in residence at the Steep Holm inn with his wife Mary. Their sixteen-year-old granddaughter Polly, and a niece Roselle, aged nineteen, were with them for a while, but they now had only one servant, James Capel, who also helped with the fishing. Frederick Henry was still running the boats, while his wife managed the Claremont Refreshment Rooms – back in the hands of the Harris family. The Steep Holm inn was by this time fifty years old, and its position only just above the beach made it very vulnerable to damage by storm. Grandson Frank Harris, in an interview when he was aged eighty-three, still remembered that the house was 'that old we couldn't get any plaster to stay on the ceiling . . . we'd wake up in the morning and we'd find it on our bed'. When the easterly gales raged, the water 'Twould fill all the yard up and half the house sometimes . . . coming over the wall you see. We'd have to run down and open up the scuppers and let it out and open up the doors and let it away!'

Botanists from Wales

In May 1883 a party of some fifty persons from Cardiff Naturalists' Society visited the island, primarily to see the Steep Holm peony and to seek and list other rare plants – but also to enjoy themselves on a rather special kind of annual outing. The paddle steamer *Nelson* was hired for the day; arrangements were made for the ferry boats which would be needed when they reached the island; and a specially booked caterer and staff organized afternoon tea on the plateau. Ashore, at the inn, a 'black eyed maiden' (Roselle or Polly?) was charged by the landlady, Mrs Harris, to guide members of the group to where the peony plants were growing: 'We pass up the steep path; whence diverging we clamber downwards among privet, clematis and smyrnium [alexanders], down ledges filled with hyacinth, and odorous with the scent of the fast fading cowslips, among grasses . . . to the cliff edge' where the peony plants grew above an '80 feet' precipice. How different from the scene today! No one was allowed to touch the famous peony, but the same prohibition did not apply to the almost equally rare wild leek, specimens of which were taken to be grown in Cardiff gardens. A botanical ramble round the island was followed by tea '. . . prepared among the old buildings at the summit of the island, by Mr Chalk of Cardiff; whose good servants, what with the heat of the day, and the gypsy fire, and the labour of carrying the materials up the rocky way, are more dead than alive. The members, disposed picnic fashion, jovially fall to . . .'.

All too soon, and as still happens when steamer parties visit the island, the ship's whistle drew the party regretfully down to the beach to re-embark at the end of their memorable day. Nearly a hundred years later, during our archaeological work at the east end of the priory site, we were to find numerous cockle shells and an area of ashy deposit. Were these perhaps a legacy of the May 1883 festivities? This large group of visitors engaged its own caterers; others must have obtained food from the inn, sometimes to be consumed in the open air on fine days. A broken spoon which we found near the picnic spot, impressed with the letters 'F. HARR[IS]', is an archaeologist's dream – a find which can be extremely accurately provenanced and dated! It was perhaps similar picnic fire remains from this period, together with a crude hearth, which led members of Bristol Naturalists' Society to suggest that this was where the Victorian works foreman had his dwelling; but as we have already shown, his temporary home was the renovated 1776 tenement.

A Cholera Hospital for Steep Holm?

The faster steam ships which replaced sailing vessels during the nineteenth century allowed a rapid growth of trade and commerce between all parts of the world – but in turn contributed to the world-wide spread of Asiatic cholera. In the upper Bristol Channel the Port of Cardiff, with its extensive coal trade to the Middle East and India where the disease was common, suffered several disastrous epidemics. These were shown to originate from infected persons carried on incoming ships from abroad; and the authorities were acutely aware of the need to stop the disease from being brought into the trading ports. Isolation being the best means of checking the entry of the disease, preliminary negotiations were begun in 1883 with the respective owners of Barry Island, Sully Island, Flat Holm and Steep Holm, enquiring if a temporary cholera hospital might be established at one of those places. Steep Holm's answer was an unequivocal refusal from Col. Charles Tynte's solicitor: '. . . Col. Tynte regrets that he is unable to comply with your request as in the first place there are several people living on the island, besides children, and in the second place, the Government having a Battery of Marine Artillerymen there, might object, and it appears highly undesirable to expose these various persons to the risk of such a fearful thing as cholera. [signed] R. Bere.'

The Marquess of Bute, who owned Flat Holm, might have voiced exactly the same objections, but chose not to do so. He agreed to the building of the proposed isolation hospital on that island. His consent caused great alarm to all those connected with the farm, lighthouse and fortifications. Who would buy the lambs, fowls, eggs, butter, milk and vegetables produced there? No tourist would wish to visit Flat Holm – and what about the risk of infection to those living on the island? Forceful protests were received from Trinity House, and the army vigorously complained of the danger to personnel manning the guns. But all was to no avail. The first tented hospital came into use in September 1883, when three patients from an incoming ship were treated, one of whom died. This resulted in more objections from the military authorities and from Trinity House: '. . . relative to the landing of a cholera patient from the ship *Rishanglys* on the island of Flat Holm . . . I am directed to draw your attention to the great risk to navigation which would be incurred in the event of either of the two keepers being suddenly attacked by cholera and . . . to suggest to your Board the immediate removal of all cholera cases from the island to Steep Holm . . .'. These representations had no effect, and in 1886 a four-bed ward was constructed from an old barn. Finally a pavilion-style hospital capable of accommodating twelve beds, was built on Flat Holm in 1896 – by which time medical knowledge had advanced enough to make it virtually redundant although it remained in a state of readiness until July 1935, with the amply compensated farmer acting as caretaker.

In the early years of the hospital the question also arose of extending the use of the Flat Holm anchorage for cholera infected vessels to include any such ships bound for Bridgwater. Steep Holm was again suggested as an alternative. The proposal received a brusque reply, Capt. Jobson, the Bridgwater harbourmaster, stating that he had sailed up and down the Bristol Channel for twenty-six years or so, that the anchorage at Steep Holm was little used, and that no practical seaman would anchor there for more than one tide.

An Unexpected Court Case

Returning to the Harris saga, the final blow to the family business ventures on Steep Holm came on 30 May 1884, when two inoffensive gentlemen visiting the island inn ordered half a pint of beer and a gill of whisky. The sequel came three months later, on 25 August, at the Petty Sessional Court held at Axbridge, when Frederick Henry Harris was called to answer charges of selling intoxicating liquors without having a licence. The charge of selling alcoholic drinks was not disputed. Indeed Frederick Henry said that he and his father had done so for thirty-eight years! On the question of not having a licence, he reminded the local magistrates that the island was several miles out to sea, and not within any parish. Never before had they been asked to have a licence, or called into question for not having one. To the astonishment of the barrister appearing for the Inland Revenue, this defence was readily accepted by the Axbridge magistrates. His own well-reasoned arguments – that measured from the tip of Brean Down, Steep Holm was actually slightly less than three miles from the mainland; and that the Court at Cardiff had recently found in favour of the Crown in a similar case against the innkeeper at Flat Holm – were discounted. The charge against Frederick Harris was dismissed.

After registering dissatisfaction with the magistrates' decision, the Inland Revenue took the matter to appeal in London. The High Court case was heard on 10 March 1885, when Justices Matthew and Smith ruled that in future Mr Harris must apply the mainland laws of licensing and excise duty to his Steep Holm trading ventures. There was little future profit in having to abide by such rules. With Frederick Harris (senior) already deceased, his son left Steep Holm which had been his home for so many years, to concentrate on his cargo carrying and pleasure trip work. Under the local rules for ferrying passengers on trips to the islands from Weston, as a First Class boatman he was entitled to charge 12s for a party of twelve, and 1s for every additional person wishing to travel to Steep Holm. All pleasure boats plying for hire had to have the number of persons to be carried painted in words on the inside of the stern in legible letters. In theory a stay of not less than three hours was guaranteed on each trip.

To Flat Holm

The tenant farmer who was unfortunate enough to be living on Flat Holm when the first tents had been erected as a temporary isolation hospital had suffered substantial trading losses. In April 1881 there had been twenty-six people on that island. Master Gunner Thomas Barrett had his two young sons and a daughter staying with him, and five gunners in his charge. Head Lighthouse keeper William Dale with his wife and two sons occupied one Trinity House cottage, and an assistant keeper had the other. Henry Morgan, his wife, and eight children, their governess and a servant girl lived in the hotel, and he also farmed the land. The cholera scare was to change everything for them. After the adaptation of a farm building to enlarge and make more permanent hospital accommodation, the tenant and his family left, and by 1889 the farmhouse was in a poor state of repair. Two years later, a nurse and attendant were 'in residence' in the hotel, which they used as their office.

Although Frederick Henry Harris had left Steep Holm when the 1885 High Court case diminished his hopes of maintaining good profits there, island dwelling was his life, and he kept a shrewd eye on prospects of another lucrative tenancy. In the early 1890s he became the new farm and inn tenant on Flat Holm, where he also earned a regular salary as caretaker of the isolation hospital. His son Frank Harris succeeded him in these posts. Frank had been lucky to survive a childhood fall over the cliffs on Steep Holm which left him scarred for life; and he never forgot his grandfather's emergency first aid treatment of bathing the injuries in brandy! Again, father and son cheerfully dispensed drinks at all hours; to clash on more than one occasion with the constabulary over their right to flout mainland laws. Eventually Frank was in his turn hauled before the (Welsh) magistrates, in 1922, for serving alcohol on Sundays. Consequently voyages from Wales, to avoid strict Sunday teetotal rules in that country, lost some of their popularity – with tea becoming the strongest beverage served! The Harrises remained on Flat Holm until the Second World War, when the military evacuated the family, took over the farmhouse home, and moved Frank to live alone in a small adjoining cottage, to act as postman and boatman for the soldiers. Memories of this adaptable character were again revived when, in 1980, one of his twin sons visited Steep Holm with his family.

Despite the responsibilities of Flat Holm it had been difficult for the Harris family to abandon Steep Holm completely, and until he died in 1913 Frederick Henry Harris kept returning there to help with the boating and fishing, or occasionally to act as caretaker. He recalled that they 'ran the Steep Holm fishing from Flat Holm as the inn was often flooded at high tide', and because by the early years of the twentieth century the building had become totally ruinous. At one stage a Steep Holm peony was taken across to Flat Holm and planted in the inn garden there, where it and its successors survived for many years. Now a fine specimen is growing near the lighthouse, suitably protected from the attentions of the rabbit population.

One unique Harris connection with Steep Holm was retained by the child with the extraordinary name of Beatrice Steep Holm Ann Cooper Harris, who was born on the island in 1872, although it was not until 1884 that she was christened by one of the Bristol Channel Missioners. She was later to become Mrs Wellings, when she married a Bristol Channel pilot.

One New Tenant After Another

From 27 July 1885 the hopeful new occupiers of Steep Holm were Mrs Caroline Davies and her two adult sons, Harold and Wallace (Harrold and Wallis in the agreement) paying a rent of £35 per annum, with very flexible terms of three, five, seven or ten years for the lease. The fact that the first half year's rent was waived on the understanding that repairs were carried out supports Frank Harris's memories of the dilapidated condition of the storm-washed inn. The nearby well and the catchment tank adjoining the inn provided sufficient water for their needs. Fishing gear left on the island was taken over by the new tenants at valuation. Family traditions tell of the determined Mrs Davies going to the mainland to shop. On returning to the quayside, she found her ferryman 'dead drunk' in the bottom of the boat. Rather than miss the tide and have to stay ashore all night, she somehow sailed the boat alone. Her son stood on the island cliffs watching its erratic progress through his telescope, terrified for his mother's safety, but to his amazement and relief she managed to reach the beach without capsizing.

With the help of a maid they tried to run the fourteen-room inn as the Harris family had in the past, by advertising day excursions or holidays, boating, fishing and shooting. Wallace unsuccessfully attempted to introduce Belgian hares to improve the shooting; and the farm included cattle, sheep, goats, pigs and poultry – with the inevitable donkey. He grew oats, barley and vegetables, as well as producing his own hay. Two farm labourers were employed, possibly living in the farmhouse, and several more men were taken on for the winter fishing, when as much as two tons of fish could be caught on one tide. Cardiff market took large quantities of cod, sprats, whiting, skate and conger.

But the island did not live up to the family's dreams, and after only a year their stock and equipment was sold to yet another new tenant, Thomas Henry Waite-Hall, of the Crown Inn, Glastonbury. For £250 he acquired 'furniture, fittings, utensils, 4 head of cattle (3 heifers and a steer), 5 goats, 10 pigs, hay, the yawl or cutter called *Lance*, and 4 other boats'. Waite-Hall was a good hotelier, and a letter of 20 August 1887 from a well-satisfied guest described his very pleasant stay at the Holm Hotel, as it was then known:

The isle . . . can be often reached in calm weather without any fear of discomfort by yacht - as the *Daisy* and *Osprey* – by boat, or by Mr Perry's small steamer. I passed over in the *Daisy* managed with skill by Mr Harris who has the reputation of being one of the most experienced and safest sailors on the Severn Sea. I found good accommodation at the Holm Hotel and can truly say that Mr Hall's cheap tariff is an extra inducement to those who, like myself, are not blessed with a superfluity of this world's goods. A nice sitting room, a good piano, good plain board, and decent lodging can be obtained at about half the usual seaside charges. Mr Hall's sister is a very attentive and obliging hostess and is indefatigable in her efforts to make her visitors comfortable.

On exploring the island I found that it consists chiefly of a plateau covered with thick short grass which evidently in favourable seasons furnishes nourishment to a small flock of sheep; in fact the present flock of 60 or so Hampshire Downs and the cow and calf give proof of the truth of this assertion, and the goats of the island seem to be thoroughly in their element. . . .

The lessee of the island has in a room of his hotel some dried petals of that very rare flower, the single peony, which blooms here in May or June, and which is so valued by botanists. . . . I returned from the Steep Holm invigorated by the health-giving ozone, and never felt better than now. The return trip was made in Mr Perry's steamer, and it took 20 minutes to land at Knightstone, the sea being as calm as a pond. . . .

Mr Waite-Hall should have been on the brink of another successful Steep Holm tenancy to rival that of the Harris family, but despite his ability to provide excellent service and accommodation something went wrong. Were his charges too modest to cover his expenses? Were there too few tourists sampling the delights of the island? Did a poor season or two demolish his hopes of a thriving farm? Or, remembering what Frank Harris had said about the inn being built too close to the sea for comfort, was it flooded once too often? The inn closed, the farming ceased and the buildings were left empty, to fall into a sorry state of disrepair. Despite the presence of the remaining gunners, considerable damage was caused by vandals. The rabbiting rights had been let to Banwell Brothers, of the Swan Hotel in Weston, but unauthorized shooting became a problem. On 23 May 1891 Mr Roland Perry, the agent, was forced to put an announcement in the press that no one would be allowed to land on the island without a written authorization from the (remaining) lessee, the army.

A Fishing Tragedy

During the winter fishing season Roland Perry engaged local boatmen to remain on the island, to look after the stall nets on the beach and to tend cod-lines set out about 400 yds off shore. The small punt which he provided for this purpose does not seem to have been adequate for work in the strong tidal currents around Steep Holm.

On 23 December 1893 Joseph Ellard, husband of Violetta, and George Fisher were out fishing the cod-lines in calm weather. They cleared the north lines, then came ashore for some stones to sink the middle line opposite the beach. A third fisherman, William Hayden, who was on shore mending nets, watched them row around to the south side. Ten minutes later a sudden squall alarmed him, for the sea instantly became turbulent and the little punt was out of his sight. He hastened up to the plateau, but could not see the boat. Corporal Reed, one of the garrison soldiers, believed it to be safe in the lee of the island – but it was not seen again until it was found in Berrow Bay two days later. Ellard's body was washed ashore on Brean Sands six weeks afterwards, on 13 February 1894. At the resulting inquest it was established that the men were experienced boatmen, who had no chance of survival in those conditions with such a small boat. Joe Ellard is remembered for building some of Weston's fleet of 'flatners'. To us, his death that Christmas seemed particularly tragic, when we discovered that only a few years earlier two tiny children had been buried in Weston cemetery: Florence Blanche Ellard, 19 August 1885, aged five weeks; and Violet Bessie Ellard, 19 February 1887, aged four months.

The derelict inn, 1930s

A Last Distant Glimpse of the Military

The rule about obtaining written authorization from the army before landing on Steep Holm was taken seriously by the organizers of an 1898 excursion enjoyed by members of the Geological Society. Their report is carefully prefaced with the words 'Leave having previously been obtained from Col. Tyler, the Commandant of the district . . .' From the description of their visit we also learn that already the inn was 'now ruined'. Before many years had passed it was to become quite derelict. It was certainly roofless and windowless by 1910.

From Steep Holm the Geological Society went to Flat Holm, and when crossing the dividing channel in their steamer, the *Merrimac*, they passed a small steam launch conveying General Sir Richard Harrison on what must have been one of the last tours of inspection of the two island forts. Perhaps feeling slightly snubbed, they recorded: 'Our flag was dipped by way of salute, but met with no response. . . .' Did the worthy general have too many problems on his mind when he failed to order an acknowledgement of their courtesy salute?

Chapter Sixteen

INTO THE TWENTIETH CENTURY

By contrast with the exciting events of the nineteenth century, the start of the new era was an anti-climax for Steep Holm. The farm was idle; the inn, which had been built in 1832 with such high hopes of profit, was derelict. The corporal and his small caretaker force of soldiers were soon to pack up for another posting; and the gun batteries, constructed at such enormous cost and with so much human effort, were to be abandoned. A scrap metal merchant who dismantled and took away the gun carriages found it unprofitable to remove the heavy weapons. With the civilian buildings mainly ruinous, and the War Department continuing to hold a lease on the fortification areas, the likelihood of attracting new tenants for Steep Holm was remote.

Occasionally adventurers sailed to the island, ignoring the old 'No Trespassers' notice on the beach; and Weston guide books continued to publish tables of boating charges for visits 'of not less than 3 hours'. Among these explorers were pupils from Brynmelyn School, Weston-super-Mare, founded in 1881 by genial botanist and local historian F.A. Knight, with his friend and co-teacher John Lawrence. Before 1900 Francis Knight was suffering from ill-health and had retired from teaching, to concentrate on writing books, of which *Seaboard of Mendip* is one of the best known; and John Lawrence had previously left the school. But the tradition which they had started of summer picnics combined with botanical expeditions for the children continued under the new headmaster, H.E. Landon, who was soon to acquire a personal but regretted niche in Steep Holm's history.

Strangers Are Introduced to Steep Holm

Cardiff Naturalists' Society also continued to make regular visits to the island, and on 25 May 1907 thirty-four members arrived, including Robert Drane, one of the Society's founders, who had no inhibitions about introducing a new species of wildlife to someone else's property. In his diary he afterwards wrote: 'The main reason for my own going was to take six of Millais' Orkney Voles, *Evotomys orcadensis* and liberate them on the island so as to form a colony of this new and northern species, so that at some time hence someone may be surprised [to find] it there.' (The Orkney Vole was not recognized as a separate sub-species until 1904.)

This experiment must have failed, for no positive sightings of voles have since been recorded on Steep Holm. The diary entry continued:

> The special plant of the island, the *Paeonia officinalis* (*mascula*) was there in bloom and our party was pledged before landing not to touch it *but think of it*, some miscreants had been there an hour or so before us and had gathered some (three) of its blooms and then threw them aside as they descended to join their boat so that we found them lying by the pathside and brought them home. I had one and Dr E.T. Vachell had the other two. We saw two Peregrine Falcons on the wing, they breed there annually and are as regularly robbed: also two Ravens, five Cormorants which nest there, and quite a number of Herring and Lesser Black-backed Gulls, also breeding and their eggs found freely. We saw also a tame pigeon, some Rock Doves, a white rat and some Rabbits. Amongst the plants we found the Leek *Allium ampeloprasum*, Tree mallow. . . . There has been no inhabitant on the island for several years. We were there from 4 to 10 o'clock p.m. during which time I kept two traps set for any local mouse or vole but caught nothing.

The bird sightings make familiar reading, as does the wanton spoiling of peony blooms. Much more intriguing – what was the 'white rat' which he saw on Steep

Cormorants on north cliffs – one adult with chick on the lower nest; two eggs in the upper nest, photographed in the 1950s

Holm, where no rats or mice have been recorded? An ornithologist, the Revd F.L. Blathwayt, who visited the island during the previous month, wrote in his diary: 'Went to Steep Holm with Sylvie, – had to row all the way there, and sailed back with very little breeze. Sea smooth. Hot sun.' – an unusually placid spring day! He recorded seeing the peregrine falcons nesting on the north cliffs, a pair of ravens with young near the old inn (with their nest not far above sea level), shelducks, a kestrel, herring and black-backed gulls, and several varieties of small birds – a familiar list to birdwatchers today.

The Sleeman Family Arrives

Col. Blandy's October 1908 letter to the Rt. Hon. Charles T.H. Kemeys-Tynte (8th Baron Wharton), giving notice to terminate the military lease of Steep Holm as from April 1909, at last allowed new occupiers to take over. In May James Sleeman, who had lived at the coastal town of Portishead since about 1890, and who was soon to move to Millend Mills, Eastington Maltings, in Gloucestershire, negotiated for and was offered the tenancy. The maltster did not wish to rent the island for his own residence, but for his nineteen-year-old eldest son (also called James) who suffered from tuberculosis, and who had been recommended to take a sea cruise. As this would have been too expensive the prescription was changed to the largest possible dose of sea air – and where better than Steep Holm, now available at a modest rent of £30 per annum, payable at half-yearly intervals? With the youngest son Thomas also having infected lungs, the family made arrangements for the two boys to live on the island with their brothers Jack and Oliver, their sister Madge and an aunt. One of our correspondents, writing some years ago, described the somewhat unusual complete abandonment of the Sleemans' mainland family home: '[They] lived in a house in an isolated terrace [South Road] at Portishead, down a rough road overlooking the site now occupied by the Power Station. A few years before the Kaiser's war they took the tenancy of Steep Holm, hired a tug, and put all the furniture, etc., on board, and the whole family migrated to the island. They abandoned their house in the terrace and never returned. . . . In the 1920s and 1930s it was derelict with broken windows and holes in the roof, falling into decay.' In fact the whole family did not go to the island, for the father commenced his malting business in Eastington, making the long journey to see his children as often as possible; but it seems strange that he allowed the old family home to fall into total disrepair.

The twenty-one-year lease of Steep Holm specified that 'the occupier . . . with all convenient speed put into repair the dwelling house [Farmhouse] with the outoffices used in conjunction . . . and the Barracks . . . and the buildings now standing and being upon the Island (other than the old building formerly used as a Hotel and the old cottage formerly used as a Store room which old buildings the Lessee is to be at liberty to put into repair if he so chooses).' This infers that the inn and either the tenement or Cliff Cottage were no longer considered priority for repairs, and also that work on both the barracks and the farmhouse was already necessary. In fact, when the family finally moved in – not until 29 December 1909 – they chose to make the cavernous but probably better maintained barracks their home, rather than the more compact farmhouse. Their decision may have been influenced by the far more plentiful water supply from the underground tank at the rear of the army buildings, and the ample, airy space for separate accommodation – but it could not have been easy to heat the large barracks. A donkey carried stores from the beach; and a marine winch, positioned above the pebbles, was used to haul small boats to safety beyond the reach of high tides. Goats were kept to provide the fresh and very necessary nutritious milk for the invalids; and fowls were housed in the 'Government offices', with gulls' eggs being collected in season. The underground ammunition stores proved to be perfect for keeping potatoes in good condition. More disappointing, they found the rabbits unfit to eat and a nuisance – for these long established residents enthusiastically welcomed the change of diet provided by newly-planted garden produce. The lads, anxious to restore grazing pasture, retaliated with snares and shotguns. The lucrative fishery was an essential source of income, quite apart from the best of the catch providing regular meals – and becoming vital if supply boats were forced to turn back when it was impossible to land goods, and Madge had only one more loaf in the locker!

Soon the family was to make headline news, for the *Daily Chronicle* sensed a good story, sending its local reporter and photographer to bargain with John Watts to take them to the island in his sturdy flat-bottomed boat. Front page pictures and an article extolling island life appeared in March 1910. But by the time the *Daily Mirror* photographer and reporter arrived in 1912, only Madge and James were living there, still with the goats, fowls, donkey and a spaniel – who had to be kept chained in case he mistook their pet Belgian hare for one of the island rabbits. There was a well-stocked bookcase of frequently read volumes, and tea was dispensed to the visitors, who were impressed by the courtesy of their hosts and the unexpected comfort of the barracks home. Although for a while delighted with the isolated life, the Sleemans found that lack of contact with the outside world was a drawback to island domicile. Being accustomed to 'modern' mainland living, then deprived of the benefit of speedy communication, caused frustration when having to rely on a bonfire, or heliograph, in the hope that someone would see their signals.

By 1913 Madge and her brother had left, for the bracing sea air and exercise had so benefited the invalids that first Tom, then James was able to return to the mainland; where Madge kept house for her father at Eastington, while James helped with the business. Among local men employed by the Sleemans for the main winter fishing season, Frederick Henry Harris makes a re-appearance – as caretaker of the island in early 1913. In his spare time he partially repaired Cliff (or Smugglers') Cottage for use as a net store. By then an old man, he was happy to tell tales of his father 'brewing and distilling' using barley grown on the island; and to show visitors the nooks and crannies where contraband goods used to be hidden. He died shortly after these last reminiscences, and his friend Capt. J.R. Brueford, who had operated

The Daily Mirror

THE MORNING JOURNAL WITH THE SECOND LARGEST NET SALE.

No. 2,770. Registered at the G.P.O. as a Newspaper. MONDAY, SEPTEMBER 9, 1912. One Halfpenny

ISLAND KING AND QUEEN: BOY AND HIS SISTER WHO LIVE ALONE ON A LITTLE ISLAND IN THE BRISTOL CHANNEL.

Madge and James Sleeman in their island home, featured on the front page of the Daily Mirror, *1912. The beach (lower right) is reached by a sloping path bridging a gap in the rocks. A ladder is to one side of the path, and on the other there is a winch, formerly used for hauling up boats but during the Second World War relocated above the steep path to South Landing*

trading schooners until he was injured in a shipwreck off the Irish coast, looked after the island for a few weeks – but soon returned to his pleasure boating from Weston to the two islands. Steep Holm was once more uninhabited, with a notice on the beach: 'This island is private property and it is forbidden for anyone to trespass on it.' For the time being the Sleemans had abandoned the island, but they left the donkey and the goats to graze at will on the plateau, with furniture, fishing and trapping equipment being locked in the barracks in case any of the family wished to return – for they did not relinquish their twenty-one-year lease.

Thieves – and Trespassers!

While living on Steep Holm the Sleemans had tried to enforce the rule that anyone wishing to land there should ask for permission; but there was so much disruption that consent to visits had to be withdrawn. Many times interlopers tried to force their way on to the island, and when the family departed people landed without restraint, with local boating advertisements encouraging the practice. Most visitors wished only to enjoy the scenery and the wildness of the place, or to view the abandoned forts; but inevitably some were intent on stealing or causing senseless damage.

In April 1914 James Sleeman (senior) went to the island to find that the barracks had been burgled. Every door and lock in the place was smashed, windows were broken, every drawer and cupboard had been forced open, and the roof had been damaged by stone-throwing. Silverware stolen included serviette rings, a teapot and a biscuit barrel. A copper kettle and a brass dinner gong were also taken, with a lead weight from the grandfather clock, a plate camera, a brass pump from the hand fire engine, a large swing fishing net, and a whole armoury of shooting equipment. The police were asked to investigate, and P.C. Carter went to the island on 18 May. It so happened that Brynmelyn schoolchildren embarked on their annual expedition to Steep Holm that same day, to explore the island and study the flora under the supervision of their headmaster, Mr H.E. Landon. He also took his little daughter who still recalls that visit.

Mrs Olive Hallam told us that if she had not actually been there to vouch for the truth, it might have been a chapter in schoolboy fiction. After swarming over the island looking for botanical specimens, the fifty boys were called together to sit on the grass and picnic baskets were opened. When her father stood up and leaned over to open a bottle of beer for himself, one of the Sleeman goats quickly spotted a tempting target. Mr Landon was butted, the beer was spilled, and the boys were convulsed with laughter! That was by no means the end of that eventful day, as P.C. Carter arrived during the afternoon to investigate the burglary at the barracks. Several boatmen, who had sailed a fleet of boats across to the island, were discovered at the top of the path to the beach awaiting the return of their charges. Mr Landon, his daughter and the boys were still having tea; the constable was invited to join them – and he gladly accepted. Tactfully he failed to notice any joyriding by the boys on the back of the old donkey. Nor did he observe them collecting birds' eggs – but he did see that they had picked common blue flowers (bluebells) such as 'grew by the acre' in Weston Woods.

Another Court Case

When P.C. Carter reported back to Mr Sleeman he also happened to mention his picnic with the school party. Within a month the worried headmaster was taken to court by James Sleeman (senior) for trespass. After an adjournment to allow time for the lease to be produced, the case resumed in July. Boatmen admitted having always taken parties to the island, saying that they could not read the 'Private' notice. The prosecution commented that people had some extraordinary idea that Steep Holm was a sort of no man's land (they still have!). Despite Sleeman's contention that the schoolboys had wantonly trodden down the peonies and collected leaves and flowers, P.C. Carter's evidence cleared them of this charge. There was an 'end of term' atmosphere to the case, and having sharpened his wit on the various lawyers and witnesses, the judge had little patience with James Sleeman's claim for £20 compensation for trespass and damage. He awarded damages against the four defendant boatmen of 1s each, with the costs of the first hearing having to be borne by James Sleeman. Mr Landon had to pay 1s and other costs, after undertaking not to visit the island again without first obtaining permission – and from that day Brean Down became the future venue for Brynmelyn School's summer expeditions into the estuary.

World War

The light-hearted approach to the Brynmelyn court case heralded the end of yet another era, for the First World War began within weeks – on 4 August – and James Sleeman (junior), having overcome tuberculosis, was to be killed in the fighting. As far as Steep Holm was concerned, all was quiet for over a year after war was declared. The Sleeman family, of course, still held the lease; but in December 1915 the island was requisitioned by the Admiralty 'for the duration'. Coastguards were stationed on the rock, sweeping sea and skies with their field glasses, and signalling to Barry when necessary; but having few war duties, they occupied some of their spare time by observing and reporting on sightings of migrating birds.

The earliest recorded Steep Holm ghost story belongs to this era, when a Cardiff lady was staying in the barracks with Mrs Smith, housekeeper to Tom Sleeman, who had now returned to live on the island. The coastguards were billeted elsewhere, probably in the farmhouse, and Mrs Case described the barracks as partitioned into separate rooms. Her bedroom window was wide open one warm moonlight night when she was awakened by the sound of steady tramping of feet on the gravel outside. She jumped out of bed but could see nothing, although the tramping still went on. She wondered if it could be the coastguards on watch, but next morning her hostess assured her that it was not the coastguards. She and Tom Sleeman had often heard this sound. It was the footsteps of monks who had lived in the priory hundreds of years before!

Yet Another Court Case

James Sleeman (senior), plaintiff in the trespass case of 1914, was in 1917 himself answering a charge. The National Insurance Scheme had been introduced in 1911, and for several years he had failed to pay any contributions for the island's boatmen and fishermen. His solicitor's rhetorical question, 'How many of us actually do stamp employees' cards regularly every week?' does not seem to have helped his case, for Sleeman was fined 10s and ordered to pay all the contributions due.

Tom Sleeman's Tenure of Steep Holm

It took until 26 August 1919 for the Admiralty to decide that it was no longer necessary to hold the island as a coast watching station – more than nine months after Armistice Day; but Tom Sleeman, five years younger than his brother James, had already returned to Steep Holm during the war, with Mrs Smith as his housekeeper, and her young son. It must have been some time in the early 1920s that two young ladies surprisingly obtained permission to stay on the island for several days, taking their own food and blankets, and living in part of the barracks which was not normally used. Many years later, one of the girls told of the voyage.

They met Tom Sleeman, a taciturn man, at Knightstone Slipway, Weston-super-Mare, and boarded his boat. He started to row to Steep Holm, pointing the bows of the vessel well to the north of the target. Curious, and still full of enthusiasm, the girls asked him why he did this. Rowing hard across the current, he glowered at them before barking one word: 'Tide.' Cowed into silence, his passengers endured sea water washing around the boards, soaking their shoes, and becoming deeper each moment. At last they nervously drew Tom Sleeman's attention to this, to have an empty tomato can tossed to them between rowing manoeuvres, with another single gruff word: 'Bail.' They did – and those were the only two words which he spoke during the whole voyage – until to their great relief the girls were landed safely. Like so many later visitors, the sea crossing made such an impact on their memories that their adventurous stay on the island could not be remembered nearly as well!

That episode seems to sum up the character of Tom Sleeman in his younger days, although some forty years later he became more garrulous; and we listened with fascination to his voice in a recorded interview with Harry Savory. He told of goat breeding for milk, with the young kids being good meat; of market gardening, sheep, and poultry-keeping; of rabbit snaring by moonlight; fishing, net making, and net repairing. He recalled that when the ranks of stall nets were set on the beach (fifty of them in three tiers) the lowest row was usable only on the very big tides, when sea levels ebbed far out. Working with the tides he fished at all hours of the day or night.

Fishing stakes and nets on East Beach at low tide in the 1930s. The derelict inn can be seen, and Cliff Cottage is just visible above

Large shoals of sprats were the principal catch, and these were sent to Cardiff for sale, being transported in a small (engineless) pilot cutter owned by his father. This single masted sailing boat 16–18 ft long, and named *Edith*, was used also for carrying provisions to the island, and for 'exporting' garden produce and rabbits to Weston. To his brothers the rabbits had been a nuisance, but to Tom, on his return to Steep Holm, they were a source of profit. He remembered them as 'small, but good', for there was plenty of grass on the island plateau, so that 'it was like walking on velvet'. How different from the rampant scrub which has taken over since the Second World War! The formerly reticent islander described how he had watched the peregrine falcons teaching their young to hunt, and how he took shelduck eggs, which were 'good eating, better than hen's eggs' by using a crooked stick to roll an egg out – as the bird would not lay again if a hand was put into the nest.

Was it the same old billy goat of Landon fame, which always watched for a chance to corner Tom Sleeman, but never managed it? On one occasion, when the barracks needed painting, men were brought to Steep Holm one evening and shown what needed doing, before spending the night in Cliff Cottage. Early next morning they were due to start work, but did not appear for breakfast. Tom walked down to investigate, and found the goat standing guard outside, with the frightened men having been unable to sleep as he butted the door at intervals during the night, and refused to let them out!

It had to be Sleeman who told the next ghost story of the island! Moonlight was best for tending the fishing nets at night, and his dog, happily chasing rabbits near Garden Battery, suddenly showed signs of terror, refused to move and had to be carried back to the barracks. After that first time he would not go past the battery at night. Elaborating on Mrs Case's First World War story, Sleeman told of often hearing a 'sentry' marching up and down on the pebbles spread outside the barracks 'but did no one harm'. Could it have been his own donkey, or the goat, testing their master's nerves? Tom Sleeman knew how to tease his listener, with a good story of the only time he actually 'saw' a ghost. As he hurried down the path past Cliff Cottage early one morning to tend his fishing nets, 'a great white thing loomed up and wrapped itself around me. I can tell you, I wasn't half scared'. Then he admitted that it was just a sail drying on the rails outside the cottage that had been suddenly lifted by the wind!

Poachers and Robbers

In 1928, some time after Mrs Smith had returned to the mainland and with two years of the lease still remaining, Tom Sleeman gave up island life to become a fishmonger's assistant in Weston. His Steep Holm property was left unattended for long periods, and the boating fraternities on both sides of the estuary inevitably took advantage of 'The Hermit's' absence; which was an open invitation to poachers who soon became too confident. It was probably Harry Cox, the dedicated bird-warden of Brean Down, with his habit of sweeping both sky and sea with a telescope, who first noticed the two small sailing boats which had anchored overnight off Steep Holm's East Beach. Tom Sleeman was alerted, and accompanied by P.C. Hanham he set off for the island, in Frank Watts (senior's) motor boat. As they drew near the intruders' anchors were hurriedly lifted, and they set sail for the Welsh coast – but there was little wind, and they were quickly overhauled. As the pursuers gained, the four occupants of the *Whitewing* appeared to be throwing objects overboard; one of which, floating back to the motor boat, was seen to be a volume of *Encyclopaedia Britannica* – stolen from the barracks. Two of the fleeing passengers carried sporting guns, and there was a dog in the boat. Later a sack containing ten dead rabbits was found on board, providing sufficient evidence to convict all four persons for trespassing in pursuit of game. Two of the six occupants of the second boat to be chased also carried sporting guns, and one sack contained four live rabbits.

The court case was heard early in 1930. Frank Watts, who said he had tried to retrieve a sodden encyclopaedia from the sea, 'but it had slipped from my hand', took Constable Hanham and Tom Sleeman back to Steep Holm immediately after the chase on 15 September 1929. They found a pickaxe which Sleeman did not recognize on a garden seat outside the barracks. This tool had been used to break into the building. In the dining room were five remaining volumes of the encyclopaedia – the others were missing. One of the defendants admitted taking a book from the 'ruined house' as it 'seemed a pity to let such a good book spoil'. He was fined an extra 10*s* on top of the 10*s* fines plus costs levied on all defendants who had given their correct names and addresses to the plucky constable who had boarded the boats in mid-Channel. Those who had given false names and addresses were fined 12*s* 6*d* for causing 'a good deal of trouble' in tracing them.

A decade later Joe Walford, a Second World War soldier, was saddened to see valuable old books piled outside the barracks. Could these have been the remainder of the Sleeman library?

A Removal from Steep Holm

In June 1930 the Sleeman's twenty-one-year lease of Steep Holm expired, and Tom finally relinquished his island retreat, five of the younger local boatmen helping him to move house. Heaving the cumbersome furniture from the barracks to the beach and loading it on to waiting boats was no easy task, as Alfred 'Juicy' Payne recalled to us nearly fifty years later. On the day all the local boatmen had come to an agreement – the youngsters would do the heavy work involved in the removal while the older men touted for the easier 'round the bay' trips – afterwards to share out all takings equally. This arrangement was by no means uncommon and usually worked very well. But this time a strong on-shore breeze made the sea so choppy that there were no customers for the bay trips. After slaving all day, the five young men found that theirs was the only money earned – and took home 9*d* each!

The epilogue to the Sleeman occupation of Steep Holm took place at Stroud County Court later in 1930, when the 8th Baron Wharton was awarded £81 damages against James Sleeman (senior) in respect of dilapidations which had occurred during the family's tenancy. He had failed to abide by the contract of twenty-one years before, that the buildings would be kept in reasonable repair. Unchecked ivy growth had sent tendrils under some slates and gales had dislodged others, causing leaks in the barracks roof. These may have been long-standing problems due to neglect. But despite the tenants being blamed also for broken windows, this damage was surely the result of vandalism after Tom Sleeman had returned to the mainland to live.

Repairs – and a New Lessee

Before the island could be re-let it was necessary to make urgent repairs to the barracks roof; and, as a practical measure, the south windows were modified. Work was also needed on the bridge above East Beach. Years before a part of the path at this point had been washed away in a storm, and the gap had been bridged by heavy wooden beams and planks which needed regular replacement. This time 'unclimbable' iron railings were to be erected at the approach to the bridge, with a flight of shallow steps leading to a locked gate. A new 'No Trespassers' notice was erected yet again.

The Barracks in the 1930s. The large windows have been boarded up and smaller glazed frames inserted. There are only two doors to the main building. During the Second World War the second window to the right of the doorway dated 1867 (left) was converted into an additional door, and the two buildings were joined by a brick kitchen

Instructions to the builder carrying out the work were typical of general island practice. Slates needed for the barracks were to be obtained from disused military side-arms stores. To reduce the size of the south windows of the former master gunner's quarters an interior partition was to be removed, so providing the necessary tongue-and-groove boarding for infill panels, and leaving only small apertures. As far as practical, the 'new' opening window frames were to be taken from the long derelict farmhouse. Most of the other south facing windows were to be boarded up completely, with unwanted glass being salvaged to repair damaged panes at the back. Robbing old structures to build anew was an economy measure, but it did not save time. Repairs were not completed for several months. In 1931, before the work was finished, there was a further raid by a group of Welsh poachers. This time the lessee happened to be on the island, and he arrested the intruders to keep the court busy with another case of trespass.

Harry Cox

The new tenant was Harry Cox, F.Z.S. (Fellow of the Zoological Society), a well-remembered personality in the Weston-super-Mare area. Born at Stow-on-the-Wold, Gloucestershire, he had developed a keen interest in natural history while living in the Cotswolds; and on coming to Weston to live, in 1911, he was at once attracted by the isolated Brean Down headland, with its bird population and rare plants. It was at his instigation that the Bird Society (later the Royal Society for the Protection of Birds) acquired the promontory in September 1912 and had it scheduled as a bird sanctuary, subsequently appointing Harry Cox as its warden.

From his home at Bella Vista, Clifton Road, Weston-super-Mare, Cox, regularly travelled the winding roads which are still the circuitous route to the Down, often camping out for several days in the little iron shed which he constructed for himself there. At night the gleam of his oil lamp shining through the window was clearly visible from Weston sea front, and is one of the many memories which old Westonians have of him. Studying and protecting the flora and fauna, he acquired a considerable local reputation, enhanced by the photographs which he took to illustrate his lectures and articles. Although in demand as a knowledgeable and humorous guest speaker at meetings, he sometimes forgot that his audiences wished to return home at a reasonable hour! This was the man who was to extend his conservation activities to include Steep Holm. For the first time the island became principally a nature reserve. Harry Cox was determined to protect the wildlife and rare plants from unwelcome visitors; and when he was not there, the 'No Trespassers' notice and locked gate were made more effective by his constant surveillance of the landing beach from his Brean Down eyrie. Publicity gained by uncompromising court cases which he brought against unauthorized visitors helped to spread the message that in future people must land on the island only by special favour; but despite his natural antipathy towards poachers, rabbit-shooting parties were encouraged – under his strict supervision – although they were often disappointed with their 'bags'. He was harsh with over-enthusiastic botanists. On one well-remembered occasion an invited party had been allowed to view the peony. Afterwards he alleged that someone had picked a bloom, and scolded the visitors unmercifully before escorting a subdued group back in the boat. Yet on occasion he gave favoured friends peony seeds or even plants as souvenirs of their visits.

Cliff Cottage Inhabited for the Last Time

Harry Cox seldom stayed on Steep Holm for any length of time, preferring to be on Brean Down, and to escort visitors across the water when necessary. He wrote in 1933 that the island was not inhabited except in winter when a few fishermen employed by him lived there. For the last time winter fishing was carried on from Cliff Cottage – once elegantly built as a smaller imitation of the contemporary 1832 inn. Now it was reduced in size, with a shanty-style roof, to provide a temporary

Fishermen on East Beach, nets on 'Gooseneck', mid-tide, in the 1930s

Cliff Cottage in use for the last time, as a fishermen's store with nets drying outside, in the 1930s

home – while still being used as a net store. Sprats, whiting, cod and skate were caught in considerable quantities. Just a few years later this modest dwelling was once again in ruins; the fallen roof littering the floor, window glass shattered, but with the words 'Home, Sweet Home' still traceable above the fireplace. From this last attempt to profit from the Steep Holm fishery a salmon trap of withies was rescued, and kept in the barracks – until in recent years it was broken up and used by visitors as kindling for the fire.

Transient Adventures of the Gillards

Rents from the winter fishery helped to offset expenses; and in 1934, for a while, Harry Cox sublet a part of the barracks to a young family who could live permanently on the island and act as deputy wardens. Mr and Mrs Francis Gillard from Winchester, were accompanied in their short-lived adventure by their fourteen-month-old adopted daughter, by Mrs Gillard's young brother, and by a friend who was a soldier just home after service in India. During the voyage out to the island on 'housewarming' day, Mrs Gillard was thrilled at the prospect of living on a small remote island away from mainland hustle and crowds, and she talked

The Gillard family start their sub-tenancy on Steep Holm in 1934. Harry Cox takes the child from her mother with Francis Gillard looking on. The boat is loaded with their luggage as it grounds on East Beach

romantically of 'sleeping on the cliff-top with the sound of the sea always in our ears'. They had plans to keep goats and to grow all their own vegetables: had no one told them of the hungry rabbits? It was arranged that if help was needed a large white board would be displayed on the cliffs where Harry Cox could see it through his telescope. In an emergency the reverse of the board, bearing a large black disc on a white background would be similarly placed. But, of course, there were difficulties. At first they had to rely totally on stores taken with them, which were replenished when conditions allowed. Supplies were delayed, or were spoiled by sea water. Sometimes boats arrived but were unable to unload their cargo as surf thundered on the beach. Provisions were used more quickly than anticipated – and, predictably, mist or driving rain prevented their message board from being seen.

Three months after their optimistic arrival, Harry Cox received a message that one of the islanders was needed urgently at Winchester. The sea was too rough for him to make the journey to Steep Holm in a small boat, but he ingeniously solved the problem of communicating the message by persuading the captain of P. & A. Campbell's pleasure steamer *Waverley* to divert course en route from Weston to Cardiff. She approached the south cliffs close enough to allow a message to be shouted through a megaphone – but no one could leave the island in those conditions.

A few months later, on a Sunday afternoon in September 1934, members of the Gillard family gained the distinction of being rescued by Weston's new lifeboat on its first service mission. Still too new to have been officially named, the *Fifi and Charles* was called out when the Gillards' vessel suffered an engine failure, and was drifting helplessly in a choppy sea. Under the direction of Coxwain Fred Webb, the lifeboat towed the vessel back to Anchor Head having rescued its occupants. Shortly afterwards the Gillards returned to a more predictable existence on the mainland.

Another Sub-Tenant

From local people we learned of Mr Harding, who married Miss Hunt, a tailor's daughter of Burnham-on-Sea. He ran a thriving charabanc service, then sold out and took the sub-tenancy of Steep Holm in 1936. The family moved to the island with the intention of keeping sheep and tending the fishing; but this was another ill-fated venture. Within a year their boat was damaged on the beach, Mr Harding was marooned for several days, and ambitions of making a living on the island came to an end. So, once again, Steep Holm and the vagaries of the sea had defeated efforts by mere humans to make a permanent home on its rocky plateau; and it was left to the wildlife, under the supervision of Harry Cox, who occasionally permitted selected parties to enjoy conducted tours, or even to stay for a few nights.

Observations of Birds and Flora

James Sleeman, when making a comprehensive list of Steep Holm birds in 1916, had said of the puffin: 'Some ten years ago the Puffin was a well known islander. It was last known to breed on [the] island during the Spring of 1909.' The Revd F.L. Blathwayt revisited the island with a group of Bristol Naturalists on 2 May 1936, after a break of twenty-nine years. When recording his 18 April 1907 sightings in his diary he had added a comment that the boatman had reported seeing 'numbers of Lundy Parrots (Puffins) . . . in July among the gulls on the cliffs. . . . Guillemots also were to be seen around the island in Winter.' On his later visit of 1936 he was again fortunate to have 'A perfect day.' This time he travelled in the motor launch *Quest*, and as before circled the island to check on the colony of cormorants: 'About 10 nests apparently & to me light-breasted non-breeding birds. I should think 10 pairs of breeding birds about the mark.' He was guided by Harry Cox to a Peregrine Falcon's nest: '. . . after a rough scramble but without rope, and saw the 4 eggs in a very suitable recess in the rock. On the ledge were feathers of birds chiefly pigeons . . . with rings on them!' Apart from recording his estimates of the quite small numbers of great black-backed gulls, he commented on 'the *enormous* increase [in herring and lesser black-backed gulls] since 1907 . . . breeding all over the island . . . almost everywhere . . . Cox thought numbers were 2-1 in favour of Herring but I should think the numbers were about equal and in all from 600 to 800 pairs but this is only a guess . . . many full clutches of eggs . . .'. From the boat he noticed five ravens, the 'three young about as big as the parents', and 'about 20-30 pairs [of Shelduck] on cliffs and sea'. In all he estimated seeing twenty species of birds on the island. Of the flora he noted that the peony was 'well grown and strong . . . to the N. of landing beach and well *above* it. In one spot was a good patch of a half dozen or so plants showing about 10–12 buds . . .' with the 'Great Garlic [wild leek] . . . on the cliffs to S. above the landing beach . . .'. What astonished him most was the alexanders: 'The most striking change botanically since my last visit was the *enormous* increase of this plant. The whole available surface of the island except part of the N. top and a few other parts seemed covered with it flowering most luxuriously and pervading the air with its sweet sickly scent. . . . It is smothering the island and the small migrants are hard to spot as they take cover in it. Brambles, Privets and elders also abound and some smallish *Sycamore trees* at W. end.' Like so many other observers, he confused his compass bearings, for these trees grow only above East Beach, as do the 'Wallflowers, yellow . . . on parts of the old buildings and rocks at W. [again, east] end'.

Last Years of a Pre-War Haven

Newspaper feature writer Ron Bailey was another visitor accompanying Bristol Naturalists' Society members on a similar visit during the nesting season. He afterwards recalled hordes of sea birds rising as the boat approached the beach; the trek to the island plateau, past the ruined inn and cottage; angry gulls swooping to the attack as the visitors threaded their way around nests which littered the ground; and the Victorian barracks which Mr Cox used as his temporary home when staying on the island.

Benches apparently used by the soldiers were still in the building – and a little gallery of pin-up pictures of shapely actresses, with tiny waists, bustles, and 'hour-glass' figures. Surely these keepsakes had not survived from the days of the last soldiers to be stationed on Steep Holm, as Ron Bailey suggested? Were they perhaps Edwardian postcards collected by the Sleeman family?

Bristol Naturalists' Society for several years obtained permission to camp in the barracks while conducting their annual studies. Published as a comprehensive report in 1939, this work has been invaluable to later researchers. Such groups, wishing to stay for a few nights, lived in the sparsely furnished main room of the barracks, which again became the theatre for more ghost stories. Stranded yachtsmen also contributed stories of sleepless nights and apparently inexplicable sights and sounds in the barracks. When on the island Harry Cox himself lived in a small room, formerly part of the master gunner's quarters, with a few 'rough pieces' of furniture, and his bed strategically positioned above a trap-door in the floor – to discourage nocturnal 'visitations'! The 49,000-gallon underground water tank was more than adequate for the needs of the warden and his visitors. He never used the old well, which, he said, 'yielded a very limited supply and looked more suitable for a lotion than a drink'!

To celebrate twenty-five years of caring for Brean Down, Harry Cox headed an appeal by the Royal Society for the Protection of Birds, sent in September 1937, to

A Christmas card sent by Harry Cox commemorates his joining H.M. Coastguard. Rudder Rock is pictured before the erection of the searchlight post above the arches

all those 'friends and sympathizers who have at various times accepted his hospitality at either Brean Down or Steep Holm and who have enjoyed his guidance and benefited from his expert information about those remote places and their occupants whom he knows and loves so well . . .'. This appeal was targeted to enrol 250 new subscribers to the Society.

A new structure, albeit a small one, was erected on Steep Holm in 1939. An Ordnance Survey triangulation pillar was positioned on the whaleback curve of the plateau to mark the highest point at 256 ft above sea level.

As ominous portents menaced world peace Harry Cox, veteran of the First World War, continued to be warden of Brean Down and Steep Holm. By Christmas 1939 he had become a member of HM Coastguard Coast Life Saving Corps, at the age of seventy. When asked if he wished to be supplied with mortars and maroons in case of emergency, as his island predecessor had been, he answered: 'If I wanted assistance I should light a fire or run up a flag.' However, he did condescend to have a wireless on his Brean Down base. But soon the peaceful atmosphere of Steep Holm, under the strict supervision of its dedicated warden, was to be shattered by the bustle and noise of yet more hurried building operations; and only a short time was to elapse before the old barracks was to resound to the voices of many more soldiers than the island had ever before seen.

Chapter Seventeen

WAR COMES TO THE ISLAND

Emergencies on Steep Holm

The outbreak of hostilities meant that, as in the First World War, coastguards were called in to man Steep Holm as a watching station. Even before the Admiralty's formal requisition order, sent to Harry Cox on 27 January 1940, three elderly ex-Merchant Navy men had been detailed for this duty. A dynamo-powered signal lamp, lit by vigorously pedalling a stationary bicycle, was their method of communication with the mainland; and above the beach a new notice flanked by barbed wire warned that under the powers vested in the Admiralty, no unauthorized person was allowed to land.

As winter drew on, air temperatures over the whole country plummeted, and life in the old barracks became intolerable – despite periodic motor boat deliveries of coal from Weston by fifty-seven-year-old Frank Watts (senior). In January 1940, for the first time in living memory, Blagdon Lake, nestling in a deep valley on Mendip, froze over; at Weston the sea spray turned to ice particles; and wet salty sand on the beach actually froze, to form a massive skating rink. It was not surprising that in such severe conditions the Steep Holm coastguards suffered from exposure, and one became seriously ill. Alerted by the signal lamp on 1 February, boatmen Frank and Ted Watts managed to reach the island and land under extreme difficulties, to find fifty-eight-year-old Harry Phillips suffering from double pneumonia, with a dangerously high temperature making him delirious. To get Mr Phillips back to the mainland quickly was essential, but an attempt to use a door as a stretcher to carry him to the beach failed. The boatmen were forced to return to Weston to summon help. Sea conditions prevented an immediate return, but next day they were back on the island with ambulance officers and a collapsible stretcher. This time, despite fierce currents and a swell which threatened to wash the boat on to the rocks every time it neared the beach, the coastguard, wrapped in blankets, was successfully taken aboard, and an hour later landed back at Weston.

In 1987 we were fortunate enough to meet his daughter. She detailed the events of that first wartime crisis on Steep Holm, and told us that she came to see her father several times as he recovered at Weston (old) General Hospital. She flew with her mother from their home town of Cardiff to Weston Airport in a twin-engine de Havilland Dragon biplane, which was a very expensive way of visiting, each return flight costing 9*s* 6*d*. At the outbreak of war Weston aerodrome had been requisitioned by the Air Ministry, but afterwards the Weston–Cardiff air service was allowed to reopen for a short period. Later the Dragons and Rapides were impressed into the Royal Air Force as communications aircraft.

Frank Watts (senior) had another adventure on Steep Holm when he holed his vessel trying to land coal and other supplies for the island coastguards. As he steered for the safe pebble beach, cross currents threw the boat off course, and a wave lifted the bows before crashing it down on a submerged rock. Water flooded in, and food supplies had to be hastily offloaded. When the tide receded, coastguards and boatmen worked together to bail out sea water and rescue sacks of coal. It was a race against time to uncouple and remove the engine and gearbox before the next tide came in, so that the lightened vessel could be dragged up the beach for temporary repairs. Frank Watts's son (also Frank, and owner of the present ferry boats for the island) told us how he came home on leave from the R.A.F., and assisted in towing the damaged boat back to Weston with a tarpaulin wrapped around the hull to keep it afloat.

The Army Takes Over

In May 1940 the disaster, and miracle, of Dunkirk brought this country to the brink of invasion from the French coast. The Admiralty requisition of the island was taken over by the army; and as part of the Severn defences Steep Holm and Flat Holm, with Brean Down and Lavernock were re-fortified. Once again Steep Holm was to be the scene of massive construction works, and this time the job was undertaken by soldiers. But even in this greatest emergency, it was to be 1941 before building could start. Meanwhile air raids on England had begun. The industrial cities and ports of the west were prime local targets, but Weston did not escape being bombed with incendiaries and high explosives.

It was against this background of tension and danger that Mark VII 6-in breech-loading guns – between thirty and forty years old, from warships which had been scrapped long ago – were withdrawn from armament stores at Cardiff, by the Royal Artillery Regiment. Civil engineering tradesmen who had recently been conscripted into the army found themselves drafted into a special military construction unit of the Royal Engineers, part of whose task would be the re-arming of the two Holms. Ex-soldiers from both regiments who served on Steep Holm at this time have never forgotten the extreme physical strain of working under harsh island conditions; the problems of tide and rough seas; the dangerous cliffs; and the narrow, twisting trackway to the plateau – a neglected path which had collapsed in some places, and at others was partly blocked by fallen rocks.

Mr J. Graddon, before his call-up for the army, had been an architect. He became one of the small team of specialists attached to the Royal Engineers directing the positioning and construction of the new military works to be built by the Pioneer

Corps on both islands and the two promontories, as well as at Portishead. Years later he recalled his wartime island experiences, remembering, for example, R.A. officers who were sometimes angry because they were not saluted – there was no time for such finer points of discipline – and whose 'advice' on the siting of gun emplacements was disregarded for practical reasons. For instance, one of their suggested positions would have placed the battery observation post in line of fire! But officers and men generally worked together, and all looked like navvies in the heat of the summer of 1941.

Indians and Guns Arrive

A small Indian Army contingent with mule teams arrived, and without their help in the initial stages the work could not have been completed within the timetable. It was the mules, brought to the island by tank-landing craft, who carried and pulled much of the heavy equipment to the summit; and it was also to be the mules who dragged up the first of the 6-in guns. The animals were stabled in the ruined farmhouse on the plateau, tethered to heavy iron rings removed from one of the Victorian gun batteries. Mule shoes, some specially made for giving the animals a better grip when climbing up steep slopes, have been found in debris on the priory site and elsewhere, and are now on display in the barracks. Regimental Sergeant Major Adams thought the Indians a fine lot of men, though with a different lifestyle from the English. Live sheep had to be transported to the island especially for them. These were killed and cooked by the Indians, and R.S.M. Adams remembered with pleasure the plates of curried food which they shared with him: 'believe me, an Indian, when he cooks a curried mutton, he makes a really good job of it!'

From ex-Sgt Harold Underhay, Royal Artillery, we learned how men from his detachment at Cardiff had been detailed to help with the shipment to the island of component parts for four of the heavy guns – barrels, shields, mountings, and operating mechanisms – all being carried on tank-landing craft. The first problem was getting everything ashore safely, with the treacherous tidal conditions. Artilleryman Reg Stone, an ex-grocer called up in 1940, was one of the men who accompanied the guns on the sea crossing from Barry Dock. He recalled in 1978 how they coped with unloading the guns in a rough sea off Steep Holm's beach:

> Cables were slung around them, and they were dumped into the water, to be hauled ashore a couple of days later when the sea had calmed down a bit. There were three lay-bys on the long haul up the cliff path, and we manhandled the guns up to the first lay-by using block and tackle. Afterwards the Indian Regiment with their mules dragged the guns up to the top on trolleys. The winch operated railway to the top had still to be built by the Engineers. With much of the construction work still to be done we had to sleep in tents; no Nissen huts had yet been put up and the old Victorian barracks were used at that time by the officers.

We were told of one 6-in gun barrel which, having been pulled laboriously almost to the top of the path, broke loose from its fastenings, to roll, slither and crash all the way to the bottom again. As with most of these memories of times long past, the aftermath of the accident could not be recalled. Mr Stone stayed on Steep Holm for only three weeks on this occasion, although two years later he was to return as N.C.O. in charge of a gun team. Ironically, one of the jobs he found himself doing after his first island visit was erecting Nissen huts (so badly needed on the island) at the mainland base at Cardiff.

Construction Starts

Whenever they could be spared from other tasks men were put to work on modifying the Victorian barracks. The two main buildings were joined by a brick-built kitchen, and a separate Victorian machine shop at the west end was connected to the former master gunner's quarters. The south-facing windows which had been boarded up during the early 1930s were partly bricked up, leaving the upper sections to be fitted with reinforced glass. A sergeants' mess Nissen hut was erected parallel to the main barracks room, and linked to it by a short passageway which effectively blocked the most easterly entrance to the main building. To allow general access a new doorway had to be made, by cutting away the stones below a window. This upset the symmetry of the Victorian front, but the alteration was so skilfully disguised that over the post-war years no one spotted the change; until we noticed something different about a pre-war photograph, which showed only two doors to the main building, whereas now there are three! The installation of electricity was another innovation, and there was even a cold store with cork-lined walls. With two large cooking ranges, the barracks was to be used both as the island headquarters, and as the NAAFI canteen. Many pieces of the familiar stamped crockery have been found scattered around the island.

New Gun Emplacements

The Victorian batteries not being considered suitable for mounting the 6-in guns, new emplacements were needed; and with the extra buildings required to house searchlights, generators, and diesel winches – as well as men and officers – construction work was on a scale similar to that of the Victorian fortification era; and so, once more, the face of the island was to be irrevocably changed by the threat of invasion. Instead of being spread more or less evenly around the perimeter of the island plateau as the Victorian batteries had been, the new concrete emplacements were grouped in just two pairs: Steep Holm South above the south-east corner of the island, and Steep Holm North at the north-west corner. With the Victorian military engineers having previously chosen the same advantageous situations for their own Garden and Summit batteries, partial destruction of these two earlier double gun emplacements was inevitable.

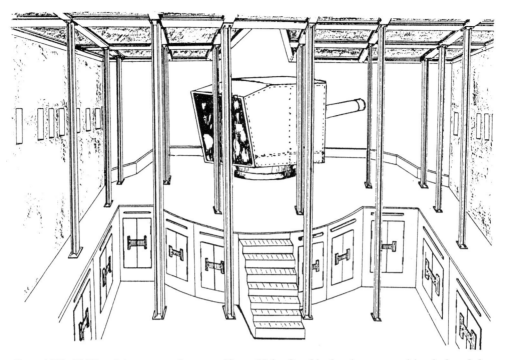

Second World War 6-in gun emplacement 'Steep Holm South', showing ammunition lockers below gun on mounting, protective concrete walling and 'plastic armour' roof supported on network of girders

A large and ugly concrete structure of blast walls and ammunition lockers was built behind each of the 6-in gun platforms. Unlike its Victorian counterpart, the modern gun was carried on a pedestal firmly bolted to the concrete, instead of resting on a revolving carriage. The eastern half of Garden Battery was completely buried beneath the new emplacement, and its 7-ton cannon (already cut into two sections in 1903) and pivot gun are missing – almost certainly removed from their former positions. One ex-soldier said he thought one or two old guns were sent for metal salvage when the re-fortification work started, but there is no firm evidence that they were taken from the island, so they may yet be found. The western barbette of the Victorian double battery was smothered with earth and rubble to the top of its parapet, to raise the level sufficiently to erect a concrete base for a sighting or instrument post, and a small shelter to be used by the gunners while on watch. Underneath the infill this half of the old battery was relatively undamaged by the new works; except that what might remain of the Victorian underground ammunition stores became inaccessible. In 1903 this battery's 7-ton cannon had been rolled to the ground below the barbette, and an attempt made to cut off its barrel. The scar can still be seen on this, the first gun that is now noticed on reaching the top of the path and upper steps from the beach. To complete Steep Holm South a second gun emplacement was erected at a lower level to the west of the first, with a flight of steps leading down into the gun position from the south perimeter path.

At the other end of the island, the Summit Victorian gun battery was badly damaged by another hastily erected defensive position – Steep Holm North. Here a 6-in gun emplacement was built over the north-eastern half of the earlier double gun battery, completely destroying it. The 7-ton cannon was rolled away, and is still perched beside the path close to the cliff edge. The Georgian pivot gun, with part of the 'racer', was taken out and left lying in the undergrowth. This seems to prove ex-Sgt Graddon's point when he said that none of the old cannons would have been buried beneath the concrete gun emplacements. One such gun has been discovered beneath the concrete base of the island's battery observation post, but such a building is subject to considerably fewer stresses than a gun emplacement, and we see no reason to contradict the expert technician who actually worked on the fortifications in 1941. A deep incision in the old Georgian cannon from Summit, near the rear of the barrel, suggests that an attempt was made to cut it up for Second World War salvage – or perhaps it was accidentally cut during work to modernize the gun position. The scrap metal merchant in 1903 could hardly have scored it in this way while it was still buried deep in the ground. Foundations for another Second World War emplacement at Steep Holm North caused further damage to the Victorian Summit site, piercing the brick barrel roof of one of the underground stores and partly filling it with a cascade of concrete and rubble. The access ramp and steps to the mainly preserved old barbette were also spoiled, although its guns and racer were left intact and the second ammunition store is still accessible.

The concrete sighting post, or instrument pillar, for use with the two 6-in guns at Steep Holm North, stands within an open, semicircular brick structure situated on top of the Victorian raised defensive bank at the rear of the old Summit gun battery. In the past this protective brickwork has been wrongly assumed to have been built during the Second World War, but close examination of old photographs and maps proved that the brickwork was built between 1886 and 1903 – obviously as a lookout and signalling point for the *Arrogant* bombardment of the nearby Rudder Rock battery in 1898. A 1913 article specifically refers to this feature, hard by the Summit Battery. In 1941 the Second World War construction engineers recognized the value of this excellent viewing point, and mounted their modern instrument pillar within it. There was no such protective brickwork around Steep Holm South's sighting post, but at each of these positions a small shelter was built to the rear. Ex-Sgt Graddon told us that originally the Second World War emplacements and guns were all open to the sky, until, as an afterthought, roofs of 'plastic armour' were added. These prefabricated slabs of tar and pebbles faced with iron sheets were set into frameworks of iron girders – each hurriedly erected in a day – as a protection against machine-gun fire from low-flying enemy aircraft. No one had much faith in the roofs, but they were never tested by enemy attack; in the event they withstood frequent firing practice, and remained in position until many years later.

Searchlight Posts

Besides the construction of these four emplacements, a similar number of searchlight posts were built low down on the cliffs, to the great peril of the men carrying out the work, not with the intention of seeking raiding aircraft but to sweep the sea, looking for torpedo boats or surfaced enemy submarines which might attempt to creep up the estuary under cover of darkness. One of the searchlight posts was constructed below and to the south-west of Tower Rock, with a long since eroded approach path. Another is at South Landing, and easily the most accessible, while the third, perched perilously upon Rudder Rock, is now out of reach – for the fixed vertical ladder has rusted away. The fourth clings to a rock pinnacle projecting from the north cliffs. Both at Rudder Rock, and for the North Cliffs searchlight, flights of concrete steps had to be built over the cliffs, with handrails on each side. To see this last searchlight post involves a descent down 208 narrow steps (now without handrails) which in places fly out clear of the steep rock face. Those brave enough to attempt this are rewarded by close-up views of the largest breeding colony of cormorants in the south-west.

Gun emplacements, searchlight posts, generator houses, a Battery Observation Post (which partially obliterated the Victorian single gun battery at Rudder Rock), nearly thirty Nissen huts, for use of officers and men, and the installation of light anti-aircraft guns: all had to be completed with extreme urgency.

Rudder Rock searchlight post camouflaged in 1943. An official war artist painting by Ray Howard Jones

A Pier, Quay, and Railway

From the start of the re-fortifying it was obvious that for this work, and also for the subsequent efficient running of the island as a military base, improvements had to be made to landing facilities and to the access route to the plateau. Plans were drawn up for a girder-type pier projecting seawards across East Beach. At its landward end a stone quay was to be built against the cliffs, connecting with the foot of the old zig-zag path. A railway to the top also had to be built. All this, although essential, was an additional time and labour-consuming operation.

The pier was to be approximately 120 yds long, and at its seaward end some 50–60 ft high, with wooden beams to protect ships coming alongside. Working on the beach, the first sappers immediately found themselves contending with the problem of the twice daily tides, which continually refilled with pebbles and silt the deep holes which they were laboriously digging for the foundations of the pier supports; and freshly laid cement was often washed away before it had time to set. As construction progressed the men were frequently working up to their waists in chill water. Building the 14 ft high stone quay at the foot of the cliffs was a little easier; the concrete plinth was laid, and facing stones for the retaining walls were obtained by the time-honoured island custom of taking them from elsewhere – on this occasion, by removing dressed stones from the walls of the Victorian Laboratory underground stores, other old gun sites, and the former side-arms stores.

Another group of sappers had the difficult task of straightening and improving the irregular and uneven path which originally had been cut in the early 1830s from the beach to the plateau. A firm three-legged zig-zag track emerged, wide and strong enough to carry a 1 ft 11½ in narrow gauge railway line, with space for points and winch houses at the intersections and at the top. For this the 1832 inn and Cliff Cottage had to be largely demolished; rock outcrops were cleared, using explosives; and the outer edges of the trackway were reinforced, or, in places, built up.

It was to be March 1942 before work on a totally different type of landing jetty at South Landing was undertaken. Here a stone-built series of steps and platforms was constructed from low water mark to the old lime kiln above this tiny beach, with a narrow gauge railway linking it to the perimeter path. Curiously, none of the ex-Army personnel can recall this landing ever being used. Even today it is utilized as little as possible.

Personal Memories

Fred Brueford, gunner, and son of ship's captain J.R. Brueford, who had lived on Steep Holm for a while in 1913, was serving on the island during the fortification works. Although not a construction engineer, he was detailed to help with building the pier; and he long remembered the tough conditions under which they all lived and struggled to complete tasks during exhausting shifts. The Indians were still dragging supplies to the top with their mules, for the railway was not yet ready; and everyone, sometimes grudgingly, had to help with the work of the engineers 'as there was all the building of the sites to be made'. Other ex-servicemen were inclined to express their views in much stronger terms! One even maintained that he was happier after being posted to 'Rommel's desert' – a different world where he was not constantly reminded of his Weston home, so near and yet so out of reach. Poor Sgt Stickler of Penarth! He would wake each morning and look towards his home town where he could almost see his wife hanging clothes on the washing line. To him, life was grim enough on Flat Holm, but Steep Holm was 'about the worst place I had ever been in my life'.

Infantryman Eddie Long of Tetbury had served with the Glosters in France. After bitter fighting during the retreat of 1940 he was one of 981 soldiers evacuated from Dunkirk by the former paddle steamer *Waverley* (later sunk on minesweeping duties). Following a brief spell in a rest camp he was seconded for construction duties on Steep Holm from mid-1941 until late spring 1942. On a return visit fifty years later he vividly recalled the regular processions of Indians with their panniered mules carrying coal and other supplies to the top of the island. To us, his description was a reminder of the Victorian military donkeys using exactly the same method for transporting stores. During his nine months on Steep Holm, the zig-zag part of the railway was completed, but trucks filled with sand and cement still had to be manhandled along the track from the Tombstone winch house points to the construction areas. Eddie has never forgotten the hazards of building the steps leading down to the searchlight post at Rudder Rock – and the even more notorious 208 steps flying out over the sheer north cliffs.

'Conditions on Steep Holm in 1941 were diabolical,' said ex-gunner Cyril Stickland. Of all his various wartime experiences – including being wounded at Amiens – he said that the short period which he spent on the island was among the roughest of the war. He was another who remembered sleeping uncomfortably in tents on the summit, and he confirmed other memories of the supply boat being unable to land provisions. There was one period when they were completely cut off for thirteen days which happened to coincide with his birthday. By then they were living on 'hard tack' (hard baked ship's biscuit), made a little more palatable with a spoonful of jam. To wash they stripped and sluiced themselves with cold water from a can. 'It was a good job we had mules on the island,' he said, 'otherwise we might have gone without water as well; but the mules needed a lot to drink.'

Disease!

The water supply was a real problem. It was not just that the large garrison (and ongoing construction work) required more water than could be provided by the old well and the 49,000-gallon Victorian catchment tank at the barracks. Disaster in the form of contamination had struck the island water early in the re-fortification period. Typhoid had been brought to Steep Holm by one of the muleteers, a carrier of the disease. It was Ivor Swarts, for many years a crew member of Barry lifeboat, who commented about the health of the men on Steep Holm in 1941 when, as well as the British troops, there were 'Indian Army soldiers on Steep Holm, with mules going up and down the cliffs, taking up guns and supplies. I saw them going there in the early part of the war, on a landing barge. Soldiers that were there had a pretty hard time, with a lot of illness and disease, through bad water and sanitary problems.' At least one man is believed to have died, and after the typhoid scare the use of island water was forbidden. All water supplies had to come from the mainland in barrels and 'hundreds of 4-gallon cans'. Two of these cans are now on display in the barracks.

When Gunner Stickland was posted away from Steep Holm the 6-in guns had not been mounted, but he recalled helping to haul up some parts using the still unfinished railway. He especially remembered one of the bogies tipping sideways off the rails, to balance precariously on the cliff edge with its gun cradle cargo in jeopardy – but later to be rescued. What seemed to be unending complications meant that to complete Steep Holm's re-fortification within six months, or even a year, was an impossible task, and much work remained unfinished at the end of 1941. But, in the urgency of war, the guns of Steep Holm North and Steep Holm South were then officially considered ready for manning by Nos 188 and 189 Coast Batteries respectively.

Lt L.R. Fisher, and Capt. J.R. Brougham were two of the 189 Battery officers who reported to the island at that time, and in 1978 Mr Fisher recounted some of his experiences:

We went to Steep Holm in January 1942 to man 189 Battery. The guns were already on the island and became operational shortly after our arrival. While the guns were in position, and we had successful practice shoots, work was still being done on the construction of gun houses and ammunition recesses. Further work was also necessary in the construction of searchlight emplacements which, for anti-ship purposes, had to be almost at sea level.

Life on Steep Holm was somewhat limited but we were busy training and helping with the construction work. Our accommodation, both for sleeping and mess, was in Nissen huts. All supplies, including water, had to be sent from the mainland, and this was done by two motor barges which operated from Barry, where our Regimental HQ was situated.

The Royal Army Service Corps operated its own fleet of requisitioned small vessels for ferrying personnel between both islands and the mainland. For supply purposes they were augmented by two old Thames-type barges – the *Peter Piper* which supplied Steep Holm, and the *Snowflake* which went to and from Flat Holm. With the completion of the pier, and the island's new water storage arrangements, boats bringing fresh water to Steep Holm were able to couple their hoses to a long pipe leading to large tanks which had been constructed alongside Cliff Cottage. From there, other powerful pumps forced the water up to the main storage tanks newly situated on the plateau - nearly 250 ft above sea level, and sufficiently above roof height of the barracks and Nissen huts to provide the necessary head of pressure for taps and latrines. The concrete bars which supported these tanks may still be seen, with remnants of the piping.

Flat Holm's Defences

Almost simultaneously with the re-fortification of Steep Holm, similar large scale military engineering was taking place on Flat Holm: a pier, railway, gun batteries and searchlight posts were being built, with Nissen huts and command posts.

In the Victorian period the guns on both islands had been of the same type, although the method of mounting was different. In the Second World War the guns themselves differed. Whereas Brean Down, Steep Holm and Lavernock all had 6-in ex-naval guns, suitable only for coast defence, the Flat Holm garrison was primarily a part of the anti-aircraft defences of Cardiff. Lt. Fisher explained:

> During the summer of 1942 I was transferred to 146 Coast Battery under the command of Major Benger. This was one of two batteries situated on Flat Holm. These batteries were each comprised of two 4.5-in A.A. guns, and up to this time had been manned by A.A. personnel [351 H.A.A. Battery]. . . . Since they were situated in the Channel, and in the middle of Coast Artillery Batteries, it was decided that they should be manned by Coast Artillery. So we became operational A.A. gunners. . . . However, although we were operationally A.A. we now became experimental coast batteries using the A.A. guns, so that we had a dual function.
>
> The dual role training and practice shooting was interesting, but the only actual firing against the enemy was in our A.A. capacity.

As late as March 1944 army records for Flat Holm show: 'Enemy aircraft engaged by 146, & 205 Coast Btys. R.A. 6 targets at heights 12,600 feet–28,000. Speed, 300-350 m.p.h. Direction of approach S, & N, & S/W to N/E. No observed results. 109 rounds expended.' Major Benger wrote down many memories of his wartime experiences for the Flat Holm Project, and its supporting Society. On the mainland he had helped to train the men of 188 and 189 Batteries before they were posted to Steep Holm, and occasionally had reason to visit that island in the course of his duties, although he never served there.

Sgt Walford Remembers

The second half of 1942 saw all the officers and men of Nos 188 and 189 Batteries on Steep Holm being replaced with fresh units. As a 'farewell' gesture red lead paint was used to scrawl over the wall of the Rudder Rock underground shell store:

Sgts Joe Walford, Harold Underhay and Reg Stone, with a 6-in coastal gun behind, during the 1940s

R.I.P	189 BTY
A A	
GNRS.	W. COLLINS
GNR. J. HEARSEY	M. FAIRLEY
F. GREEN	T. BONNER
W. DULY	

Ex-Sgt Joe Walford, whose father, Corporal Walford, had escorted an army donkey back to the mainland at the end of the Victorian military occupation, was a member of 366 Battery which took over from No. 189. The new unit was largely comprised of local men, Reg Stone and Fred Brueford being among his comrades.

Joe Walford served with the artillery at Cardiff, Portishead, Brean Down and Steep Holm; and if Flat Holm had had 6-in ex-naval guns instead of the 4.5s he would probably have served there also. After we met, he wrote to explain in detail the operation of the pier and railway system:

The pier was constructed using bolt together stanchions, cross-braced with lengths of approximately 12-in diameter piping welded together, and was about 120 yards long. At the seaward end it was 50–60 feet high; with a diesel crane for hauling supplies ashore and for shipping returnable goods. I suppose that the rise and fall of sea level, at spring tides would be in the region of 44 feet, and this meant that at low water the loading and unloading took considerably longer time.

All supplies brought ashore on the jetty were loaded on to narrow gauge rail trucks and pushed to the bottom of the first incline. There a number of trucks were coupled together to form a small train and a wire hawser attached to the first. The trucks were then pulled up the first incline by a diesel winch, thus completing the first stage of moving the supplies to the top of the island. The second stage was completed in exactly the same way; and again, until all supplies were at the top. Then a small diesel engine pulled the train across the island to the appropriate storage bases.

When all the stores and personnel were ashore, and only then, were outgoing stores and personnel allowed on the jetty, to avoid congestion. In this way a turn round of the ship could be completed within an hour if the tides were favourable. Many times, owing to rough weather, the vessel would come within throwing distance but not be able to tie up; and, much to the disgust of people waiting to go on leave, would turn round and make for Cardiff (with the cheers of the soldiers [on board] knowing that they would have extra leave in Cardiff, or at home if Welshmen).

The rough weather could, and very often did, maroon the island for days and weeks on end. One ENSA party came for a night's entertainment for the troops and spent eight days – which we were very pleased about. Urgent supplies under these conditions were dropped from the air by Lysander aircraft.

German aeroplanes used to lay parachute mines in the Channel, and some ships from Avonmouth were blown up. Sometimes loose mines were seen floating in the water nearby. Passing Steep Holm, German planes flew so low that we could look down on them, and the island's light anti-aircraft guns could not be depressed sufficiently to take aim.

The four 6-in ex-naval guns for coast defence purposes were mounted in two batteries. They came from a First World War battleship, or cruiser, and had been adapted for shore use. The pedestals were bolted down to the concrete bases; and the turrets had been replaced by metal shields mounted on a light steel framework. Including the N.C.O. in charge, the crew needed for each weapon was nine, or ten, men. At night the duty watches for each gun rested in war shelters, and took it in turns to do sentry lookout duty on an hourly rota basis. None of these 6-in guns, with their 12,500 yards range, had to be used in action, but, of course, we did have firing practice – against targets towed by the Navy. At night these dummy shoots could be quite fun.

Whether the crews of the navy towing vessel (the *Hasler*) found the night practice sessions such fun is open to conjecture!

Mr G. Chesterfield, a specialist officer from Gunnery Instruction Section, added his objective comments about the ex-naval guns: 'The point about naval guns being used on Steep Holm (as in dozens of other places around our coasts) is that they happened to be available. These guns were, of course, armaments of numerous ships that had been scrapped but stored away by the Navy. In 1940 when invasion became a possibility these were the only guns that were readily available – apart from the fact that we had better uses for new equipment. Most of the guns were thirty years old, or so, and none the worse for that, although they were certainly not as effective for firing from land as proper coast artillery equipment.' In comparison with the Victorian cannons, these ex-naval guns, apart from the additional range, fired 100 lb armour-piercing shells, using $11\frac{1}{2}$ lb canvas cartridges.

Joe Walford told us more of his experiences:

While on Steep Holm I had ear trouble, and transferred to the searchlights. The emplacements were in remote and difficult places, low down on the cliffs to be close to the sea; and in the dark the steps and paths leading down from the top of the island could be quite dangerous. The emplacements were very uncomfortable and lonely places to be; especially in rough weather, and at night, when they were manned by one person – whose sole companions to help him pass the time, and keep awake, were books, a home-made crystal set radio, and bits and pieces for model making. When the searchlights were switched on it was not easy to pick up the ships; and you also had to be careful to keep the beam away from the guns' line of sight. The lights could be manoeuvred manually, or automatically from the Battery Observation Post.

Years later we were told of wartime residents of Brean being kept awake by the sweep of Steep Holm's south cliffs searchlights – made more prominent by the strict blackout regulations then in force. But to continue with Joe Walford's story:

The searchlight detachment supplied all the electricity for the island; for Officers' Mess, Cookhouse, and men's huts, as well as for searchlight and gun emplacements, and for the Battery Observation Post.

Although ample light was provided within buildings very rigorous blackout restrictions were observed outside; which made travelling about the island after dark very dangerous. We lost some men in this way, falling over the edge.

Some ex-soldiers remembered that they were banned from eating gulls' eggs and that the rabbits were unpalatable, but in Sgt Stickler's time on the island 'There was one good sport and that was getting the gulls' eggs. You could always pick up gulls' eggs on the floor, but if you wanted a lot the one thing to do was [to go] over the cliff . . . by means of a rope . . . [I] could fill up my shirt or battle-dress . . . but you had to be very careful, because the gulls would attack you, and many a time I've seen men come up with the eggs all smashed in their shirt.'

Sgt Walford wrote:

> Seagulls' eggs abounded in their thousands, and we always had two for breakfast. They were quite good to eat; as large, but not as strong as a duck's eggs. We did keep a couple of pigs at the old inn site [also at Cliff Cottage] off the waste from the cookhouse; but the venture was only partially successful, as we could not let them roam, and the sites proved too small.
>
> On the cliffs many hawks' nests were found, with the bones of forty odd racing pigeons per nest. All the leg rings which were recovered were sent off to the Racing Pigeon Association; who acknowledged with a letter of thanks and quite a donation – which was much appreciated by those on a shilling a day.

Perhaps it was at this stage of the war that the army decided to shoot the peregrine falcons, as they had developed a taste for carrier pigeons.

Commanding Officer Jones

The new commanding officer for Steep Holm in January 1943 was Capt. W.G.M. Jones who, thirty-five years later, was to pay a nostalgic return visit to the island. 'The gulls and their eggs were the same,' he later said. 'The views were the same, but naturally the whole atmosphere of the island had changed – as had the vegetation.' Later, he wrote:

> In 1943 there were broad and level paths, and a flat piece of ground (grass, I think) which could be used as a small parade ground. Usable paths ran across the top of the island. The establishment was approximately five officers (including a resident Medical Officer who was called Capt. Dick – if I remember rightly) and 130 other ranks to man the four 6-in guns and the searchlights.
>
> I do not believe that the batteries were constantly manned, as at many Coast Defence sites. One could reasonably expect warning of any attack, and the number of men available could not possibly provide twenty-four hour manning for four 6-in guns. The guns were always prepared for action morning and evening, when corrections would be worked out for wind, tide, etc. Firing practice at towed targets would take place both by day and night.

Capt. Jones confirmed that pigs were kept in Cliff Cottage – to the extent of kindly sending us a photograph of the well-fed animals. The sty was 'Built by TEA, AHH, AH, CW, Nov. 1942', according to graffiti in the little walled enclosure attached to the ruined cottage. His letter continued:

> One tried to safeguard a portion of the island as a bird sanctuary. A mutiny might well have been caused had one tried to enforce a rigid prohibition on the lifting of gulls' eggs. In those days a gunner was only paid three or four

Pte. Haynes, R.A.M.C. barbering Lt. Curtis outside a Nissen hut at Split Rock, 1940

shillings a day and marriage allowance was very low, so the eggs not only helped the rations of the island, but were also a considerable source of income. It was organized by one or more N.C.O.s who paid a penny for each egg. They in turn sold them for two pence to the skipper of the boat. He sold them for three pence to the Barry shops, who sold them for four pence. Everyone made a penny an egg!

I heard later that on one occasion a soldier was nearly killed near Rudder Rock, as he tried to collect eggs from the cliff. Whether he had climbed down, or whether the rope broke, I do not know, but I believe it was touch and go before he was saved.

I remember the peony patch well. It was flourishing – a mass of healthy plants about ten yards square. They were coming into flower as I left to go to Portishead.

A great advantage of the island was that no Senior Officer (such as the Commander, Severn Fixed Defences, who was stationed somewhere along the Severn's north coast, and at this time was Col. Ferrard) could drop in on one without warning!

Communications

Among specialist officers from Headquarters who regularly visited the two islands was Mr H.C. Gifford, of Western Command (Severn) Signals. His special concern was the efficiency of communications, and of the extensive military telephone network which had been set up in the upper Bristol Channel area. Laying submarine cables to connect the Barry Headquarters with the two islands and Brean Down had been another of the re-fortification tasks. Roughly 3 in in diameter, each cable contained about twenty-five pairs of telephone wires, protected from the sea water by a rubber and hessian casing and armoured with an outer covering of spiralling steel wires. On the Welsh side of the Channel, the cables came ashore at St Mary's Well Bay, on the Sully Island side of the beach. Both here and on the two Holms they sometimes became exposed on the beach, and needed to be reburied hastily for security.

The cables still run beneath the sea, although now long out of use, and are occasionally caught in ships' anchors. On Steep Holm, where they come ashore at East Beach, they are sometimes uncovered when rough seas wash away the deep layer of pebbles – only to be covered up again with the next change of tidal conditions. The former telephone cable distribution hut can still be seen on the first section of path from the beach. For communication between the island's Battery Observation Post, guns, and searchlights a separate generator-powered cable telephone was used.

The End of War in Sight

To relieve the stress and tedium of life on Steep Holm, concerts were occasionally held in the barracks. R.S.M. Adams remembered that ENSA parties arrived after a rough crossing 'in no fit state to sing' but after a time they 'got their land-legs, and would go on stage as if nothing had happened'. With wicked humour, he said that the entertainers were given a hearty supper of fried gulls' eggs – not the best preparation for their return trip, but it was difficult to refuse well-meant hospitality!

The whole direction of the war had changed by the beginning of 1944. With a German invasion of this country no longer feasible, and with United Kingdom, Colonial and American troops massing for intensive training in preparation for the Normandy landings, Coastal Defence units were being reduced or disbanded. The soldiers manning the batteries on Steep Holm were being dispersed, and for a short period were replaced by men belonging to the large garrison on Brean Down. Reg Stone, the Weston-super-Mare man who had been on the island for three weeks in 1941, came back at this time, as N.C.O. in charge of the double gun battery, Steep Holm South. When this was closed down after about three months, and put on a care and maintenance basis, he took charge of the Steep Holm North battery, facing Flat Holm, until that too was shut down a few months later. With the island's military strength reduced to a mere token force, he found himself controlling thirty men, where once there had been a garrison of over two hundred.

By late autumn of 1944 Reg was back at Brean again, when the island base was finally closed down. The war in Europe was to end only six months later, and a new phase in the Steep Holm story was soon to begin.

Chapter Eighteen

LEGACY OF WAR AND A NEW LEASE OF LIFE

The Victorian fortification of Steep Holm had left useful barracks buildings, with a large underground water tank, as well as six gun batteries with their weapons and appendages scattered around the island. The Second World War left four additional and much more prominent and unsightly gun emplacements, with searchlight posts, generator and winch houses, about thirty Nissen huts, and a disused narrow gauge railway track without its rolling stock or winches. This fortification bequeathed little of practical use to the island's resources and did nothing to enhance it visually. Indeed, this latest military occupation left all the debris of a present-day army – concrete, corrugated iron, girders, barbed wire, reinforced glass, and a mass of discarded impedimenta.

Memories of a Prisoner-of-War

By far the most obtrusive structure of the 1940s was the iron girder pier which had been built on East Beach to provide unloading facilities for large quantities of stores and equipment. At the end of the war it was decided that this had to be dismantled, and the main workforce for the task was a detachment of German prisoners. Although the conflict in Europe had ended in May 1945, some captured Germans were not to be repatriated from this country until 1948. In the meantime they were delegated to occupations where there were severe shortages of manpower, such as on farms – or to clear away wartime installations.

Like so many of the prisoners, ex-tank driver N.C.O. Max Flemming could not have returned to his own home immediately even if he had been repatriated; for that was in the Russian-occupied zone of Germany. The British, French and American zones were full of displaced persons unable to return to their former towns and villages in the eastern area. Before being captured on the Belgium/Holland border by Scottish soldiers who were trying to make contact with the ill-fated advance airborne force which had landed at Arnhem, Mr Flemming was an instructor at a tank warfare training camp. He woke one morning to see hundreds of British gliders overhead, some of which landed short of their target and had their wings torn off as they came down among trees in an orchard. Subsequently, in the fighting to prevent or delay the link-up of Allied troops, he was taken prisoner with others of his detachment; transferred to a temporary P.O.W. camp in a Belgium school, and afterwards brought to Scotland where he spent a while in hospital, before being moved to Wales. In 1946 he was one of a number of prisoners-of-war helping to dismantle the two wartime piers so laboriously constructed on the landing beaches at Flat Holm and Steep Holm. When, forty-five years later, he revisited the islands with Brenda, his English wife, he reminisced happily about his experiences:

> I remember the two islands well. I have for a long time wished to revisit them, and to show them to my wife.
>
> I think it was the end of 1945, or the beginning of 1946, when I was moved to Flat Holm from Gloucestershire; and there were then about twenty-five of us prisoners-of-war living in the old farmhouse and two Nissen huts in the walled farm compound with an English sergeant in charge. We had complete freedom of the island, and the only other persons there were the lighthouse keepers. They were very friendly to us, and I went up the lighthouse tower several times.
>
> Our job was to dismantle the wartime pier and some of the other installations, although the railway had already been removed. To direct the work an engineer used to come out to the island regularly from Barry, on the supply boat which brought the rations and the mail. We had plenty of spare time, and no responsibilities. If we could not yet be repatriated, Flat Holm was not a bad place to be.

Max told us that one of his group was very clever at woodwork, and made toys from driftwood or salvage which the engineer took back to Wales to sell. A crew member of the supply boat serving the islands also remembered the trinkets and ingenious toys, such as wooden ducks or pecking chickens, which sold very quickly in a little shop on Barry Island, at a time when such luxuries were scarce.

There were nesting gulls on Flat Holm, but the engineer took Max and others in his boat to Steep Holm to collect gulls' eggs, as they were far more plentiful on that island. These were much appreciated by the work party, and those not needed were taken by the engineer for sale on the Welsh mainland. 'After we had finished the work on Flat Holm we were moved to Steep Holm; again to dismantle the pier, and some other installations. Here we lived in Nissen huts near the old barracks building. We used this as our canteen. It had two large old-fashioned iron ranges on which we did the cooking.' In 1991 Max was delighted to find that these were still in position, and that relatively little had changed since he was on the islands all those years ago. He recalled that their diet was again augmented by seagulls' eggs; and the young birds were 'delicious, like chicken'. Rabbits were also caught and eaten, although the men were more cautious of them, fearing TB infection.

The guns and the searchlights had all been removed, but the railway and pier were complete, with all the lines, diesel winches, cables and little trucks. All this was still in working order. We used the railway to take our supplies to the top, and sometimes even to carry passengers – as some of the trucks had been fitted with two low-backed seats. The winches pulled the trucks up the slope. Their own weight was all that was necessary to take them back down; a powerful brake on the winch controlled the speed. But there was one occasion when no one was looking after the winch brake, and an empty truck shot down the lower section of track, to somersault off the end on to the beach. It could have been very dangerous.

On the seaward end of the pier there was a petrol, or diesel operated crane, which we used until it was necessary to dismantle the pier itself. Once we used it to lift up a small boat which, I think, must have been swamped and sunk as it tried to come ashore through the surf. It was the tender belonging to our supply boat, which had moored at a large buoy anchored just off the island.

Water tanks at Cliff Cottage and on the plateau were still in use at that time, and Max remembered a hose connection at the end of the jetty for connecting up to the supply vessel. 'When we came to dismantle the iron framework of the pier we had to use burners; but I cannot now remember what finally happened to the pieces. They

Second World War pier being demolished, 1946. Some of the planking and girderwork has been removed, but trucks are still on the railway line

Hans Messner and Max Flemming, German ex-prisoners of war, on the remnants of the Second World War pier which they helped to demolish in 1946. The ruined inn, with its garden wall, is in the left background

were just rusty scrap metal. Much of the wood from the decking would have been burned, or thrown away.'

On arrival at Steep Holm on his nostalgic return visit, Max was interested to see that some of the stanchions remain piled up beside the path above East Beach, still not rusted away. On a second visit to Steep Holm with his ex-German Navy friend Hans Messner, who had worked with him on the islands, they were able to examine the remnants of the pier which they had helped to demolish – still visible at very low tide.

Desperate Escape from Steep Holm?

We also heard from Max the true story of the great escape from one of the islands on a log, which had made national newspaper headlines at the time, and about which many different versions have been told since. Laughing, he explained that this was not an escape attempt at all; and Hans, who travelled from Cologne to revisit the two islands in 1991, confirmed his version of the adventure which so nearly ended in disaster. The 'log' on which the 'escape attempt' was made, was actually a small raft, made quite openly by the prisoners, with the tolerant English sergeant in charge knowing what they were doing. After all, the war was over, and what was the point of trying to escape at that stage? In their spare time they collected thick planks from Steep Holm's dismantled pier decking, and fastened them together with some of the disused bolts and metal clamps. The Germans had time on their hands, and the raft was a 'fun thing' for floating in shallow water just off the beach – preferably when the sea was absolutely calm, and at the end of a rope! This was no *Kon-Tiki*, having neither steering oar nor sail, and relying on simply fashioned paddles for both direction and propulsion. As they grew more accustomed to the primitive craft, there were young men's dreams of trying to cross the five miles or so to Weston, to sunbathe on the beach there; but both Max and Hans were positive that the near-tragic voyage which did take place was a foolhardy attempt to paddle to Flat Holm on the flood tide, to get some English cigarettes from the lighthouse keepers, before coming back on the next ebb tide.

It was a beautiful day, with apparently ideal conditions when two of them set out – to be swept past the corner of Steep Holm in the tide race before being sucked into the deep water channel between the two islands. To their dismay, there was no slackening of speed until they found themselves well to the north of both islands. It was becoming dark; the weather changed to stormy; and they were hungry, wet, cold and very frightened. Fortunately they were seen by the crew of a lightship off the Welsh coast, and eventually rescued by lifeboat while clinging to a buoy in a desperate state. When the escapade was discovered, the prisoners on Steep Holm did their best to cover up for the English sergeant in charge of the group, feeling rather sorry for the trouble which he faced.

Unlike most of the stories told by British soldiers about the early days on Steep Holm during the war, Max and Hans had very happy memories of the time spent on both islands in 1946. Although far from home, and with an uncertain future, they were under little pressure, so able to relax and enjoy life. When the work on Steep Holm was finished, the men were dispersed to other centres, mainly to assist with farm work. In 1948 the only remaining prisoners-of-war in the United Kingdom were those who had elected to stay in this country to be employed in agriculture. Max did return to Hamburg then briefly to eastern Germany, not being too keen on a farming career; but being even less in accord with conditions in the Russian zone of his country he applied for permission to re-enter England where he settled, marrying Brenda, and has remained here ever since.

Back in Civilian Hands

With the war ended, the heavy military equipment removed, and the pier demolished on the advice of boat owner Frank Watts (senior) – although Harry Cox felt that the giant structure would have been useful – Steep Holm came back into the legal occupation of Harry Cox, by then an old man. In 1939 he had prided himself on becoming a member of HM Coastguard at the age of seventy. Now he was entering the last years of his life, and although he still travelled the lengthy route from Weston to Brean Down, he was unable to care for the war-ravaged island as effectively as he had in past years. Steep Holm was cluttered with debris; Nissen huts were still in position; and tons of rusty iron girders that had formed the supports of the dismantled wartime pier remained at the foot of the path from the beach, or strewn among the pebbles and rocks. This was a restoration problem which few people would care to tackle, and to add to the devastation trespassers smashed the windows of the barracks, broke down doors and damaged the old buildings, as well as causing havoc among the Nissen huts.

A Very Short Tenancy

When Harry Cox died in 1949 his lease of Steep Holm still had two years to run, and his executors offered the island to let. Farmer H.P. Dungey leapt at the chance of renting a remote island, and perhaps sharing it with a few like-minded enthusiasts interested in birdlife, fishing, sailing and other such pleasures. Alas for his high hopes! At Easter 1950, after only a few months as tenant of Steep Holm, he was the subject of another front page newspaper story in the doleful history of shipwrecks. His boat was smashed to pieces on the beach, and he had the humiliating experience of having to be rescued. Landing on East Beach in the immediate post-war years was more hazardous than ever before, because the iron and concrete base supports for the pier had not all been removed; and although the comparatively light stanchions had been piled on the stone-built jetty, a number of heavy girders still littered the foreshore. As late as 1969 an official report was to record that 'the waters near the beach are full of old military equipment, and can be dangerous'. Even now, despite many post-war attempts to clear the beach, low tide still reveals rusted girders sprawling across the rocks and pebbles.

A Trust is Formed

Each year, from 1946 onwards, ornithologists had obtained permission to visit the island to record the ups and downs of the bird population; and in 1950 and 1951 members of the Bristol Folk House Archaeological Club arrived to clear vegetation and debris from the site of the medieval priory, and commence trial excavations. When the lease held by Harry Cox's executors came to an end on 29 September 1951, Lord Wharton would have liked to have sold the island, but failing a reasonable offer his agents were anxious to find a body of appropriate character and standing which would be willing to rent the island on a long-term basis. Initial approaches were made to Mr Edmund Mason, a lecturer of the Folk House Club, who had been taking his students to Steep Holm for tuition in archaeological fieldwork. Being small in comparison with some of the county associations, and appreciating the need for botanical, archaeological and ornithological representation, the Club decided that other, bigger societies with wider interests and skills should be approached to participate jointly in any new lease which could be arranged. With Ted Mason acting as 'honest broker' between solicitors, his own

Club and leaders of other groups, the result was the multi-discipline Steep Holm Trust which was to lease the island for twenty-one years from 25 March 1953, at a rent of £26 per year. As with Mrs Davies when she took a lease of Steep Holm in 1885, the first half year was free of rent; in her case to compensate for the inn being in urgent need of repair, but this time because the whole island was in such a state of dilapidation. It was during this period of negotiations that the island was scheduled as a Site of Special Scientific Interest because of its unique flora.

Under the terms of the lease, the Steep Holm Trust would '. . . use the island for the purposes only of archaeological, scientific and educational purposes approved by the landlord, in accordance with the rules for the time being of the Bristol Naturalist's Society, the Somerset Archaeological and Natural History Society, the Folk House Archaeological Club of Bristol, and the Mid-Somerset Naturalists' Society [the four constituent organizations] and not do anything on the island to interfere with its preservation as a sanctuary for birds and wildlife, and its use for ecological and archaeological research, and for educational and research purposes of a like nature . . .'. The rent charge was divided between the four parent societies in proportion to their respective memberships. As the barracks were 'in too advanced a state of dilapidation to put or maintain them in good repair' the usual repairing clause, making the tenants responsible for such expenditure, was considered inappropriate, and so omitted from the agreement.

A gigantic task faced the new Trust. In the years since there had been any regular occupation of Steep Holm, visitors had commented that the gulls and the plants had quite taken over the island; while the barracks had become derelict. Windows and doors were smashed and many roof slates were missing, resulting in damage to the rafters. Paint had blistered and woodwork was rotted, with plants decorating what remained of the gutters. The War Office had made little or no attempt to demolish and clear the numerous Nissen huts, one of which was directly in front of the main building of the old barracks; and these huts were already in an advanced state of decay, with fitments removed or destroyed. A visiting reporter spent a weekend with one of the first groups to work on the island after it was leased by the Trust. He described the rusted Nissen huts as 'caved in or on the verge of collapse', and was horrified with the conditions in which he was expected to 'live and sleep rough'. After seeing 'every inch' of the island, experiencing the cold sea wind which buffeted across the exposed plateau, and huddling round a makeshift fire in the leaking barracks, he heaved a sigh of relief as the boat finally pulled away from Steep Holm on the return journey. With his nerves jangled by the continual day and night shrieks of thousands of gulls, he commented: 'The birds can have it. I never want to see or hear another seagull.' Another reporter wondered why the volunteers endured such privation: as we ourselves know, only an enthusiast could begin to understand!

In the first year of the Steep Holm Trust's tenancy, Ted Mason told of trampling through the broken down huts, and of clattering over rusted fallen corrugated iron sheeting. On the jetty there was a huge heap of some 40 tons of girders from the

Rows of Nissen huts west of the barracks in 1953

former pier, almost blocking the pathway from the beach; and he was to report that although on the mainland the stanchions would have had considerable scrap value, the various dealers approached could not undertake the prohibitive transport costs. East Beach was still a dangerous landing place, with military debris being shifted by the tide and deposited in unsuspected positions. By exerting tremendous effort, Trust members levered and rolled several of the more perilously positioned stanchions up the beach and over a ridge of rock, where it was hoped that they would be less of a hazard to the ferry boats; but it was beyond their resources to clear the heavy metal completely from the beach.

Deploring the depredation wrought as a result of the war, co-Trustee Mr Harry Savory of the Bristol Naturalists' Society (which had been responsible for the pre-war Survey of Steep Holm) pinpointed the obliteration of some of the more picturesque and rare Victorian defences, and the entombing of part of the twelfth-century priory foundations beneath one of the Nissen huts; as well as destruction of the pre-Victorian inn and Cliff Cottage, and disfiguration of the East Beach area. Even so, he saw that although these were matters of aesthetic consideration, they were of little moment as far as the island's birdlife and plants were concerned. Certainly the birds were thriving. Cormorants were nesting in good numbers; and if the breeding gull population had not quite reached the explosive proportions of a few years hence, visitors to the island were in no doubt that they were not welcomed

Aerial view of East Beach from the south, at mid-tide, showing Tower Rock (left) with Second World War gun emplacement above, and three winch houses on incline railway. The stone-built quay has a generator hut (now demolished) and a brick-built store. The beginning of the track passes the ruined inn and zig-zags through the sycamore wood

by the thousands of herring, lesser, and great black-backed gulls, which rose above the island in huge whirling clouds as the boat approached, screaming their defiance; and, when the explorers landed, fiercely defending their territory. On the ground, nests occupied every scrap of space between great stands of alexanders, nettles, brambles, elder and privet. How quickly the island had reverted to nature, around the gaunt decaying ruins which stretched skywards from the vegetation!

Repairs and Restoration

Although the lease had not stipulated any repairs, the Steep Holm Trust's first priority had to be to make one of the island buildings habitable for work parties. The barracks were occupied by gulls, with rotting boards deep in guano, and quite open to the weather. For the first two seasons the most practical place for the volunteers to stay was one of the generator huts left by the army. Despite having only a concrete floor on which to lay sleeping bags, this building had the luxury of a roof in good repair and some intact windows, although the hinges of the iron doors had long since rusted solid, and everyone had to climb in and out of a rear opening. Mr Peter (later Sir Peter) Scott, founder of the Slimbridge Wildfowl Trust, was a supporter of the Steep Holm Trust, and on one overnight stay to take part in a broadcast he was highly favoured by being allocated one of the concrete generator beds on which to lay his sleeping bag!

Of the work confronting the Trust, Ted Mason commented: 'A builder backed out after accepting the job [of repairing the barracks] on the grounds that it was too difficult to come from the mainland, so we had to revert to voluntary labour.' As a first step towards having habitable quarters, the gaping windows of the barracks were covered with wire netting to prevent the gulls from entering, with sufficient panes of armoured glass being rescued from Nissen huts to keep out some of the weather. Doors were repaired, fitted with locks and repainted. Gradually new floorboards, rafters, guttering and slates for the roof were brought over from the mainland, and a good supply of tools was locked in a store; but with volunteers being able to spend only weekends on the island it was a long and strenuous project. Ivor Hodges, one of the workers, set himself the task of reglazing all the windows, which he finally completed in 1960. But the new windows were attacked by vandals to such an extent that constantly broken glass eventually had to be replaced by John Barrett, this time using plastic sheeting.

As soon as the main restoration was achieved, and the barracks were once more fit for habitation, beds and mattresses were purchased and transported to the island, with crockery, a portable cooker, lighting and basic furniture. There was emergency signalling apparatus, with specialist equipment for the group of ornithologists in their own workroom, and even a small generator. But annual reports show that throughout the Trust's tenancy the old barracks and the wartime flat-roofed kitchen which connected the two Victorian buildings needed constant repair, especially after winter storms and depredation by vandals. With the pressures of having to make the dilapidated barracks weatherproof, work parties were hard-pressed during the first year, but they cut down large bushes which had smothered the ruins of a number of derelict Nissen huts, before removing these wartime eyesores. One of the first huts to go was that which had so disfigured the front of the Victorian barracks building. Where it was found that slow worms were sheltering beneath fallen corrugated iron sheeting this was left for their benefit. Gulls habitually nested in abandoned hut fireplaces, so not all of these were demolished. Timber was collected and stacked for firewood, and, as had happened so often in the past, a new notice was painted and positioned by East Beach, warning off unauthorized visitors.

Regular path clearance, tending the water supply, disposing of as much of the wartime debris as possible and repairing the barracks became unending routine tasks. Intruding bushes were removed from the area near Cliff Cottage where the peonies grew, and the precious plants began to regenerate.

The Water Supply

Fresh water was a problem. With the Victorian tank behind the barracks having been left uncovered by the army, and later being provided with only an old wooden door balanced over the access manhole, this underground reservoir had collected a great variety of debris, as well as the corpses of birds which had been trapped inside; and with recollections of the typhoid scare, the water was considered unsafe. The only alternative source was the old catchment well above East Beach. This had become hidden among bushes and, having no lid, was choked with rock scree. After laboriously clearing a path to the well, removing the scree and cleaning out the cavity, this was to become the Trust's normal drinking water supply (supplemented by canisters filled before leaving Weston). Courses of brickwork were laid, and a new heavy metal lid was specially made to size, brought from the mainland, and with considerable difficulty positioned and fastened over the well. Until shortly before his death, Harry Savory was a self-appointed 'water-carrier', filling two portable churns on a milkmaid's yoke (which remained in the barracks for many years) and struggling up to the island headquarters. For washing and other purposes, a large galvanized tank was placed to catch water from the barracks roof. Later, samples of the water in the Victorian tank were tested for bacteria by the Public Health Laboratory, and found to be within safety limits if boiled, so this much more plentiful supply was brought into use. One hazard was that the wooden makeshift lid was sometimes left open by those drawing the water; and apart from the danger that a child might fall into the tank, this allowed contamination – on one occasion necessitating reopening the catchment well for a while.

A Memorial is Erected

Members of the Steep Holm Trust felt that a great deal was owed to Harry Cox who had cared for the island before the war, and that there should be a permanent memorial to his years of dedicated wardening. A Second World War sighting post was still in position at Steep Holm South, above the infilled barbette of the Victorian Garden Battery. What better place for a simple bronze memorial plaque to be fixed, where it would not be obtrusive, and from where at that time there was an excellent view of Brean Down, where Harry Cox had spent so many hours in peacetime, and during the war? Arrangements were planned by the Trust and by Harry Cox's relatives and friends, and a subscription was started. Plant growth and the last remnants of the small war shelter were cleared, its concrete base being left as a viewing platform. The plaque was made and fixed in position, and on 10 June 1957 a large Union Jack draped over the post was removed by Harry Cox's son John, to reveal the plaque – and the letters 'H.C.' fixed to the top of the monument. Attending this simple ceremony were many friends of Harry Cox, and a rather special guest – Frank Harris, then eighty-six years old, on what was to be his last visit to the island which had been his home as a child.

Impressions of the Trust Years

As the seasons came and went it became apparent to Trust workers that maintenance and coping with visitors had to take priority over other projects, such as archaeological work on the priory site, which was severely curtailed. With the formation of the Trust, Ted Mason had hoped to be able to concentrate on his favourite pursuit on Steep Holm, and for several seasons he struggled to continue with investigation of the outline of the priory walls, but his overall responsibilities became too onerous to allow any archaeology after the 1964 season. He, Harry Savory and others delved into the history of the island, and collected memories of those connected with its past, besides spending many hours lecturing and encouraging interest in the Trust.

Complete demolition of the remaining Second World War structures became impossible because of other urgent tasks. Nevertheless, by the end of 1960 Trust representatives were able to report that good progress had been made. In a letter to Harry Savory, one of the enthusiastic Trust workers commented: 'The tidying up of the island has really had an effect. When the last of the Nissen huts has gone we should consider demolishing some of the brick built eyesores.' But to clear all the devastation, and restore Steep Holm to its pre-war condition was too great a task for the labour force, whose weekend visits often had to be cancelled because the small open motor boat was unable to reach the island in rough seas. The same writer's revised opinion only a year later was: 'It was sad to see how obtrusive the military installations still remained despite all the work that had been put into clearing them up.' Nevertheless, the eastern gun battery of Split Rock was largely cleared, including the blocked entrance to the underground ammunition stores; and somehow the 7-ton gun was levered over to clear rubbish from beneath it. The annexe to the inn was also shovelled free of a tremendous amount of rock and debris with which it had been filled during the cutting of the railway track during the war.

In its first year, the Trust had received a grant from the Society for Promotion of Nature Reserves; voluntary labour continued to be provided by Trust members who often met their own expenses; but boating charges had to be paid, and there was the continual need to purchase equipment and materials. Donations and fees from visitors were essential to keep the Trust operating.

Every year schools, colleges, societies and individuals with projects to complete, or specialist interests, came to Steep Holm. Visitors normally had to be limited to no more than twenty-four (two boatloads) at one time, and were always kept under supervision, with a leader being appointed to be responsible for each group. Mrs Dorrien Mason became the busy Secretary to the Trust, and received many appreciative letters – even from as far away as Israel. She earned the envy of her children when she was marooned with a party of Cardiff naturalists who had travelled by Campbell's steamer from Wales, to meet her and the ferry at Weston and spend the day on Steep Holm. The weather changed within a few hours, and as her husband and children tried to reach the island in the afternoon the boatman was forced to turn back into the easterly gale, with much bewailing from two saturated youngsters sheltering beneath a tarpaulin: 'It's not fair – we've never been marooned!' The pleasure steamer returned to Wales without the Steep Holm group, who were faced with a complicated journey home on the following day.

A visitor with a college study group left a graphic account of a three-day stay one August, describing the stowage on the small motor boat of a party of twelve's luggage; the pauses for regaining breath on the steep path, while watching the 'miniature boat' moving homeward across the sparkling sea; allocation of rotas for cooks and orderlies in the barracks; mortality among the gull population; the beauty of the island and its wildlife. He was awed by the pathetic military remains, once so polished and well-tended – and still more impressed by the journey home! On an extremely hot day the baggage was taken down to East Beach. The boat was late and the waves began to crash threateningly on the pebbles. A signal from the boatman indicated it was no longer safe for the little craft to pick them up from there. All the gear had to be carried back up the path and down to South Landing. They boarded without mishap and set off, 'punching our way through the waves' with the sunlit island soon behind them. Suddenly the sun disappeared, and as they came around from the shelter of Tower Rock, 'the sea ran high as we crouched in our rocking boat which dug her nose deep into the trough of an oncoming breaker. Wave after wave poured into the boat and I decided I was no sailor.' After eventually landing at Weston, wringing out his clothes, and warming up with a cup of coffee, the adventurer decided that he had enjoyed the experience, and was looking forward to the next trip – which, on the whole, is the reaction of most visitors today.

Regular requests from researchers resulted in published reports which were compiled with the co-operation of the Trust. One of these experts was Dr Cuillin Bantock who first studied the evolution of the island's banded snail population in 1971 and 1972, before finishing his project in later years, and publishing his findings in 1978. Other projects included an intensive programme of investigation into environmental problems in the Severn Estuary; with studies of parasites, crustaceans, sediments and marine organisms all taking their turn, along with the more general observations of plant, animal and birdlife.

The Gull Research Station

To monitor Steep Holm's bird colonies, and others passing through on migration, the Trust had formed a separate ornithological section, initially known as the Gull Research Station, which had links with the Severn Wildfowl Trust. As a result of one count of nests, reports began to circulate among birdwatchers on the mainland of strangely marked seagulls, with red tail feathers. Some birds had been over-anxious to return to their nests before the red paint used to distinguish nests had dried! The team's name was to be changed in 1970 to the Steep Holm Ringing Group, and published reports remain its main claim to fame – as well as a tendency to become the subject of newspaper stories when members were marooned.

A Sad Blow for the Trust

Harry J. Savory's sudden death in June 1962 created a vacuum in the Trust. As naturalist, photographer, caver and enthusiastic trustee, he had been a stalwart who was difficult to replace. He and four others, all with the name 'John', had explored and named 'Five Johns' Cave' on the north cliffs, and with his rock climbing experience he had investigated other caves around the island; but in particular 'H.S.' had produced some superb photographic studies of the island's birds, and had made the care of the Steep Holm peony his special concern. It was his regular clearance of rock and scree, sycamore saplings, privet and other encroaching vegetation which had saved the plants from near extinction; for when the Trust first leased the island there were no more than a dozen plants. In the year of his death there was the most magnificent display of blooms seen by Trust members, the 'peony glen' reaching a peak of perfection in 1966, when over fifty blooms were counted. Two years later there were more than 100 healthy plants.

Robbery!

Trespassing and the accompanying petty pilfering was often an annoying facet to island management; but in 1965 Trust members were devastated to find that thieves had broken into the barracks and stolen their generator, lamp, crockery, cutlery, food and fuel stocks. Apart from being without basic supplies for a while, having to purchase further stores and equipment depleted the finances when resources were badly needed to pay for repairs; and the generator was not replaced.

The Last Years of the Trust

For many reasons 1969 will stand out as one not to be forgotten by members of the Steep Holm Trust. The Victorian guns were classified as being beyond doubt the 7-ton version of the Mark III cannon and 'more important than the Georgian cannons used as pivots'. For the first time it was officially recognized that Steep Holm and Flat Holm between them possessed a rare collection of weapons of that type, still remaining in association with their original batteries. In the same year disaster struck in the form of *botrytis paeoniae* – a grey mould fungus peculiar to peonies. Kew Botanical Centre advised contacting the Ministry of Agriculture, and Dr A.G. Walker came to inspect the plants. His report was discouraging: this was a fungus capable of over-wintering in the root stocks, a disease favoured by damp conditions and was not easy to control. Dr Walker became a voluntary advisor on all the island plants, and when several of the woodland peonies were found to be infected with rotting tubers, John Barrett transplanted a healthy seedling to a drier situation on the island plateau. This plant grew to be for many years the main specimen peony, being located behind the base of a former Nissen hut to the west of the barracks, in a small specially created 'garden' area. One of the reasons why the peonies in the 'glen' near Cliff Cottage had failed was that the sycamore wood had become a roost for thousands of starlings, and their droppings had contaminated vegetation and the ground. To add to the problems encountered, the breeding gull population had expanded to such an extent that in spring and early summer Steep Holm was becoming uncomfortable for birds and humans alike. A census of breeding gulls in 1956 had counted some 3,550 pairs of herring gulls. By 1969, when the Gull Research Station took part in the nationwide 'Operation Seafarer', 5,400 nesting pairs of herring gulls were estimated. The lesser black-backed gulls had remained static at around 600 pairs, but the great black-backs had decreased from seventy-four pairs to thirty-nine pairs.

Lord Wharton, an ex-R.A.F.V.R. officer, died childless in July 1969, aged sixty-one, having spent most of his post-war years living in Switzerland. Succession to the title and to his estates passed to his sister Elizabeth, who became the tenth holder of the baronetcy while living in Portugal. Reports on all aspects of the Trust's work on Steep Holm had been sent regularly to Lord Wharton's agents, and the baron had taken an interest in the history and archaeology of the island. Ted Mason wasted no time in informing the baroness of the progress of all the island projects – at the same time mentioning that the lease had only a few years to run, and enquiring about the prospects of an extension or renewal of the term. An unanticipated problem then arose, because firmly, if mistakenly, the baroness formulated the idea that Steep Holm's ancient priory was a sixteenth-century foundation of Greek Orthodox monks which, never having been deconsecrated, must have a still extant altar stone. On this supposition she concluded that for the altar stone of the church to be disturbed by archaeologists would be sacrilege. With the baroness living abroad, and all correspondence being through her solicitors in London, it was difficult to explain the true position – that Steep Holm's religious house had been Augustinian, not Greek Orthodox, and that it had been closed by authority of the Bishop of Bath and Wells as long ago as 1260. The subsequent 700 years had seen both civil and military occupation of the site, with the old structure on many occasions becoming a 'quarry' for other buildings, so that all that remained were much disturbed lower foundations of walls. Somehow the baroness remained unaware, or unconvinced, of the true position, and even before the time came for re-negotiation of the lease to be considered, or for a fund to be launched for the purchase of Steep Holm, she had ruled out any question of the Trust being allowed to continue in occupation of the island beyond the stipulated twenty-one years. Despite resolute attempts to reach a compromise, its work and tenure of Steep Holm were to come to an end in March 1974.

Meanwhile, with the baroness's agents looking for a suitable purchaser, or a larger association to take over the running of the island, an approach to the Landmark Trust resulted in its chairman, Mr John (later Sir John) Smith, being escorted around Steep Holm in May 1973 by a representative of the Steep Holm Trust. In correspondence after the visit Mr Smith praised the work of the Steep Holm Trust, and confirmed that an offer to purchase had been made by his organization to the owner's agents. Seemingly the offer was not acceptable, for in February 1974 – after reading various press reports about prospective new owners – he was again writing to Ted Mason asking for information on progress. A month later he wrote another letter to say that he had not heard from Lady Wharton's solicitors, that the matter still seemed to be in abeyance, and he was not sure how to proceed. By that time a rival purchaser had appeared on the scene, one which was to achieve more success in its negotiations.

Chapter Nineteen

THE ALLSOP MEMORIAL ERA BEGINS

S etting up a Trust to administer some form of memorial is not unusual. For such a Trust to have the ongoing responsibility of maintaining an island is indeed rare.

Kenneth Allsop, a Yorkshireman born in 1920, was a reporter for the *Slough Observer* before enlisting in the R.A.F. in 1940, and marrying in 1942. While on a battle training course in 1943 he injured his knee, the resulting complications leading to amputation and keeping him in hospital until 1945. By 1948 he had returned to journalism as a feature writer, and in the 1950s he entered the world of television, where he quickly became popular with viewers. His lifelong fascination with birdlife, and in particular with the peregrine falcon and other birds of prey, led him to become an uncompromising crusader for conservation of wildlife generally – particularly when controversial environmental issues arose in the post-war years; and he lectured tirelessly to arouse similar enthusiasm in others as he saw the world of nature which he had known and loved rapidly degenerating.

The best-seller *Adventure Lit Their Star* was his first published book, in 1949. Other novels appeared at intervals. *Fit To Live In?*, one of the 'Connexions' series of booklets, was aimed at alerting schoolchildren to what was happening to their countryside; and his regular *Daily Mail* column was the inspiration for his classic *In The Country* – a diary of wildlife around the Dorset mill which had been the family home since 1970, and where he died tragically in May 1973.

In the autumn of that year, Kenneth Allsop's family and friends were disheartened by their failure to purchase part of Eggardon Hill, in Dorset, to be kept as a wildlife sanctuary in his memory. When they were unexpectedly offered the chance to buy Steep Holm, the memorial monies at their disposal were far below the amount needed for an immediate realistic offer. But Baroness Wharton was sympathetic; approving their plans she generously allowed time for the launch of a fund-raising appeal – and even permitted occupation of the island in anticipation of future purchase.

Kenneth Allsop Memorial Committee members made their first visit to the island on 4 November 1973, while the Steep Holm Trust was still the legal occupier; and Ted Mason and John Barrett of that Trust explained features of interest and importance. To the surprise of the Committee this was not just an isolated nature reserve, but a place rich in military relics, and with an unexpected history of its own – although presenting far greater problems than they had foreseen.

Steep Holm's vegetation does not look its best in November, and the visitors were taken aback by Second World War remains which still disfigured the island. Nevertheless, they were impressed by the opportunities open to enthusiastic guardianship. Kenneth Allsop had never had any connection with the island, but this would be a fitting memorial to someone who had never shirked a challenge – a place needing protection and enhancement and, above all, known to have been a nesting site for the peregrine falcon, his favourite bird.

A Public Appeal is Launched

With the memorial funds being only a small fraction of the asking price for Steep Holm, a nationwide appeal for donations was made, spearheaded by John Fowles and John Percival. Meanwhile it was announced to the media that the island was being purchased as a memorial to Kenneth Allsop, and that Peter Rees, an ornithologist of Puncknowle, Dorset, would be taking up residence on the island to act as its warden.

The Steep Holm Trust's lease ceased in March 1974, and very shortly afterwards Baroness Wharton died. Her eldest daughter, the Hon. Mrs Myrtle (Ziki) Robertson, who has since succeeded to the title, visited Steep Holm during the summer of 1974 to see the progress being made by the new occupiers. She was impressed by what she saw, and with great generosity was to agree to a very substantial reduction in the asking price for the island.

Money was the major hurdle. In addition to the initial purchase, funds would be needed to pay the warden, to meet ferry charter fees, to purchase a boat, and to allow for repairs and improvements. But more than eighteen months after the launch of the first appeal, the balance sheet for 24 September 1975 was to show that donations had totalled only £12,441 – a long way short of the amount needed to buy the island.

A Warden Moves In . . .

While all the fund-raising activity was taking place, the barracks was being adapted to provide a home for Peter Rees, who started his resident wardenship in August 1974. Ambitious plans were put into action, starting with proposals to re-activate the wartime underwater telephone. The end of the cable running beneath Steep Holm's East Beach pebbles was easy to trace. On Brean Down, Army Signals men with detectors followed the termination there from the old fort to the cliff edge and the sea. But all was in vain, as a considerable length of offshore cable had been removed for its scrap metal value; instead an expensive radio telephone had to be installed. Much later this was to be replaced by hand-held radios.

In the initial surge of enthusiasm which usually accompanies a new venture, and thanks to the publicity generated by a flow of glowing media reports, many individuals and organizations were to volunteer their services. In the first year of management under the new Trust much progress was made in tidying up Second World War military remains – as well as with the never-ending tasks of path clearance and maintenance of the barracks.

Peter Rees's first report of March 1975 said that 118 volunteers were actively helping, with fourteen weekend working parties having been mustered during 1974. The Trust had acquired its own inflatable boat which, fitted with a powerful outboard engine, had already made a score of journeys to Steep Holm laden with equipment and supplies. An up-to-date list of plant species for the island had been started, and a check list of bird observations was being maintained. The new enterprise had made a good start.

. . . and Moves Out

For all the optimism the problem of fund-raising would not go away, and was to cause a serious setback early in the history of the Trust. Despite the massive reduction in the asking price for the island, the purchase would absorb virtually all the funds, leaving no surplus to pay a full-time warden. Peter Rees returned to the mainland in June 1975, to find a letter giving him a month's notice. He was to be replaced by part-time non-resident warden Rodney Legg. It was now a desperate question of cutting costs. Before long the boat would have to go, with the Trust turning back to traditional island transport provided by the Watts family of boatmen, who had served a succession of island tenants over several generations.

Purchased At Last!

The formal purchase of Steep Holm was completed in 1976; the Hon. Mrs Robertson's munificent gesture being to sell the island for the amazingly low figure of £10,000, raised by donations. The Allsop name had not lost its magic appeal, and his widow Betty, sons Tristan and Fabian, with daughter Amanda, stayed in close association with the project. The continued preservation of this little island as a nature reserve caught the imagination of many supporters, as Steep Holm came into new ownership for the first time in 143 years. Inevitably the early enthusiasm of large numbers of volunteer helpers would wane, but in its first two years of occupation, the Kenneth Allsop Memorial Trust was able to claim encouraging progress in its campaign to tidy and renovate Steep Holm. It was yet to discover, like its predecessor, that ambitious proposals to clear away all intrusive features and restore the island to its 'natural beauty' would be impossible to achieve.

Clearing Gun Sites

The best preserved of the island's Victorian gun batteries is at Split Rock; still with its two 7-in cannons and most of its masonry intact. This was destined to become the Trust's military showpiece, and a scheduled Ancient Monument. Members of the former Trust had already cleared part of the emplacement, but shortage of labour had prevented completion of the work. In 1975 the batteries were again tidied, with the remaining Nissen hut debris being shovelled away, and remnants of the accompanying Victorian side-arms store were located in the following year. Situated on the raised area in front of the two Victorian batteries is a concrete pad with a ring of bolts. This is one of several laid down on Steep Holm in the Second World War as bases to which anti-aircraft guns were fixed. With the Georgian pivot guns, Split Rock has relics from three different periods of military history.

The other three double gun sites have not survived in such good condition, although Laboratory Battery suffered less than Garden and Summit, both of which were badly damaged by having 6-in gun emplacements built over them.

Of the single Victorian gun sites, the Tombstone area had been used as a wartime supplies dump; with coal being tipped at the nearby head of the railway and sand which had been stored within the parapet almost smothering the giant cannon. Volunteer help came to the aid of the Trust in 1976, clearing tons of sand and debris, to once more reveal this barbette, with its cannon, pivot gun and 'racer'. The entrances to underground stores choked with vegetation were also made accessible, and collapse of the zig-zag path below Cliff Cottage was repaired by building a short section of dry-stone retaining wall.

Moving a Monument Reveals Another Gun Site

One early project involved moving the wartime sighting post on which the former Steep Holm Trust had fixed the Harry Cox memorial in 1957. This concrete post had been left as positioned by the army until the new enthusiasts heaved it a few feet to rest upon the parapet of the western half of the Victorian Garden Battery. The bronze top plate was lost, and the letters 'H.C.' were broken off. Later these were recovered and are now displayed in the barracks. The memorial plaque affixed to the post to commemorate the respected former warden still remains in place.

Beneath the post's extended concrete plinth, which had supported the wartime shelter for gun crews on duty, was a mass of soil and rubble that the army had heaped on top of the underlying nineteenth-century fortification, so that their ranging equipment might be mounted at a more effective height. This infill was shovelled away to reveal once more the western barbette of Garden Battery, still intact, and seen for the first time since the 1940s.

Monks' Well

Other workers cleared the earth and scree which had once again cascaded over the iron lid of the old catchment well above East Beach. However, this was not (as they believed) the first re-discovery of the well since the 1940s. In the intervening years scree had been regularly cleared by members of the former Steep Holm Trust, who themselves cut access steps and built up the brickwork before designing, commissioning and fixing the heavy iron lid which prevented debris and animals from falling in.

Fixing A New Memorial Plaque

A priority task was to remind every visitor of the reason for the island's purchase by the new Trust. Kenneth Allsop's daughter Amanda had said of her father: 'Conservation was his life and this [island] will be the perfect memorial.' A large slate, once part of a floor in Parkhurst Prison, was cut to size, suitably engraved and packed for its journey across the water on 21 August 1976. There were anxious moments in the choppy waters of the tide race off Steep Holm before it was landed and somehow heaved up the insecure ladder from the beach. Fortunately this heavy burden had to be carried only as far as Cliff Cottage, where it was intended that it should be fixed within a niche beside the great stair-well arch. When the wrappings were removed the slate was found to be just a fraction too big! Instead, it had to be cemented to the wall alongside, where it is less well protected, but perhaps more obvious to those climbing the path.

Activity at Rudder Rock

Clearance of encroaching vegetation around the Rudder Rock Victorian single gun site was tackled several times by the former Steep Holm Trust – to be repeated yet

Stan Rendell (below) and Bob Wood haul the heavy slate memorial tablet to Kenneth Allsop up the shaky ladder from East Beach, 21 August 1976

again by volunteers assisting the new Trust. This was another military site on Steep Holm to be scheduled as an Ancient Monument. Already modified by the 1898 installation of a stone plinth, concrete apron and metal shield for the HMS *Arrogant* test bombardment, the battery had been half buried beneath a 1941 concrete battery observation post; and its 1869 cannon – moved from position for the bombardment test – was lost.

Island warden Rodney Legg scouted around at intervals in a vain search for the gun. After seeing a pre-war photograph which showed its position in the 1930s he and his helpers were spurred to greater efforts. But trenching with pickaxe and shovel into the edge of the scheduled area near the battery observation post still did not locate the missing gun – until Stephen Tripp, a regular worker for the Trust, loaned his metal detector to Mr Legg one day in 1981. A massive signal indicated a large metal object beneath the concrete floor. Although this base was far less substantial than those supporting the Second World War coast defence guns, it was some weeks before the thick layer was chipped away sufficiently to show the great cannon (minus one trunnion) lying in its concrete 'grave', where it can still be seen today.

Victorian 7-in 7-ton cannon beneath the concrete floor of the Second World War battery observation post

Demolition of Gun Emplacement Roofs

For us, the most spectacular week of the Trust era was in October 1985, when we accompanied cases of explosives and detonators, in the charge of three cheerfully efficient young men from the Royal Ordnance Factory, Puriton, to the island. Their task was to demolish the dangerously unstable roofs of three of the four wartime gun emplacements, and although we had intended having a 'quiet' week concentrating on our archaeological work, we found ourselves drawn into the routine of count-downs and reverberating explosions at half-hourly intervals, which sent clouds of evil-smelling black smoke across the estuary.

Yet another press and TV day brought an assortment of journalists and technicians, who sought to capture in sound and vision the 'big bangs' which brought the roofs down, more or less to order. A year later there was a second memorable week of controlled explosions to cut the girders into smaller sections; although even then it was not easy for Trust workers to move away all the heavy debris from the emplacements. But at last these were clear and safe, and have since been popular picnic places for visitors.

Only the lower south emplacement has been left with its rusting girders and a few 'plastic armour' panels still in place for the benefit of military historians who may view it from above; but access to this relic has been blocked to avoid danger to over-enthusiastic explorers.

Operation 'Cannon Lift'

During wartime demolition of the eastern half of the Victorian Summit battery to build a modern 6-in gun emplacement, both old guns were removed. The 7-ton cannon was dumped on the nearby cliff edge, and its Georgian pivot gun was dug out and rolled away, to be left lying in undergrowth in the great 'ditch' behind the site. For forty years it remained there, often hidden in the vegetation. A group of Trust workers felt that the old cannon should not be left rusting where few visitors even noticed it, so they tugged and levered it across to a nearby Nissen hut base, with the ambitious intention of dragging it around the island on rollers to the barracks where it could be displayed to advantage. An ingenious plan but, with more than 2 tons to pull across rough ground and through dense vegetation to the other side of the island, an impossible task! The cannon became stuck in the narrow gully leading out of the defensive ditch, and there it stayed for another five years. At this point Ken Cass, vice-chairman of the Trust, had a different idea for tackling the problem. He appealed to No. 707 Naval Air Squadron, Yeovilton for help. The Navy co-operated wholeheartedly, and a Westland Sea King helicopter piloted by Falklands veteran Lt. Jerry Spence was dispatched to Steep Holm on an initial reconnaissance, before returning one glorious September day in 1986.

This time two powerful Sea Kings arrived. With press and television well respresented, Lt. Spence landed on the plateau with his machine stripped of all

Sea King helicopter from Fleet Air Arm base at Yeovilton, piloted by Lt. Jerry Spence, with winchman leaning out of the door, lifting a Georgian cannon from the gully behind Summit Victorian gun battery, 25 September 1986

possible fittings. First the shackling of the trapped Georgian cannon was overseen by the air crew; then, with only the pilot and winchman on board, the Sea King took off again for the short flight across to the gully. After an anxious moment the cannon – weighing very close to the maximum lifting capacity of the helicopter – swung in the air and was taken cautiously across to the barracks. It was lowered gently on to the carriage, and the trunnions were eased into their slots by the ground crew. Would the wooden sleeper construction take the strain? It did, and the spectators cheered. The day could not end there. Jerry Spence landed his Sea King again, and came with his crew to the barracks for refreshment not knowing that a surprise had been prepared. The Trust was about to celebrate the occasion by attempting to fire the old cannon! A wooden replica shell, with a carefully calculated small charge of gunpowder, was rammed down the bore, and everyone was pushed back to a safe distance. With a satisfying BANG! the wooden shell and the accumulated dirt of almost a hundred years was fired from the barrel. There was no second chance for those who had missed their photograph! Pessimists were proved wrong. The carriage did not collapse; the gun did not split; and the wooden shell splashed into the sea half a mile offshore, to be retrieved by boatman John Watts. It was later brought back to be displayed in the barracks. The deep cut in the old cannon was filled, and the weapon received a

The Georgian cannon, safely lowered on to its specially constructed wooden carriage, fires a wooden shell out to sea

coat of black preservative paint. It has since provided a popular focal point for adults and children – the present record being eighteen youngsters balanced on the barrel!

Other Helicopter Landings on Steep Holm

The first known landing on Steep Holm by helicopter took place in 1973, when Ted Mason accompanied a visitor who wished to inspect the plateau at close quarters from the air. The pilot of the privately chartered helicopter from Weston Airport first took them on a circuit of the island, then hovered a few feet above the ground, looking for a suitable landing place free from obstructions which might damage the rotors. Finally he landed upon the tiny grassy patch close to the Victorian farmhouse, by which time strong cross winds were blowing over the plateau; so only a hasty ground inspection was allowed before the frail craft took off again for the flight back to Weston.

In September 1980 two helicopters buzzing around brought Trust workers running out of the barracks. It was the start of an unexpected adventure, for they were enrolled as additional actors in an Indian film drama, having flights around the island as filming progressed, with boatman John Watts acting out a 'rescue' of 'bodies' dropped from above.

Since the memorable Sea King cannon life, an R.A.F. Puma ferried tons of sand and cement, which were dropped on the plateau in 1990; and we hope there will never be another occasion when the yellow Air Sea Rescue helicopter has to land to pick up a casualty, as happened when a young Trust member injured his foot and was transported to hospital in 1991.

Chapter Twenty

ADMINISTRATION OF AN ISLAND

Barracks Innovations

All is not excitement and adventure, even when trustees with a sometimes unconventional approach are involved in running an island; and day-to-day routine matters must necessarily occupy a large proportion of time and energy. As in the days of the former Steep Holm Trust, it was found that the old barracks needed urgent and continuing renovation. Soon volunteers led by Doug Tripp and his family were repairing the main roof; and yet again new windows and doors were fixed. The eastern building was at first thought to be beyond repair, but workers brought this almost derelict structure back into use.

Workers installing a replacement fanlight above the barracks door (until the Second World War one of the windows)

In the summer of 1982 Chris Maslen and Jenny Smith lived on Steep Holm with their ducks and geese for six months. They persevered with the gigantic task of ripping down the unsightly and damaged lath and plaster inner ceiling of the barracks, revealing an impressive framework of much more attractive beams and cross braces. On the walls the drear brown and cream colour scheme was replaced with a Wedgwood blue and white combination which vastly improved the interior appearance. The old building had been transformed, and soon there were to be display cabinets and information boards filled with objects and photographs illustrating the island's archaeology, military history and wildlife – with a special display in honour of Kenneth Allsop. Beds, many of which had been inherited from the former Steep Holm Trust, were relegated to smaller rooms, which were later fitted out with bunks – just in case a boatload of visitors was stranded overnight! The gleanings from jumble sales which had furnished the barracks were replaced by new tables and comfortable chairs. A well-stocked souvenir counter to accompany a snack bar was in response to demand from a completely new style of tourism on the island.

Problems with the Water Supply

Despite new guttering and drain pipes being fitted to the barracks roof, there were continuing worries about the lowering water level in the 49,000-gallon underground

A group of schoolchildren enjoys the comforts of the renovated barracks; displays around the walls illustrate aspects of island history and wildlife

reservoir. After a choked concrete channel was located and cleared the problem became worse – until during a thunderstorm it was seen that the newly cleared channel was acting as an overflow for blocked filter beds. These were cleaned and filled with fresh material. At last the reservoir began to refill, and a variety of debris and wartime impedimenta was cleared from inside the tank, with the former wooden trapdoor being replaced by a fitted metal hatch. At first water was drawn from the tank by the tedious method of dangling buckets from ropes; a small hand pump was tried, but was scarcely less tiring and slow. This was replaced by a portable motor pump capable of forcing the water up to a large header tank perched upon the flat roof of the wartime kitchen extension to the barracks, to provide a head of pressure for taps and cisterns.

Toilet facilities at the barracks became totally inadequate; and on a hot and fortunately calm July day in 1984, six of us, helped by the boatmen, filled Frank Watts's new (cabinless) boat with 300 breeze blocks. Offloading on the island meant stacking the 3–4 tons of blocks in shallow water before carrying them up the long path to be stacked outside the barracks, ready to be transformed into a four-cubicle 'ladies', which never fails to delight female visitors surprised to find such luxury on a 'desert' island.

A Robbery and New Security Measures

Like previous occupiers of Steep Holm, the Trust was soon to learn that pirates still roam the estuary. There is an ever-present hazard of unauthorized landings and vandalism. Even more serious, thieves broke into the barracks during May 1980, to escape with food stores, emergency rescue equipment, and souvenirs valued at some £700; and had the effrontery to sign the visitors' book 'The Robbers' before leaving. Until this episode Channel travellers had been trusted to respect the 'Private Property, no Unauthorized Landing' notice. Reluctantly the Trust had to resort to Harry Cox's method of restricting entry to Steep Holm – by erecting a gate above East Beach; and the river police patrols keep a watchful eye on the island.

Beach Improvements

What was once easy access to the path from East Beach to the plateau had been made difficult by the construction of the towering wartime quay, on the southern end of which stood the empty shell of a small generator house. After climbing a portable ladder, there was an awkward gap between the building and the cliff. To allow easier passage for supplies this structure was soon demolished by the Trust. It was to be some time before the insecure ladder was replaced by a wooden stairway and handrail which was bolted to the wartime quay; but even this innovation had drawbacks, being far too steep, and difficult to reach when the sea washed away the pebbles from around its lowest step. Chris Maslen tackled the problem with groups of helpers working between tides. After shovelling away tons of pebbles to expose bedrock, a raft was laid as a base for concrete steps. These were completed in 1987 and have remained in use ever since – except for a short period early in 1990 when they had to be partially rebuilt after a violent storm undermined the foundations and tore a gap in the top landing.

A quarry firm had been called in to blast away a huge overhanging and unstable portion of rock which threatened to fall from the cliffside. Later there were further explosions in an effort to clear obstructions which were a hazard when beaching the ferry boats. Those of us working on the priory site 200 ft above the beach were startled when an unexpectedly large explosion threw chunks of rock so high in the air that they rained down around our heads!

'Big Boat' Days

Many of the improvements to Steep Holm's amenities have been in response to needs which had never before arisen. Apart from larger local ferry boats allowing more visitors to land from Weston, a surprise development was that pleasure steamer operators showed interest in including the island in their itineraries.

On Saturday 27 September 1980 the M.V. *Balmoral* brought 200 passengers for a two-hour stay – a visit which coincided with the inaugural issue of the Steep Holm philatelic service. Betty Allsop and John Fowles were kept busy autographing attractive first-day covers decorated with the first set of four island stamps. For the Trust the visit was a success story, but the *Balmoral* was in danger of being sent to the scrap yard.

First day cover for inaugural issue of Steep Holm stamps, signed by John Fowles and Betty Allsop, and dated 27 September 1980

In the Bristol Channel, despite the interruptions of two World Wars and the consequent losses of ships called to service, the operation of purpose-built pleasure steamers had flourished from the 1880s until the late 1950s when their popularity waned, causing enormous trading losses. Ship owners Messrs P.&A. Campbell Ltd went into receivership in 1958, and although a reduced White Funnel fleet continued to operate, scheduled services were drastically cut. The *Cardiff Queen* and *Bristol Queen* – pride of the paddle steamer fleet – were scrapped prematurely in 1966 and 1967, and a proud era had ended; leaving Campbell's with just two small conventional motor vessels. As these were incapable of sailing the more demanding routes, the fast post-war cruise ship *Balmoral* was acquired in 1968, after twenty years of successful sailing in the Solent. For twelve years she operated the Bristol Channel ports, but profits were minimal, and Balmoral was to complete her 1980 season principally by ferrying to Lundy, before languishing at Bristol and Avonmouth for eighteen months while her fate was decided. She narrowly escaped the breakers' yard by being purchased for use as a static floating restaurant in Scotland. It seemed that a miracle was needed to bring back pleasure cruising to the Bristol Channel; but fate was about to intervene. The paddle steamer *Waverley*, built on the Clyde, and launched in 1946, had been cruising the lochs and waterways of Scotland for many years, until she was withdrawn in 1973. Rescued

P.S. Waverley *waiting for M.V.* Weston Lady *loaded with passengers returning from the island, 1987*

by enthusiasts and thoroughly overhauled she came back into service, to carry an astonishing 120,000 passengers in 1975. Despite this phenomenal success the Scottish sailing season was short, and from 1977 onwards her operations were extended by bringing her to southern waters, and eventually to the Bristol Channel. At first she was in the Channel for only a few days on her travels around the coast, so it was decided to extend the service by introducing another vessel to the area – the *Prince Ivanhoe*, which, on 20 May 1981, cruised through thunderstorms to land almost 300 people on Steep Holm. A second set of island stamps with covers was on sale already, on the theme of butterflies, designed by Gordon Beningfield, in conjunction with the similar Post Office issue by the same artist. Visitors scrambled to buy these unusual souvenirs. By this time a genuine old wall postbox had been acquired, and a full postal 'carriage' service was operating from the island.

Coincidentally the ferry boat then owned by Frank Watts, and used to transport passengers from the *Prince* to the island was also called *Ivanhoe* – and by one of those strange chances of the sea, both vessels were wrecked soon after that momentous first visit; the *Prince* when she struck an underwater obstruction off the Welsh coast on 3 August 1981, and the smaller boat when she was swept from moorings at Birnbeck in a force 9 gale on 19 September and battered beyond repair

A unique view of the Prince Ivanhoe *with the island ferry* Ivanhoe *approaching to take on passengers to land on Steep Holm, 1981. The photograph was taken from below Tower Rock, with Calf Rock to the left. Both boats were wrecked in separate incidents before the end of the season*

on the rocks of Sand Point. For a while only the graceful *Waverley* came to Steep Holm a few times a year. A record 700 people were landed on 27 June 1983, with some staying longer than anticipated when tidal conditions stranded them for a short while. Enthusiasm was maintained for the renewed novelty of pleasure cruising; and the replacement for the ill-fated *Prince Ivanhoe* was none other than the beloved *Balmoral* returning to her home waters in 1986, sporting new colours. Since then both ships have called regularly under the experienced direction of Captains David Neill and Steve Michel, with many faithful supporters returning again and again to savour the magic of Steep Holm.

The Island Ferry Boats

With public awareness and interest in Steep Holm so much increased, the island's ferry boat *Jane* had become too small to cope with demand. The *Ivanhoe* came into service in 1976 and endured an adventurous career until her lamentable end.

Her replacement was the personal favourite of ourselves and many other regular workers – the *Weston Lady*. Carrying sixty-eight passengers and an increasing variety of cargo, she took us on many memorable voyages before meeting a similarly dramatic but far more public fate than the *Ivanhoe*. She was drawn up to the top of the slipway at Weston for her annual refurbishing when a ferocious storm coincided

Silver Spray *and* Weston Lady *at East Beach, ready to take visitors back to Weston-super-Mare, 1988*

with one of the highest tides of the year early in the morning of 26 February 1990. The *Lady* was lifted from her trolley, and sailed crewless along the flooded promenade, to the astonishment of sea-front residents. As they watched, the boat seemed to make a desperate attempt to climb the promenade wall and return to her natural element. Her keel was ripped away, and when she crashed into a shelter more than a quarter of a mile from where her last voyage had started she began to disintegrate into the many pieces afterwards found strewn along the opposite pavement as the water subsided.

Previously, with the *Lady* backed up by Frank Watts's second boat, the *Silver Spray*, more than 100 people could be taken to the island from Weston. Although moored in the harbour when her sister vessel sailed to her doom, the *Spray* survived, and until 1993 she was the Trust's only means of transport, carrying just forty-five passengers, and gaining quite a reputation for her behaviour in rough sea conditions.

The Island Wildlife Stamp Issue

There were two more issues of the stamps and covers – one of which portrayed the mammals of Steep Holm. A friendly hedgehog and an obliging rabbit presented no difficulties for the island photographer; how we managed to photograph two shy Muntjac deer is a story in itself. Had we waited for them to pose, there would still be

Remains of Weston Lady *scattered along Weston Promenade after being wrecked in 1990*

no complete set of mammal stamps. But the ever-resourceful Rodney Legg transported a male and female to the island, and we spent an hour positioning them exactly as we wished – for these were of the stuffed variety, and purchased at an auction sale! The male still stands guard above the east barracks doorway, so that no one need return to the mainland without having seen at least one of the elusive Steep Holm Muntjac deer – although genuine sightings are becoming more frequent.

HMS *Steep Holm*

The fourth set of stamps depicted famous ships of the estuary, and HMS *Steep Holm*. A visitor on 28 May 1984 was surprised and delighted to see his old ship so unexpectedly illustrated on an island stamp and cover. Charles Reeves told us of how he had served aboard her for eleven months at the end of the Second World War, dropping depth charges to demolish wartime wrecks on the sea bed. During this exercise they even managed to damage a police station and waterfront houses when clearing obstructions from a harbour!

Project to Rebuild the Inn

During the Second World War military occupation of Steep Holm, the walls of the derelict 1832 inn had been demolished by the army. Close to the path, all that now showed was the bare outline of the rear of the building. On the seaward side, where the ground level was lower, broken walls were mainly obscured by the heaped rubble which largely filled the building and its small garden. At the beach end of the ruined inn gaunt walls of the later annexe stood poised above the rocks; but the fingers of random stonework pointing skywards around great gaps that were once windows seemed on the verge of collapse. Already much of the rubble had been removed from within these walls by the former Steep Holm Trust, but to rebuild this unstable structure was a new idea. During preliminary work further remnants of the original inn building were partially revealed, and attention was diverted from the annexe to clearance of the earlier rooms. Tons of rock and debris were removed, to show that lower walls, room plans and steps, even a fireplace and flagstone floor, remained. This became a much more challenging project, and since then most of the energies of Rodney Legg, his deputy warden and helpers have been directed towards the rebuilding of the inn in random stonework. The new structure will be totally unlike that of 1832, although resting upon the original foundations; and the aim is to use this building as a depot, available to visitors awaiting the arrival of the return boat.

Mechanization Returns to Steep Holm

For years we thought longingly of how the disused railway track might be brought back into use, as we all struggled up the zig-zag path from the beach to the plateau laden with heavy stores. There seemed little hope that the Trust, with such limited funds, would ever be able to modernize its methods – until Mrs Philippa Bowkett came to the island with a young people's group. She was appalled to see the weighty goods which had to be carried by hand from the beach to the barracks, and immediately determined to do something to help. Within eighteen months her tremendous efforts had raised £1,600 – sufficient to buy a Honda Power Carrier in time for the 1991 season; which not only eased aching arm muscles, but once doubled as an ambulance to transport a young Trust casualty from the barracks to the Air Sea Rescue helicopter on the plateau.

Observing and Caring for Wildlife . . .

Trust volunteer Tony Parsons, veterinary surgeon and naturalist, has the responsibility for recording the natural history of Steep Holm. His work has resulted in many new sightings, and it was entrancing to be eye-to-eye with the first Siberian yellow-browed warbler ever to be recorded on the island, nestling in Tony's gentle hands. Injured animals and birds which have been tended by him include a young raven which was mobbed by gulls, and post mortems on casualties among the Muntjac deer, hedgehogs or birds have provided valuable information on diet and causes of death. Like the Muntjac, hedgehogs and pheasants were introduced to the island in the early years of the Trust, with varying success. Rabbits, the 'oldest inhabitants' of the island, have been devastated by myxomatosis several times, but a few somehow survive to rebuild the population. Slow worms can often be seen slithering across a path, or sunning themselves after a shower. There are no snakes, rats, or mice, and although a live lizard was found by the former Steep Holm Trust in a heap of sand imported by the military during the Second World War, there has been no further record of this accidental introduction. Harry Cox, in the 1930s, said that bees sometimes followed the boat across to the island from the mainland. These were probably bumble bees: John Atkinson, the Trust bee expert, points out that honey bees would be reluctant to fly so far over water.

Of the birds, the herring gulls have decreased dramatically since the early days of the Trust, and the lesser black-backs have taken over, while the great black-backs remain fairly constant; but the total reduction in the numbers of gulls has resulted in a healthier environment. Ravens still sometimes breed, and are frequently to be seen flying along the south cliffs. Cormorants and shelduck are thriving, and there are many smaller birds either resident or using the island as a resting point while migrating. Kenneth Allsop's favourite bird, the peregrine, has also bred on Steep Holm during recent years, but appearances are erratic – and like the buzzards or herons which occasionally venture into this stronghold of gulls, these birds have to withstand or out-fly concentrated attacks from the fearsome black-backs, protecting their young against predators.

. . . and Plants

Despite centuries of man's depredations on Steep Holm, a remarkable number of plant species survive, and occasional 'new' varieties are recorded. The future of the peony seems assured, for although the status of the truly wild specimen is precarious, efforts are being made to re-establish a colony of plants in the sycamore wood. The peony removed from the glen by the former Steep Holm Trust when *botrytis* struck in 1969 still flowers near the barracks; and on the priory site several fine plants coexist with the wild leek. To improve the plateau vegetation, nearly 150 whitebeam trees were planted in 1989 on its southern slopes.

Nature's wonderful contrasts of tree mallow and scurvy grass on the east cliffs are enhanced by the vivid yellow of wallflowers, and the delicate henbane flower always attracts attention. Patches of hemlock, the dark glow of sea lavender and masses of alexanders all have a beauty of their own. They also provide mute evidence of the stubborn ability of many species to survive for centuries, sometimes despite great odds; or perhaps to lie dormant for years until the right conditions lead to a surprise reappearance. There has even been the discovery on Steep Holm of a previously unknown form of lichen.

Over the years the struggle for survival triggered by population explosions has been demonstrated – and it is not just the birds which are affected when their numbers reach epidemic proportions. Normally quantities of blackberries may be gathered each autumn, but in 1985 the lackey moth caterpillars peaked to such an extent that they destroyed their own food supply, and the brambles were stripped. There were few blackberries that autumn – and, until nature's cycle was able to restore the balance, few lackey moths.

Island Archaeology

The prospect (or first experience of) a 5-mile sea voyage in sometimes rough conditions soon separates prospective team members from those who are hardy enough to bounce off the boat at East Beach and help to unload passengers and stores before carrying archaeological equipment to and from the priory site.

Following preliminary work in 1976, and a general survey of Steep Holm in 1977, we started a programme of archaeological research and conservation on the site of the Priory of St Michael in the following year. After clearance of scrub, top priority was to divert a well-trodden path which was contributing to damage by running diagonally from the south wall to the eighteenth-century tenement to the north-west. The area within the scant remains of scarcely visible priory walling was a depressing sight, littered with debris from two army Nissen huts which had been built, one encroaching on the north and the other to the south. Trenches had been dug here and there and left open, and we soon discovered that a wartime water pipe had been laid across the east end of the building. Walling at the south-east corner had disintegrated to such

Excavating at the west end of the priory site, 1986. Mike Smith and Terry Gore are working beside a wall which was formerly part of the Victorian navvies' huts. Barry Westwood and Joan Rendell are excavating to the north of the priory north wall. Behind them the walls and doorway of the former medieval warreners' room can be seen; beneath the stones (right foreground) priory burials were found

an extent that rebuilding by stone-masons was necessary before backfilling of old trenches could be completed. The most easterly part of the site had been so disturbed that it was decided to limit the archaeological work in that area to levelling the ground and seeding it with grass. There is little grass on the island, but within four weeks of planting, in September 1979, a thick sward appeared, several inches high. Who would cut this mini-hayfield? There was no problem; for except in myxomatosis years the rabbits have been efficient grass cutters, although they do indulge in unauthorized digging! Two years later the area which had been badly disturbed by the water pipe was grassed, and archaeological work has since concentrated on the west end of the site, which had been less damaged by wartime activities.

Highlights of our work on Steep Holm include the tremendous breakthrough of proving a Roman occupation, and of finding evidence of prehistoric use of the island. The rediscovery of the lost feature which we believe to have been a signal station was a thrill; while the priory excavations and our research have uncovered much of the history of Steep Holm – and of its people.

Experiments in Photography

One pioneering experiment that was directly connected with the archaeology was kite photography. Our efforts to photograph features from a low-flying light aircraft could not produce the kind of detail which was required from the overgrown terrain of Steep Holm. Rolls Royce Technical College postgraduates of 1982 accepted the challenge of attaching a radio-controlled camera to a parafoil box kite 4 ft square, with inflatable air pockets to create sufficient lifting power for the attached camera and equipment. To control the kite a lightweight winch was designed. After initial trials on the mainland, the breaking strain of the line was doubled to 200 lb. On the first two days scheduled for island photography there was insufficient wind to lift the heavy kite. On the third attempt it was blowing a gale, and the boatmen were extremely reluctant to leave their safe mooring, but were persuaded to plough through heavy seas and land us on East Beach amid surging surf.

This was the weather that the kite needed. The radio operator sent his signals aloft, to take photographs from differing heights controlled by the winch. The first films were changed, and there was an atmosphere of euphoria. Then disaster struck. A sudden gust sent the kite dipping before it soared skywards. The line had snagged and snapped, allowing kite and camera to drift out of control across the island

Kite photography: one of the photographs taken before camera and kite splash-landed in the sea — showing the priory site with Nissen hut bases to north and south, outline of 1776 tenement walls (top centre), part of the Victorian Garden Battery with overlying Second World War 6-in gun emplacement, the corner of a second wartime emplacement and paths cut through scrub

before plunging into the sea. Dr C.A. Ralegh Radford, who was acting as adviser on the priory site, was startled to be suddenly deserted as everyone dashed down to the beach in the vain hope of rescuing the camera and radio equipment. Good low level views of the priory area were obtained from the first films; but despite carefully calculated tests, the line had not been sufficiently robust to withstand island conditions.

Final Impression

Television personality Johnny Morris may have wisecracked that he was 'lucky to be alive' after coming into the barracks and reading the Trust's warning poster: 'Your Safety on Steep Holm Depends On This', but many visitors are drawn to return again and again, not just to experience the strange beauty of the island and admire the effortless flight of the birds, but for the unexpected bonus of perhaps glimpsing dolphins or salmon leaping out of the water, or watching seals lazily stretched out on the 'gooseneck' at low tide or sporting around the cliffs. There is much in and around this island environment which needs protection – and more of its elusive past still awaiting discovery.

How will future generations compare the thin slice of Kenneth Allsop Memorial Trust history with what is now known of previous eras? Because of the enormous problems of looking after such a mid-Channel haven, it has been said that 'the island always wins in the end'. The present volunteer members of the Trust workforce are attempting to disprove this sentiment as they grapple with the tremendous challenge of enhancing and preserving for future generations this unique memorial to one of the first pioneers to campaign for conservation of the environment.

Appendix: Summary of Geological History of Bristol Channel Area

AGE[1]	PERIOD	GEOLOGICAL FORMATIONS[2]	MAIN DEPOSITS	ENVIRONMENT	EVENTS	STEEP HOLM
10,000	QUATERNARY	HOLOCENE	Clays & peats of Somerset Levels. Alluvium along rivers.	Colder becoming temperate	Sea level rise rapid to about 3,500 BC & increasingly gradual thereafter	Joined to mainland till c. 5,500 BC
c.2	QUATERNARY	PLEISTOCENE	Fissure/cave deposits Alluvial deposits in main valleys	Alternating interglacial (temperate) & glacial climate	Sea level to −100m in glacials and 0 to +5m? in interglacials	Severn deep channel system offshore in glacials
65	TERTIARY	Includes London Clay etc. in areas to the east	Probably no deposition in area of Bristol Channel	Estuarine & deltic deposits to the east? partly derived from Bristol Channel area	Strong mid-Tertiary warping; deep erosion Widespread marine regression following the Chalk, concomittant erosion	Removal of sediment cover to re-expose Triassic Steep Holm limestone 'mount'
130	CRETACEOUS	Includes greensands & chalk	Chalk, sandstone & clay	Marine	Substantial sedimentation ending with Chalk (?200m). A period of gentle uplift & warping intervenes before the Chalk	Marine sedimentation but probable removal of some cover in pre-Chalk movements
204	JURASSIC	Includes Lias, Inferior & Great Oolites, Oxford & Kimmeridge Clays	Mudstone, sandstone & limestone	Marine	Steady sinking with accompanying sedimentation. Mendip and other islands covered during earlier part of the period	Possibly > 1km of marine sediment deposited at Steep Holm
	TRIASSIC	Rhaetian deposits	Grey/black mudstone	Strongly rising sea	Inundation of Triassic plains leaving Mendips, Broadfield Down etc. as islands	
245	TRIASSIC	Mercia Mudstone (formerly 'Keuper Marl') & Dolomitic Conglomerate (in south)	Grey/green mudstone overlying red mudstone/siltstone with salt beds / Red conglomerate or breccia (red sandstones)	Arid alluvial plains with occasional rainstorms. Salt playas at times. Scree draping hillsides & spilling on to plains	Strong erosion reducing Armorican mountain chains to isolated hill masses that become progressively worn down and engulfed in rock debris. Alluvial deposition in surrounding basins and hollows	Deep erosion exposes the Carboniferous Limestone\ which forms a 'mount' rising some 150m above surrounding alluvial areas. 'Mount' completely buried by debris by end of the period
290	PERMIAN	Unnamed red beds (under Somerset levels)	Red mudstone siltstone & sandstone	Arid mountains with surrounding alluvial tracts	Strong mountain-building movements (Armorican) accompanied by uplift	Folding & faulting of Carboniferous rocks
310	CARBONIFEROUS	Coal Measures	Mudstone, sandstone & coal	Swamp/delta	Major sedimentation accompanied by sinking of land. Shallowing of earlier Carboniferous sea finally led to establishment of freshwater swamp conditions over entire area	Sedimentation of limestone, then sandstones, & finally coal measures. sediment pile? >2km
320	CARBONIFEROUS	Quartzitic Sandstone	Sandstone & shale	Delta building out from north		
360	CARBONIFEROUS	Carboniferous Limestone	Limestone	Shallow clear tropical shelf seas		

1. Age in million years except for Holocene (10,000 years), after Geological Society of London, 1981.
2. Period subdivision given for Quaternary.

BIBLIOGRAPHY

Primary Sources

General Descriptions/Histories

c. 1625:	'Extract from an Account Book of the Manor of Norton Beauchamp', Jefferies Collection, Bristol Central Reference Library *N & Q (G)*, 1890
c. 1730:	Strachey, John, *Unpublished Notes for a History of Somerset*, DD/SH 107, SRO
1791:	Collinson, Revd J., *History and Antiquities of the County of Somerset*
1824:	Buckland, Wm, and Conybeare, Wm, *Observations on the S.W. Coal District*, GS
1829:	Rutter, John, *Deliniations of the North Western Division of the County of Somerset*
1831:	Clark, Thomas, extract of diary, *Proceedings*, BNS, 1939
1832:	Diary of the Revd John Skinner, British Library Add. M/S.33728, 1928 Ernest Baker, and 1978 KAMT
1939:	'A Survey of Steep Holm', various authors, *Proceedings* 4th Series vol. 8, part 4, BNS
1981:	*Steep Holm, A Survey*, various authors, SANHS

NB. To avoid duplication these titles are not repeated in the lists for individual subjects.

Magazine/Newspaper Articles/Reports

10/6/1695:	*London Gazette* (Norton Beauchamp advertisement)
21/4/1750:	*Bristol Oracle* (marooned on Steep Holm)
1805:	*Gentleman's Magazine* (description of Weston-super-Mare)
9/6/1827:	*Bristol Mirror* (advertisement for sale of Steep Holm)
25/1/1834:	*Bristol Mirror* (recent purchase by Col. Tynte)
16/8/1834:	*Bristol Mirror* (Steep Holm's crops and flowers)
17/4/1858:	*Somerset County Herald* (attack by bear)
19/6/1858:	*Taunton Courier* (County Court Case *re* bear attack)
26/6/1858:	*Weston Mercury* (County Court Case *re* bear attack)
29/10/1859:	*Weston Gazette* (boats damaged by storm)
3/11/1866:	*Bristol Mercury* (shipwreck of *Lucy Sarah*)
6/2/1869:	*Weston Gazette* (loss of steamer *Industry*)
7/3/1874:	*Weston Mercury* (obituary, John Harse)
18/9/1875:	*Weston Mercury* (Garrett swim to Steep Holm)
30/8/1884:	*Weston Mercury* (Harris Case, Axbridge)
3/10/1885:	*The Justice of the Peace* (Harris High Court Case)
20/8/1887:	*Weston Mercury* (letter describing Steep Holm visit)
17/2/1894:	*Weston Mercury* (drowned off Steep Holm)
20/8/1898:	*Weston Gazette* (bombardment of Steep Holm)
7/7/1900:	*Weston Mercury* (Brean Down explosion)
29/3/1910:	*Daily Chronicle* (island family)
9/9/1912:	*Daily Mirror* (island family)
5/4/1913:	*The Field* (description of Steep Holm)
23/5/1914:	*Weston Mercury* (barracks burgled)
20/6/1914:	*Weston Mercury* (trespass case)

11/7/1914:   *Weston Mercury* (resumed trespass case)
31/3/1917:   *Weston Mercury* (national insurance prosecution)
29/3/1930:   *Weston Gazette* (poachers and burglary)
29/11/1930:   *Weston Gazette* (dilapidations claim)
19/9/1931:   *Weston Gazette* (poachers)
10/2/1934:   *Weston Gazette* (sub-tenants)
26/5/1934:   *Weston Gazette* (message by paddle steamer)
8/9/1934:   *Weston Gazette* (lifeboat rescue)
23/2/1936:   *Weston Mercury* (Harry Cox lecture)
2/2/1940:   *News Chronicle* (coastguard rescued)
Also numerous post-war descriptions and news items

Geology/Prehistory

1830/32:   Sketches and notes by the Revd David Williams, unpublished
                collection, SANHS Library
1898:   'Excursion to the Mendip Hills', *Transactions*, GS

Roman

1821:   Colt Hoare, Sir Richard, *History of Ancient Wiltshire (Vol. II)*,
1960:   Lord Wharton, letter, Steep Holm Trust archives

Anglo-Saxon

1623:   Camden, William, *Britannia*

Religious History

Carved Celtic Head
Personal communications from Dr Miranda Green, Dr Anne Ross, Professor Charles Thomas and Dr
Graham Webster. Report awaiting publication from Dr Miranda Green

Early Christianity
c. 1150:   Williams, H., Caradoc's *Life of Gildas*, Cymmrodorion Record Series No. 3, 1901
1709:   Leland, John, ed. A. Hall, *Commentarii de Scriptoribus Britannicis* . . .

Priory of St Michael and its Patrons
1236:   Somerset Fines, 20 Hen. III, Vol. VI, SRS, 1892
1243:   Somerset Pleas, Hundred of Wynterstok, Vol. XI, SRS, 1897
1256:   Somerset Fines, 40 Hen. III, Vol. VI, SRS, 1892
1675–6:   Dugdale, Sir William, *The Baronage of England*
1892:   Jeayes, I.H., *Catalogue of the Muniments at Berkeley Castle*

Other Medieval Priories and General Commentaries
1269:   Letter *re* transfer of Studley Canons, CCC154, Corpus Christi College Library, Oxford
1661:   *Monastici Anglicani*, Sir William Dugdale (Studley and Worspring)

Missions
1841–3:   Diaries of the Revd John Ashley, unpublished, Missions to Seamen
1866:   Steevens, Thomas, *The Fisherman and his Net*, R.A. Kingslake, 1879

Archaeology

1930s: Sketches and photographs of BNS priory excavations by Dr L. Harrison Matthews,

held by the authors
1974:	Steep Holm Trust archaeological work 1953–61, a summary, E.J. Mason, Steep Holm Trust archives
1977–86:	Annual reports of archaeological work on Steep Holm, S.D. and J.N. Rendell, for Kenneth Allsop Memorial Trust
1982:	Cole, Geoff, 'Kites over Steep Holm', *Search*, No.18, Journal of BSA
1983:	Frere, S.S., 'Steep Holm', *Britannia* Vol.XIV, SPRS (based on our own information)

Also personal communications from Dr R. Everton, Dr L. Harrison Matthews, and Dr C.A. Ralegh Radford

Ownership/Occupation

1439:	'Raid on Norton Beauchamp Manor', Proceedings in the King's Bench Court, 17 Hen. VI (Ernest Baker transcript, *c.* 1911)
1463:	'Raid on Norton Beauchamp Manor', Proceedings in the King's Bench Court, 2 and 3 Edward IV (ibid)
1628:	Smythe, John, *The Lives of the Berkeleys*, BGAS, 1883
1671:	Bailiff's Account Roll to Duke of Somerset, SRO
1696:	Letter to Duchess of Beaufort, Marquess of Ailesbury papers, WRO
1699:	Notes of Conveyances, Norton Beauchamp, Willes papers, NRO
1730:	Will of Thomas Freke, Jarrit Smith papers, BRO
1754:	Abstract of Marriage Settlement, John Willes/Frances Freke, Willes papers, NRO.
1786:	Deeds of lease, release, and transfer, John Freke Willes, Thomas Nutt, and the Revd J. Deacle, Tynte papers, SRO
1830:	Conveyance, William Willes to John Baker, Tynte papers, ibid
1833:	Conveyance, John Baker to C.K.K. Tynte, ibid
1885:	Agreement to rent Steep Holm, Tynte to Davies, ibid
1886:	Agreement for lease Tynte to Waite-Hall, ibid
1886:	Agreement between Davies and Waite-Hall, ibid
1889:	Weaver, F.W., *Somerset Incumbents*
1914:	Lease, C.T.H. Kemeys-Tynte to J. Sleeman (snr and jnr) (for twenty-one years backdated to 24 June 1909), SRO
1931:	Specification of repairs needed to barracks etc., Steep Holm Trust archives
1953:	Lease for twenty-one years, Baron Wharton to trustees, Steep Holm Trust archives

Also inquisitions post mortem; current, dormant and extinct peerages and lists of county families

Military

1803 (24 Aug.):	Letter to the Duke of Cumberland from George Cumberland, Add.m/s 36517 BL
1860 (17 Aug.):	Notification to Col. Tynte of War Dept. proposal to construct two defensive batteries on Steep Holm, Tynte papers, SRO
1865 (10 Oct.):	Articles of Agreement for intended lease of parts of Steep Holm, Tynte papers, SRO
1871 (26 Feb.):	Lease, Tynte Devisees and Others to H.M. Sec. of State for War, Tynte papers, SRO
1877:	Jackson, Revd W., *Handbook to Weston-super-Mare*
1877:	*Treatise on the Construction of Ordnance*, RAI
1884:	*Handbook of Artillery Material*, RAI
1892-97:	Lott, L., 'Reminiscences', 24/3/59, Steep Holm Trust Archives
1898 (17/18 Aug.):	Ship's Log, HMS *Arrogant*, ADM53/12540/5930 PRO
1908 (10 Oct.):	Letter from Capt. Blandy terminating lease, Tynte papers, SRO
1940 (27 Jan.):	Notice of requisition by Admiralty, under Emergency Powers (Defence) Act, 1939, Steep Holm Trust Archives
1940–5:	Letters and records of conversations with Severn Defence personnel, private archives of

1946: the authors, the Steep Holm Trust and the Flat Holm Project

Notes of discussions with two German ex-prisoners of war who revisited Steep Holm in 1991, authors' records

Local History of the Area

1572: Lease of Ankers Head (now Anchor Head), Greville Smyth collection, BRO
1727: 'Diary of the Swordbearers of Bristol', *Proceedings*, BGAS, 1939
1789: Flat Holm lighthouse correspondence, Dickinson papers, DD/DN 246, SRO
1815: *A Memoir of Thomas Turner*, 1875 by a relative
1867–86: Collector's Traffic Return at Pier House [Birnbeck], SRO
1882: *Memories of Old Westonians*, interviewed by Ernest Baker, 1911
1900: *Latimer's Annals* (Perambulation of the Boundaries of the City and County of Bristol)
Also local directories and guides, census lists, registers and records; with church histories for Blagdon, Brean, Kenn, Portbury and Uphill

Natural History

1623: Camden, William, *Britannia*
1636: *Gerard's Herbal*, Marcus Woodward edition, 1927
1773: 'Lightfoot's Visit to Wales', diary, Vol. 43, *Journal of Botany*, 1905
1907: 'List of birds seen on Steep Holm', extract of diary, Revd F.L. Blathwayt, Steep Holm Trust Archives
1907: 'Diary of Robert Drane', unpublished, Glamorgan Archive Service
1936: 'List of Birds seen on Steep Holm', extract of diary, Revd F.L. Blathwayt, Steep Holm Trust Archives
1953–68: Reports of Steep Holm Gull Research Station

Maritime

1375: 'Calendar Miscellaneous Inquisitions Vol. III, 1348–77' HMSO, 1937
1387: 'Calendar Miscellaneous Inquisitions Vol. IV, 1377–88' HMSO, 1957
1733–82: Customs a/c books and correspondence CCR

Miscellaneous

1883: Letter refusing cholera hospital on Steep Holm, Box 323, CCR

Secondary Sources

General Descriptions/Histories

Coysh, A.W., Mason, E.J. and Waite, V., *The Mendips*, 1954
KAMT and Fowles, John, *Steep Holm, a case history in the study of evolution*, 1978
Knight, F.A., *Seaboard of Mendip*, 1902

Geology/Prehistory

Annual Reports, Severn Estuary Levels Research Committee, 1990–1
Bell, Martin, *Brean Down Excavations 1983-1987*, 1990
Dollar, A.I.J., 'Geology of Steep Holm', unpublished paper, 1935
Geological Excursions in the Bristol District, UB, 1977
Whittaker, A.W., and Green, G.W., *Geology of the Country around Weston-super-Mare*, HMSO, 1983

Roman

Boon, George, 'A Decorated Arretine Sherd from Steep Holm', Vol. LXVII, *Journal of SA*, 1977
Evans, Jane and Richards, Chris,' Ad Axium – Fact or Fantasy?', *Bristol and Avon Archaeology*, Vol. 3, BARG, 1984
Fox, Lady Aileen and Ravenhill, W.L., *Early Roman Outposts on the North Devon Coast, Old Burrow and Martin Hoe*, DAES, 1966
Harden, D.B., 'The Wint Hill Hunting Bowl and Related Glasses, *Journal of Glass Studies*, 1960

Religious History

Early Christianity
Baring-Gould and Fisher, *Lives of the British Saints*, 1872—89
Dunning, Robert, *Christianity in Somerset*, 1976
Thompson, E.A., 'Gildas and the History of Britain', *Britannia*, Vol. X, SPRS, 1979

Priory of St Michael and its Patrons
Bates Harbin, E.H., 'The Priory of St Michael on the Steep Holme', *Proceedings* Vol. 62, SANHS, 1916

Other Medieval Priories and General Commentaries
Barrett, William, *History and Antiquities of Bristol* (St Augustine's Abbey, Bristol), 1789
Hague, Douglas, *Some Welsh Evidence*, Scottish Archaeological Forum, No. 5, 1973
Patterson, Robert, *Earldom of Gloucester Charters*, 1973

Missions
Kingslake, R.A., 'Brean Down Mission' (with obituaries of T.T. and Mrs Knyfton reprinted from *Proceedings* Vol.33, SANHS, and *Weston Gazette* 1891), 1891

Military

Barrett, J.H., *A History of Maritime Forts in the Bristol Channel*, 1978
Hogg, I.V., *Coast Defences of England and Wales*, 1974

Local History of the Area

Baker, Ernest, *Weston-super-Mare, Some Historical Notes*, 1928
Brown, Bryan, *Weston-super-Mare and the Origins of Coastal Leisure in the Bristol Region*, 1978
Chaplin, Capt. W.R., *The History of Flat Holm Lighthouse*, 1960
Coward, Harold, 'The Wowwall: Some Aspects of Local Government and Drainage Early in the Fifteenth Century', *Proceedings* Vol. 124, SANHS, 1980
Guy, John R., 'Flat Holm Isolation Hospital 1884-1937', *Search* No. 20, *Journal of BSA*, 1984
Hallam, Olive, *Landon of Brynmelyn*, 1986
Kemm, Wm St J., *The Story of Berrow and Brean*, 1990
Poole, Sharon, *The Royal Potteries of Weston-super-Mare*, 1987
Simons, Graham, *Western Airways*, 1988

Natural History

Gillham, Mary, 'The Vegetation of Local Gull Colonies', *Proceedings*, CNS, 1965
Grigson, G., *The Englishman's Flora* (quoting Parkinson's 1640 '*Theatrum Botanicum*'), 1975
Legg, Rodney and Parsons, Tony, *Steep Holm Wildlife*, 1989
McLean, R.C. and Hyde, H.A., 'The Vegetation of Steep Holm', *Journal of Botany* Vol. 62, 1924
Murray, R.P., 'The Flora of Steep Holmes', *Journal of Botany*, vol. 29, 1891
Ibid, *Flora of Somerset*, 1896
Parsons, Tony, Annual Reports, KAMT, 1977–90
Rendell, Joan, 'Recent [feathered] Tenants of the Priory', *Steep Holm Magazine* no. 11, KAMT, 1989
Roper, Ida, 'Permanency in the Growth of Plants', *Proceedings*, BNS, 1915
Ibid, 'The Natural History of Steep Holm', 1915
Savory, Harry, *Report on Somerset Birds*, 1954
Sleeman, J., *Birds of Steep Holm Island*, Steep Holm Trust Archives, 1916
Storrie, J., 'Notes on the Flora of Steep Holm', *Proceedings*, CNS, 1877
Thomas, T.H., 'Excursion to Steep Holm', *Proceedings*, CNS, 1883
Turner, D. and Dillwyn, L.W., *The Botanist's Guide through England and Wales*, 1805
White, J.W., *Flora of Bristol*, 1912
Withering, William, *A Systematic Arrangement of British Plants* (5th edition), 1812
Yeatman, Revd H.F., Footnote to 'Brent Knoll', a poem, 1817

Maritime

Coombes, Nigel, *Passenger Steamers of the Bristol Channel*, 1990
Eglington, Edmund, 'A Young Fisherman in World War I', *N & Q (S)*, 1990
Farr, Graham, *Shipbuilding in the Port of Bristol*, National Maritime Museum, 1977
Harrison Matthew, L., 'The Sea Fish and Fisheries of the Bristol District', *Proceedings*, BNS, 1934
Holyoak, Jon, *Balmoral*, 1986
Hope, Iain, *The Campbells of Kilmun*, 1981
James, Nick, *Cardiff Queen*, 1988

Abbreviations

BARG:	Bristol and Avon Research Group
BGAS:	Bristol and Gloucestershire Archaeological Society
BL:	British Library
BNS:	Bristol Naturalists' Society
BRO:	Bristol Record Office
BSA:	Banwell Society of Archaeology
CCR:	Cardiff City Records
CNS:	Cardiff Naturalists' Society
CRS:	Colston Research Society
DAES:	Devon Archaeological Exploration Society
GS:	Geological Society
HMSO:	Her Majesty's Stationery Office
KAMT:	Kenneth Allsop Memorial Trust
N and Q (G):	Notes & Queries (Gloucestershire)
N and Q (S):	Notes & Queries (Somerset and Dorset)
NRO:	Northamptonshire Record Office
PRO:	Public Record Office
RAI:	Royal Artillery Institution
SANHS:	Somerset Archaeological and Natural History Society
SA:	Society of Antiquaries
SPRS:	Society for the Promotion of Roman Studies
SRO:	Somerset Record Office
SRS:	Somerset Record Society
UB:	University of Bristol
WRO:	Wiltshire Record Office

INDEX

Italicised numbers refer to illustrations